To my

BREAKING BORDERS

With my best
wishes
in friendship

Alex Harris

Dec 24/12

BREAKING BORDERS

One man's journey to erase the lines that divide.

AN AUTOBIOGRAPHY

Alexander Harris

iUniverse, Inc.
New York Bloomington Shanghai

BREAKING BORDERS
One man's journey to erase the lines that divide.

Copyright © 2008 by Alex Harris

All rights reserved. No part of this book may be used or reproduced by any means, graphic, electronic, or mechanical, including photocopying, recording, taping or by any information storage retrieval system without the written permission of the publisher except in the case of brief quotations embodied in critical articles and reviews.

iUniverse books may be ordered through booksellers or by contacting:

iUniverse
1663 Liberty Drive
Bloomington, IN 47403
www.iuniverse.com
1-800-Authors (1-800-288-4677)

Because of the dynamic nature of the Internet, any Web addresses or links contained in this book may have changed since publication and may no longer be valid.

The views expressed in this work are solely those of the author and do not necessarily reflect the views of the publisher, and the publisher hereby disclaims any responsibility for them.

ISBN: 978-0-595-45415-0 (pbk)
ISBN: 978-0-595-69446-4 (cloth)
ISBN: 978-0-595-89728-5 (ebk)

Printed in the United States of America

To the memory of my father, who forever remains in my heart as my idol, mentor, and friend. To my mother, a warm, gentle, and steadfast woman, whose wings of unselfish, endless love have protected me throughout my life. To my younger brother, who all too briefly enriched my life with companionship and affection while filling me with pride for the excellence in everything he set out to do. And to all members of my extended family, who also, without so much as a gravestone to record their journeys through life, perished so prematurely and tragically in the Holocaust.

Life is what happens to you

While **you're** busy **making other plans.**

John Lennon

It is better to live one day as a lion,

Than a hundred years as a sheep.

Motto inscribed on the Italian 20-lire silver piece

CONTENTS

ACKNOWLEDGMENTS xiii
FROM THE AUTHOR xv
CHAPTER 1   MY HOME AND FAMILY 1
CHAPTER 2   MY ADOLESCENT YEARS 20
CHAPTER 3   1939 35
CHAPTER 4   THE BORDER 41
CHAPTER 5   INNOCENCE AND FREEDOM LOST 46
CHAPTER 6   THE GERMAN SPY 52
CHAPTER 7   THE GATES OF HELL 62
CHAPTER 8   MY DAYS IN HELL 66
CHAPTER 9   JOURNEY TO BOGORODSK 76
CHAPTER 10   "LIFE IS WHAT HAPPENS TO YOU WHILE
             YOU'RE BUSY MAKING OTHER PLANS" 84
CHAPTER 11   EVGENEVKA 90
CHAPTER 12   IN THE ARMY 99
CHAPTER 13   A VISIT TO REMEMBER 109
CHAPTER 14   THE BATTLES 115
             1 The Northern Front 115
             2 The Southern Front 121
CHAPTER 15   THE POLISH INTERLUDE 128

CHAPTER 16	DISPLACED PERSONS	149
CHAPTER 17	A NEW BEGINNING	159
CHAPTER 18	EAST BOUND–WEST BOUND	169
CHAPTER 19	THE MARSHALL PLAN IN ACTION COURSE	177
CHAPTER 20	REFLECTIONS ON AMERICA	191
CHAPTER 21	THE POLISH CONNECTION	197
CHAPTER 22	GLIMPSES OF YUGOSLAVIA	208
	1 Mirko	208
	2 The Maiden Voyage	211
CHAPTER 23	PEOPLE OF STATURE	216
	1 Haskel Tydor	216
	2 The Men of Intourist	222
	3 United States Tour Operators Association	227
	4 Cord Hansen-Sturm	234
	5 Ram Kohli	238
	6 Pave and Nazli—The Rebuild Dubrovnik Fund	242
CHAPTER 24	BEATING THE ODDS	245
CHAPTER 25	THE HALLS OF FAME	250
EPILOGUE		259
IN GRATITUDE		263
RECOGNITIONS		269

ACKNOWLEDGMENTS

I couldn't have created this book without the contribution and efforts of a large number of people, to whom I offer my deeply felt thanks.

To my late stepdaughter, Ada, who planted the original idea and elicited my promise to bring it to a conclusion.

To my late friend Joram Kagan, and my stepson-in-law, Denard Clark, who insisted that my life's story be shared with others.

To Krishna Ramaswamy, who presented me with my first computer and taught me its basic use.

To members of my staff, my associates, and the various members of the tour and travel industry, who contributed to my success and enriched my life, providing me with counsel and experiences I'll always treasure.

To Don Reynolds, my friend, who in my moments of doubt gave me the impetus to continue.

To Robyn Swados and Kate Frank, who initially edited and turned my original writings into a readable format.

To Jan Rudomina and his daughter Isabella, who organized and prepared my manuscript for publication and continued guiding me through the technological wilderness.

To Mirko Ilich, Colleen Troupis, and the 34.30 Design Group, whose contribution of time, talent, and artistic advice was invaluable.

To my wife, Judith, my language mentor and counselor, who gave a new dimension to my book as she did to my life.

I offer my deepest regrets and apologies to those I have omitted due to my memory lapses and to those who might feel my portrayal didn't do them justice. I also apologize for any mistakes I might have committed in representing times, places, facts, situations, and descriptions of personalities.

FROM THE AUTHOR

Every life has a story. I have been reliving mine in fragments, reviewing the sequence of past events over a dining room table or in the comfort of the living room's easy chairs with a few close friends who, like me, survived the tragedies of World War II.

As a man who suffered mental and physical tortures, who went into combat trained to kill, I found it difficult to talk about my experiences with anyone who hadn't shared a similar past. After the passage of a half a century, time's miraculous healing capacity muted my emotions, and I began sharing my memories with a larger circle of interested friends and new close acquaintances. Listening to my stories, so different from their own, they urged me to write about them, saying they were important enough to be passed along. Some of them insisted that it was my obligation to do so. It took me a long time to overcome my shyness and self-doubt in my ability to write my story in English, my adopted language. Now that I have finally decided to publish my life story, I pay tribute to the many untold stories of my contemporaries who were subjected to similar experiences.

I pay tribute also to those who were unable to escape German-occupied Europe, those millions whose lives ended as victims of a vicious regime.

I pay tribute also to those who found themselves in the vastness of the Soviet Union, experiencing the brutality of a regime that isolated itself from the rest of the world, a regime that imposed itself on its own people and others seeking shelter from the horrors of World War II. The stories of those who survived are truly inspiring and heartwarming. These people found new purpose in the United States, a country that opened its arms and hearts to them. Some repaid this warm welcome by integrating into American democracy. Many joined a mission of breaking borders of prejudice, intolerance, ignorance, and animosity by building bridges of understanding between two hostile worlds. I'm proud to have been involved in this noble process among a group of enlightened and dedicated people, some of whom I recognize in these pages. With all humility, I wish to share with you my two lives in the Old and New worlds.

*   *   *

Although this book dwells on my personal story, it is only one of many, many other stories of individuals who have, against all odds, broken the barriers of ignominy to take a place of honor and recognition.

CHAPTER 1

MY HOME AND FAMILY

My hometown, Lodz, was unlike any other Polish city. After spending more than half a century in New York City, I cannot resist identifying some striking similarities between my two hometowns. Both are pulsating, bustling cities in which life never stands still. Except for the absence of skyscrapers, Lodz was a microcosm of New York development, and its population in the 1930s reached almost 700,000. In the 1800's Poland's government chose Lodz as the country's new textile center in an attempt to industrialize the nation. Immigrants who maintained their unique religious and ethnic identities but assimilated into the multinational industrial, social, and cultural life of the city built the history and culture of Lodz. The city prospered under this integration and interdependence, though from time to time there were heated disputes and political fights, and economic unrest would erupt in the form of worker strikes.

In the 1930s, over 40 percent of the population was composed of ethnic minorities, Jews, Germans, and a smattering of Russians and Ukrainians. Poles occupied government and communal offices and were the majority of the working class. A good many Jews became manufacturers, financial and business entrepreneurs, merchants, lawyers, and medical practitioners. Many also worked in factories. The Germans excelled as engineers, textile manufacturers, technicians, mechanics, factory foremen, and were highly skilled workers, critical to the industrial and commercial development of the city. My father was one of the Jewish manufacturers who founded a prosperous mid-sized textile factory. The Jewish population produced many citizens of international renown, such as maestro pianist Arthur Rubinstein; writer Jerzy Kosinski, well known in the 1960s as the author of *The Painted Bird* and *Being There*, and master illustrator Arthur Szyk, to name but a few.

The city's architecture also reflected the different backgrounds of its inhabitants. Neo-Gothic Roman Catholic churches, and a Byzantine Russian Orthodox church, coexisted with neo-Romanesque and neo-Renaissance palaces of the business moguls, and the neo-Baroque City Hall added to the city's picturesque panorama of styles. Completing this eclectic mosaic were red brick power plants spewing smoke from their tall chimneys, symbols of capitalist expansion as well as excellent examples of industrial architecture.

The heart of the city was *Plac Wolnosci* (Freedom Square), with a monument of General Tadeusz Kosciuszko[1] at its center. Four major streets emanated from there, forming a cross-like configuration. To the south lay Piotrkowska Street, the official main thoroughfare, with shops, attractive window displays, boutiques, cinemas, and cafes, as well as the city's Grand Hotel with its richly decorated elegant ballroom.

From the hotel, a stretch of several blocks served as a promenade called a *deptak*, where students jammed the Italian ice cream parlors, pastry shops, and cafes, paraded with their boyfriends or girlfriends, and sauntered about in the hope of meeting suitable companions.

We had lived in four separate apartments by the time World War II broke out in 1939. Our first was located four blocks from the center of town. My mother kept the five-room apartment in excellent order: clean, neat, and cozy. It was a warm and happy place, with white embroidered muslin curtains that matched the bedspreads and gently billowed at the stirring of the wind; the wooden, polished parquet floors that were partially covered by colorful Persian rugs; and the crystal chandeliers that reflected the sunlight streaming through the ceiling-high windows. The kitchen was spacious with adjacent living quarters for our housekeeper. I loved to spend time on our third-floor balcony looking down at the interior communal courtyard, with its constant flow of people who entered through an arched gate from the street that was unlocked during the day. A variety of vendors would visit daily; one could buy fruit, have knives sharpened, or buy pots and pans. Violins, accordions, clarinets, trumpets and drums serenaded us, teams of acrobats delighted us, and we observed magic tricks, and clown routines and organ grinders with monkeys or rabbits atop their instruments. We rewarded them all by tossing coins into the courtyard. Most of the performers were gypsies, while others were Poles and Jews.

On the streets, German and American-made automobiles were beginning to overtake the horse-and-buggy traffic. The sidewalks teemed with people.

---

1 General Kosciuszko played an important role in the American Revolution. He created the Fort at West Point, which helped stop the British fleet at the Hudson. The fort now houses the U.S. Military Academy.

Vendors sold soft drinks, ice cream, and fruits and vegetables on many of the street corners. Youngsters offered the passersby freshly baked bagels (*bajgle*) and pretzels (*obwarzanki*), their aroma delighting our senses. Older men dressed in knee-high boots, corduroy pants, and long, loose jackets waited at busy intersections, hoping to be hired to carry heavy loads. They would hoist them onto specially built small platforms with heavy ropes to hold the load firmly; they would then attach the cargo to their bent and aching backs. The gray buildings looked tired, but the people, rather than the buildings, gave the city its particular personality and character.

In the evening, ladies of the night took over the street corners off the main avenues. Local drunks swaying, cursing, staggering, and eventually collapsing into the gutters joined them. I was amazed at the number of Jewish beggars, who were the living contradiction of the anti-Semitic propaganda that all Jews were rich.

I'm still fascinated by the miracle of memory. When is it, exactly, that we start remembering? How do we sift through the heavy load of life experiences, the years of continuous storage in the recesses of the mind, the millions of daily occurrences, in an attempt to recall something that happened years and years ago? How can we be sure of the accuracy of conversations and actions dulled by the passage of time? Still, there are some memories that survive with perfect clarity, without any effort.

My first vivid memory of my childhood is an incident connected with a workers' strike. With the eyes and mind of a five-year-old, I didn't understand the true meaning of what I would witness. I was walking with my mother from our factory up Zawadzka Street. As we passed in front of the branch office of the Polish Socialist Party, we came upon a mob of people milling about, waving their arms, and shouting angry protests against things I could not comprehend. As we tried to make our way up the street, a troop of mounted police appeared, their sabers drawn, forcing the crowd against the edges of the sidewalks. We found ourselves pressed into a narrow passage between the line of the protesters and the walls of the buildings. My mother's grip on my hand was almost painful as she guided me along the street.

The noise of the crowd increased, and suddenly shots rang out. I noticed a few of the protesters, their faces contorted with anger, reaching into their pockets, pulling out pistols, and aiming them at the police. My mother threw her arms around me; gathering me in the folds of her loosely tailored winter coat and pleading repeatedly, "Don't harm my child. Please don't harm my baby!"

One of the men turned to her, shouting angrily, "Get out of here, woman. Get into the yard of the building. *Don't you know better than to walk the border of freedom and oppression?*"

He waved us off as my mother dragged me through the archway of the nearest building.

We found ourselves in an oblong courtyard. We entered a staircase and collapsed, exhausted, against the railing. My mother was breathing heavily, her eyes flooded with tears. I smiled at her, kissed her hand, and asked her what a border of freedom and oppression was.

She looked at me with affection in her soft, brown eyes, and answered, "Not now, darling. First let's get home safely and wait for Tata. He will explain it to you."

Little did I know that my father's explanation, which he would impart to me several times as I was growing up, would affect my entire life.

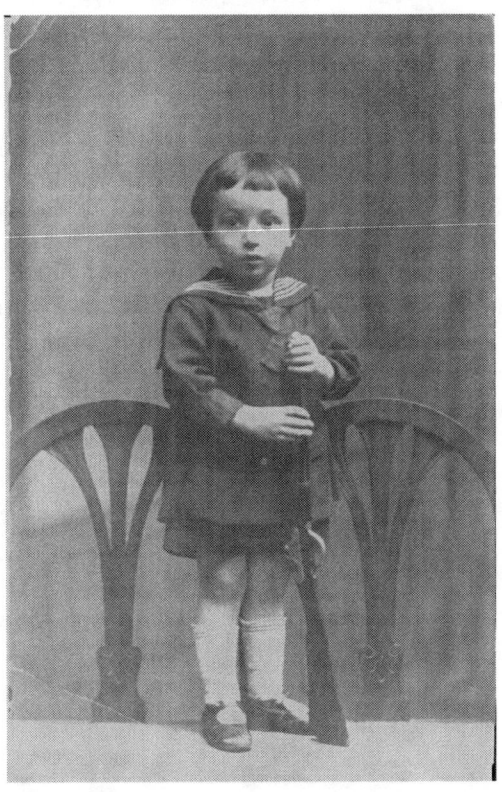

Me at age 5

"Well, well," Father said, after my mother told him of our encounter with the striking workers and the police. "Border of freedom and oppression. Hmmm."

He went to his study and brought back a thick, hardcover world atlas. For the next several hours, I would lose myself in a most fascinating lesson.

"See these dotted lines around the different shapes and colors?" he said. "These are the borders that separate one country from another. To go from one to the other, you must have a passport, which is a document with your name, picture, and other important information. The country where you were born, or the country where you live, issues the passport. You also need permission from the other country to enter it. It is called a visa. To stop those who try to cross without these legal documents, soldiers guard borders protected by barbed wires and checkpoints at various crossings."

"But the man said nothing about countries," I interrupted. "He said borders between freedom and oppression."

Our eyes met, and I detected sadness in his. What I learned then, and in the many afternoons and evenings that followed, was the difference between physical, political, religious, spiritual, and intellectual borders. I was fascinated by his stories about the persecution of the Christians during the Roman Empire, the Armenians' persecution by the Turks, the Jews and their long history of suffering, the Spanish Inquisition and the pogroms by their fellow countrymen in Eastern Europe, and the Crusaders' invasion of the Holy Land—all because of intolerance and religious hatred. My father went on to describe the differences between capitalism, socialism, communism, and anarchy, between democracy and dictatorship, between the rich and the poor, between the enlightened and the ignorant, and, finally, between freedom and oppression.

My Father Wladyslaw

I felt grown-up, and at the same time, so small, inadequate, and scared.

"You will face many obstacles in your life, son. Obstacles are like borders. So let me give you this advice," he said. "Never fear obstacles. When you face one, be confident and try to get through it. If you can't, try to go around it. And if that doesn't work, fight it and break it down."

He was articulate in conveying to me, in a simple, uncomplicated way, the deeper meaning of all of the aspects of our lives. I was in awe of the depth of his knowledge.

I didn't fully understand his message at the time, but I never forgot it. And as life unfolded, my father and his message accompanied me in all of my actions.

My father was my idol. I loved and adored him and used every opportunity to be near him. He was not the type to bounce me on his knee, carry me on his shoulders, or chatter to me in childish gibberish. But talk to me he did. Sometimes seriously, sometimes humorously, but always in an adult fashion, making sure I both listened and absorbed. I took in every word he said, asking him to explain things that were beyond my understanding. I considered the patience and attention he paid to me as an expression of his love. I followed him as he worked in his office, pacing the floor of his factory, intermingling with his workers—always with a smile and a good word for everyone. He knew the workers' spouses and their children and treated them like members of an extended family. Trying to imitate him, I became friendly with them, broadening my own little world.

My father was a patient man. I watched him speak on the phone and discuss business with people across his desk, and I never saw him raise his voice. He was always alert and always friendly.

Later, when I started school, I accompanied him on Sundays to the cafes along Piotrkowska Street, where he proudly introduced me to his friends as "my son Oles." I was proud when they said I looked just like him. I especially liked Saturday afternoons at the neighborhood bistro, where he played cards with his older brothers Moryc and Isidor. There were always bowls of delicious cold, fresh chickpeas that I loved to nibble on. I couldn't wait for the day when I would be allowed to sip beer, immersing my lips in the foam that crowned the head of the fat-bellied, frosty mugs.

I liked the smell of his clean-shaven face, his erect walk. He carried a cane as a fashionable prop and was dapper in his three-piece suit and starched white shirt, its collar embracing the perfectly knotted tie of the latest design. A gold watch chain dangling from his vest completed his handsome posture.

In summer months he wore a straw hat like Maurice Chevalier, giving him the look of a bon vivant and lady-killer. He indeed had a roving eye for pretty women and liked to flirt, which my mother tolerated with very little enthusiasm. He had a highly developed sense of humor, told good jokes, and socialized with ease and grace.

*   *   *

I had the opportunity to put his advice to test quite early. My elementary school was located four blocks from my home. I was able to persuade my mother to let me walk to school without my governess accompanying me. I was shy by nature and didn't want the other kids making fun of me by calling me a sissy for being escorted to school.

A block from my home, I had to pass a little shack where our shoemaker lived. I always waved at him as he sat by the window, bent over, hammering away at a shoe draped over a last. He always acknowledged my greeting with a friendly smile. His little son, about my age, unkempt, poorly dressed, and with a mean, hostile expression on his face, lolled about in front of the shack. One day, as I was about to walk past him, he pulled a pocketknife from his loose-hanging jacket and started waving the open blade in a threatening gesture. He blocked my way, but I minded my father's advice and crossed the street to pass him by.

This routine went on for several days. On Friday, I told my mother about it. Although concerned, she assured me that the boy's behavior was an attempt to look important, to show that he was someone with power. She was extremely comforting, assuring me that if I didn't show my fear, he would back off.

The following Monday, I confronted the boy and didn't cross the street to avoid him. I walked toward him, looked him straight in the eye, and passed him. I felt pride over my newly discovered strength in facing and crossing the first border of my still very-young life. The shoemaker's son never bothered me again. I shared my feelings with my father, who gave me a hug and a warm smile with a mysterious twinkle in his eyes. Years later, my mother accidentally revealed that my father had spoken to the shoemaker after I told her about my problem. The shoemaker gave his son a whipping, forbidding him ever to bother me again.

I loved and admired my mother for her subtle wisdom and control, which kept our family happy together. The balance between my father's romantic, dashing approach to life and my mother's down-to-earth practicality created a peaceful, harmonious atmosphere in which my younger brother Ignac and I grew up. The love and attention she bestowed upon us was unlimited. It came straight from the heart, distributed equally, almost invisibly, so natural that we took it for granted.

My mother had a distinctive, dignified appearance. In her youth, she had been a stunning beauty with a good figure and an oval-shaped face that projected beauty, warmth, and inner peace. Her brown eyes and matching brown, wavy hair blended with her best feature: her mouth, with its full, well-outlined but delicate lips. When she kissed us, we felt comfort, and tenderness. Her figure expanded somewhat out of its well-formed shape when she developed severe rheumatism in her legs, which forced her to wear elastic stockings. As a result, she was unable to walk long distances and gained some weight, making her pleasantly plump.

She established a routine, walking with me three times a week to my father's factory, where we would spend a couple of hours socializing with the workers, offering help and advice, and watching the different operations taking place.

We enjoyed walking home holding hands, chatting, and stopping to look in store windows. My only real interest was the confectioner's store, halfway between the factory and home, with its attractive display of cakes, chocolates, and candies arranged in the form of a pyramid. This was topped with a tennis-ball sized chocolate ball stuffed with crushed almonds, walnuts, and slivers of cherries and plums mixed with a moist jam. Called a *bomba*, unknown to my mother, Aunt Berta had treated me to them on occasion. They tasted heavenly. Alas, my mother wouldn't treat me to this fabulous delicacy, mindful of my weight. I was heartbroken and kept devising ways to change this agonizing situation. My childish mind invented a process of negotiation. I would refuse to walk home, insisting on riding in a *doroshka*, a horse-drawn buggy that was the city's mainstay of surface transportation at the time. My mother would have none of it. I would make faces and pretend to have pains in my legs, inventing any and every reason not to walk. I played this game for a while until we negotiated a compromise. My sudden ability to walk was rewarded with my getting a bomba every other day on the condition that I would eat only half of it each day.

My Mother Mala

As I grew, this primitive understanding of the power and skill of negotiation deepened and expanded, and the principle that one must give in order to receive remained firmly grounded in my mind. Still later, I learned that giving and receiving need not necessarily pertain to things of material value. It could apply to the needs of the other party, be it praise, recognition, esteem, power, or any other need.

In negotiations, my father was especially emphatic about never closing a deal with the other party's back pushed flat against the wall.

"When this occurs, retreat a step or two, leaving enough breathing space for the other person to profit from the deal as well, and to retain his self-respect," he said. I have lived by his words ever since.

My mother ran our household with the help of a maid who cooked and cleaned for us. A governess looked after my brother and me and did the shopping. As we grew older, our governess became my maternal grandfather's caretaker after he suffered a stroke in the aftermath of my grandmother's death.

* * *

My grandfather, Szyja (Joshua) Przedecki, was a warm, friendly, outgoing man who related well to everybody until a stroke partially paralyzed him, turning him into a semi-invalid who required a caretaker. But in his prime, he was a wonderful conversationalist, eloquent and in perfect command of Polish, German, Russian, and Yiddish. He had a great sense of logic.

Judges and lawyers often called upon him for advice. He himself could not practice law because the Russian rules, prior to Poland's independence in 1918, forbade Jews from appearing in court as attorneys. He could only act as an attorney's representative, presenting a case without having the right to argue it himself. To earn a living, he created a small textile shop with a couple of machines that produced stockings. It was my father who moved it from the cellar of an old building and organized it into a factory occupying a two-story building in the heart of the city. My father equipped the plant with facilities for weaving and coloring in addition to drying, sorting, packaging, and shipping, turning his firm into a profitable business. He assumed its ownership and earned the recognition and respect of the city's business community.

I was almost five years old when my brother Ignac (pronounced "Ignats" in English) was born. He was a beautiful baby, blue-eyed, with a head crowned with light blond hair curled into locks that gave him an angelic look. He developed into a slim, tall, athletic youngster. I was simultaneously proud of him and envious of his good looks. Being rather on the short side, and having to wear glasses to correct a weakness in my right eye, I did not consider myself good-looking. With a round face, parted black hair, and a pouting expression, my only consolation was that everyone thought I was the spitting image of my father. Ignac grew quickly. By the time we separated at the beginning of the war, he was six feet tall, a head taller than I. We loved each other, though we fought all the time, mostly by wrestling. I was cruel in these encounters sometimes, trying to prove my superiority in physical strength. We spent a lot of time with each other until we advanced in school, when the difference in age separated us. He was an excellent student earning good grades, while I was an average student with passing grades. Our school was not coed, but he was very popular with female students he met at social events. I was rather shy with girls. I developed and maintained few friendships with my classmates, feeling more secure within the intimacy of a smaller circle.

My Brother Ignac, age 2

One of the most memorable moments we shared was of my paternal grandfather's visits. Ignac and I were his favorite grandsons, being the youngest in a rather large family. Grandfather Asher Szajniak and his wife, Grandma Szprinca (Shprintsa), had four sons and two daughters who blessed them with a crop of fourteen grandchildren. Grandpa was an imposing figure of a man. Unlike his sons, who led secular lives assimilated into the Polish-speaking part of the Jewish population, he dressed in conservative, traditional Orthodox garb. His Polish, however, was impeccable, and this was the language he used with us as well as in the company of Polish gentiles. His involvement with them ran very deep. Living in Aleksandrow, a small town outside Lodz, populated heavily by

Jews, he became known as a sage. He was the spiritual leader of the Jewish community and a civic leader and arbiter in conflicts, not only between the Jews, but also between Poles. His judgments were binding and allowed no appeal. And yet, with all the respect and accolades he received, he remained humble, spending his time studying, reading, and keeping in touch with his family.

My grandfather adored nature. From an early age, every free moment during his religious studies was spent walking in the surrounding forest, studying the trees, talking to the forest rangers, and picking berries, mushrooms, and samples of different plants. He became a forestry expert and could appraise the lumber yield from the trees to be cut down. This skill brought him in close contact with the Polish gentry and nobility who owned the western forests. These powerful new friends, pleased with his manners and the fluency of his Polish, recommended him to their peers in other parts of the country, allowing him to earn enough money to support his large family.

My grandmother was a small woman who was prematurely wrinkled and shriveled. She worked hard in the house all her life and dressed modestly in simple garb, her wig sometimes worn carelessly, making her the exact opposite of grandfather's tidy look and aristocratic bearing. Yet her energy and stamina would put any younger person to shame. She was constantly in motion, cooking, cleaning, talking, and hugging us while heaping upon us every endearment imaginable.

My father was the most enterprising of all the siblings. Mechanically inclined, he left home to study electrical engineering at the Warsaw Polytechnic Institute, no mean feat at that time. Upon graduation, he returned to his hometown, Kolo, rented a hall, and, using his newly acquired skills, turned it into the town's first movie theatre. Building on its success, he constructed and managed movie theatres in neighboring towns. In one of these, Kleczew, he met my mother before she moved with her parents to Lodz. When he had saved enough, he followed them there, and soon asked for her hand in marriage. He saw the potential in developing maternal Grandpa's small knitting operation in the fast-growing textile center that Lodz had become. In time, he owned the company.

Grandmother would tell me that in the old days, as dispersed as the family became, everybody made it a priority to congregate at their house for Passover. Sitting around the table, family members exchanged stories and experiences, asked questions, and discussed problems. Grandpa Asher held court throughout, answering, interpreting, counseling, and settling minor disputes. His fairness and wisdom amazed all. Back when my father was a student, one of the relatives reported seeing him on a street in Warsaw, on a Saturday, smoking a cigarette. While everyone knew my father was liberated from traditional religious customs, the accusation still hung heavily in the air. Without batting an eye, Grandpa responded to the accusation against his son. "My dear Max, you must have made a mistake. Are you sure you had your eyeglasses on?"

Max, taken aback, turned his head in my father's direction and said, "Why don't you ask your son Wladek?"

"I don't need to do that. I know my son. He wouldn't do such a thing," replied my grandpa. What a marvel of diplomatic finesse not to force my father into a denial or a public confession, all the while delivering a mild rebuke to spare him from future transgressions. Since that conversation, my father never smoked on a Saturday in public again.

When my father started his own family, he didn't maintain a kosher home, so Grandpa wouldn't eat meals with us. Instead he enjoyed a glass of hot tea and my mother's home-baked yeast cake. He never criticized my father for being an assimilated Jew who attended religious services only on Rosh Hashanah and Yom Kippur. If our school had not had religion as an academic subject, we would be lacking any religious education.

Grandpa would bounce Ignac and me on his knees, asking us about school, our friends, and our activities. Listening to our chatter, he called us by our diminutive names, gently kissing and hugging us. I loved to return his kisses, finding his lips buried in his soft beard. He was a gentle soul, and yet there was another side to him that I came to respect.

One day, he and I were walking to my father's factory. From a distance, we noticed a group of Polish teenagers blocking the entire width of the street, weaving, pushing, pointing in our direction, and yelling obscenities. As we drew closer to them, we could hear them: "Get off the sidewalk, you lousy Jews! Make room for us! Poland is for Poles! Jews to Palestine!" I felt Grandpa's hand tighten around mine. I looked up at him, startled by the sudden change in his appearance. He had risen to a height I'd never seen. His body straightened. He gripped his cane, his knuckles tightening as if poised to strike. His eyes became cold as ice, looking straight at the gang approaching us. I couldn't believe my own eyes when I saw the gang parting, as if divided by an invisible force, allowing us to pass through unharmed. This simple display of courage and dignity left its mark on my life forever. Grandpa's silence and that look, hiding a trace of a smile, would become indelible in my mind. I have no tangible image of him, since his religious beliefs would not allow for the frivolity of picture taking, but I will carry that memory always.

When Grandpa and I reached our destination, I felt I had to convey my feelings about the incident that had just taken place. I said angrily, "*Dziadziusiu* (Grandpa), I hate these Polish hooligans!"

He sat me down in a chair, grasped my hands in his, and looked me straight in the eye. "Child, you must never allow hatred into your life. Don't hate these misguided youths. Pity them for their ignorance. They have to fill a void in their lives. Hatred is a poison that spreads and kills. Hatred leads to the destruction of peace and love. It destroys the hater, not the hated. Promise me you will never let it into your heart."

I did not quite comprehend the depth of his message, but the emotional intensity with which he delivered it was unmistakable. I responded by saying meekly, "I promise, Grandpa." He gathered me in his arms, put his hands on my head, and whispered what I perceived to be a blessing. I was moved by his love for me and was awed by the combination of strength and softness in this giant of a man.

I heeded his message on many occasions when hatred might have been the most natural response and was surprised by how much it helped me throughout my life.

My favorite uncle, the oldest, Uncle Moryc, opened a commercial laundry just a couple of blocks from our apartment. I loved to talk to his employees and stand behind the counter to collect tickets from his clients in exchange for their neatly packed laundry.

Aunt Franka, the image of my grandmother, settled into one of Poland's oldest cities, Kalisz. She supported her family by running a small business, pressing large pieces of bedding, towels, and household items on a huge mangle she operated all by herself. I hardly knew her husband, who spent every day in a small prayer house, endlessly studying and discussing the Holy Scriptures. I don't think he ever earned a penny.

Uncle Felix, the youngest, left home at sixteen and settled in Bremen, Germany. He established a furniture and carpet business and quickly became a well-to-do merchant. When my mother was pregnant with me, Uncle Felix hosted her in Bremen so she would have her delivery under the more reliable medical conditions in Germany. In 1936, he left Germany for Palestine. I didn't meet him until the late 1950s.

Uncle Izydor joined my father as plant manager of his newly built factory.

My favorite aunt, Berta, was a beauty. Unfortunately, she married a jealous and despotic man. This led to a divorce. At the time, divorces were considered scandalous, and for a while my aunt was the talk of the town. I was very much involved in her battle to gain the custody of her daughter Tola, two years my junior, a battle she eventually won. In the process, I fell in love with Tola. It was my first adolescent emotional experience, an innocent love, as we became each other's confidants, conspirators, and friends. It ended at the outbreak of the war, when I left home.

Brother Ignac with Aunt Berta and Cousin Tola

Of all my cousins, I liked uncle Moryc's son Romek the best. He worked for my father and played soccer for one of two Jewish soccer clubs in the city, Maccabi. He would occasionally take me to the matches. I remember one in Tomaszow, near Lodz, that was played against the club Lechia. Romek set up the winning goal in the decisive game to advance his club from class B to class A in the soccer league. As the game ended, riots broke out. The humiliation of a major loss to a Jewish team was too much for the hostile crowd to bear, and fans of the defeated Polish team spilled onto the field, chasing and beating up the victorious Maccabi players. The police soon intervened, and instead of protecting the attacked players, they used their clubs on them. Only after the Maccabi coach pulled a gun and fired a couple of shots in the air did the police restore order—before arresting the coach for "causing" the disturbance. Several players were seriously injured. Romek sustained a broken leg, which ended his playing career. In my teenage mind, I could not reconcile the injustice of the drama I witnessed. I was confused, frightened, and lucky to escape unhurt.

The incident left an indelible impression on me, which in my later life triggered my resolution to fight the underlying causes of bigotry, prejudice, and hatred.

Romek's two brothers, Bolek and Samek, also worked in my father's factory, but they were too grown-up for me to become close to them. There were three female cousins: Hela, Bronka, and Franka. I liked them a lot, but again, because of the difference in our ages, I did not socialize with them except for family visits.

My other cousin, also named Romek, Uncle Izydor's son and one month older than I, was my playmate. We played cowboys and Indians, police and gangsters, and other exciting games. His older sister, Bertha, would join us occasionally.

I was as distant to the family on my mother's side as I was close to the family on my father's. I didn't meet three of my maternal uncles since they had already immigrated to France and America when I was young. Uncle Maurice Harrison enjoyed an adventurous youth. He loved to travel and worked as a deckhand on various ships, exploring Europe, the Far East, Australia, and New Zealand before settling in the States, first in Milwaukee, then in a series of other mid-sized American cities where members of the Harris family had settled earlier. He wound up in Brooklyn. He and his younger brother, Max, whom he had brought over from Poland, operated a knitting mill on lower Broadway in Manhattan.

My youngest uncle, Elek, was the most intelligent and daring member of the entire family. In spite of his Jewish origin, he was awarded a gold medal at his graduation from *Gimnazium*. This was unheard of at the time considering the rampant anti-Semitism among the Russians, who occupied Lodz at that time and supervised the schools. Later, when my grandpa didn't feel well enough to present a case in court, he would send Elek to substitute for him.

All of my maternal uncles were short; none reached more than five feet two inches. Elek was barely five feet tall. After graduation, Grandpa asked him to present a case before a judge known to be particularly mean. The judge hailed from a Polish family of poor cobblers and used every opportunity to wield the power of his office. My uncle approached the bench, his head barely reaching a level at which the judge could see him. The judge announced, with biting sarcasm, "I shall not listen to you. Since when do young upstart Jewish midgets dare present cases to this court?"

"If judges with the intelligence of a dumb cobbler are appointed to hear a case, even a midget is tall enough to present it," was my uncle's response.

Tipped off by a friendly court clerk that an order was being prepared for his arrest, Uncle Elek left for France that night. He was fortunate enough to have a valid passport and a French visa, as he had been accepted to study at the Sorbonne.

My American uncle Maurice Harrison

My youngest uncle and mentor Elek, who had become Emile Paulin

After his university graduation, with honors and a doctorate in maritime law, Elek began putting his business acumen to work. He negotiated with the Polish government to become its sole distributor of Polish tobacco products in France. With this contract in hand, he approached other eastern European governments and managed to obtain exclusive rights to represent and distribute other commodities. He became quite wealthy. In all of his business dealings, he developed important connections with numerous influential French government officials and political leaders. Eliasz Elek Przedecki chose to become Dr. Emile Paulin, a journalist for the French press. His contacts brought him close to several prime ministers of France, including Schumann, Blum, and Mendes-France, as well as to General de Gaulle.

With his grasp of world economic conditions and his political connections, he established "Centralag," a company that transferred trainloads of workers from countries suffering from post-World War I unemployment to countries in need of cheap labor. He brought Polish miners to France, Yugoslav peasants to Spain and Belgium, and so on. This in turn resulted in the creation of Generaltur-Agence Generale de Tourisme, which branched out to England, Canada, and the United States after World War II.

Joseph, the second youngest of my mother's brothers, and by far her favorite, and Samuel, the oldest, were the only ones living in Lodz. Joseph owned a glove-making factory. I liked him and his aristocratic wife Aunt Lotka and my cousin Cesia. Two years my senior, she treated me as a friend, confiding in me, sometimes teasingly stirring my sexuality, causing me to imagine all kinds of romantic escapades.

Uncle Samuel was the most detached member of the family. He was always dressed sloppily; I never knew what he did for a living. After Grandpa's stroke, he would come to our home occasionally to shed a few tears, looking at his father mournfully, leaving without making any contribution toward his support.

I remember visiting his wife, Aunt Adele. She was of Russian descent and came from an aristocratic St. Petersburg family of physicians. Their apartment was filled with Russian art and was a little stuffy, but it was nevertheless a place of curiosity and wonder. A woman of medium height with a swarthy complexion, dressed in fine clothes that never revealed her real figure, she always looked sternly at us, her nephews. The crown of her black hair matched by her generous black brows gave her a severe look.

She served cookies and tea poured from an antique Russian samovar into fine, thin glasses resting in shiny silver holders. We were glad that our visits there were infrequent. Her son, my cousin Herman, whom we called Grisha, had the same swarthy looks as his mother. His black, penetrating eyes transmitted a fiery disposition and intelligence. He studied medicine in Bologna, Italy. He used to spend some of his vacations at our summer retreat, a house we used to rent from a peasant in a beautiful village, Zielona Gora, which was located at the edge of a deep forest. A meadow with a stream running through it faced us across the road. On either side of the property were fields of potatoes. I liked seeing them in flower, but I loved to dig them out when they were ripe. The feel of warm earth around my fingers gave me a strange and pleasant sensation and a small feeling of power, being able to wrest nature's fruit from its womb.

Other family members used to visit our summer place, but most of the time I spent playing one-on-one soccer with Ignac. We assumed the identities and names of the most famous soccer teams in Europe, competing and eliminating one after another, as in a real round-robin tournament, to reach the finals between the two clubs we admired the most. Our playing field was the large meadow. We played rough and tough, throwing all our energy into the imaginary tournament, sometimes suffering cuts and injuries. Yet nothing could stop us from having fun. At half time, we would stretch out on the grass or eat raspberries and blackberries that we picked off the surrounding bushes. Those blissful summers kept us happy, and the memory of them linger with me to this day.

CHAPTER 2

MY ADOLESCENT YEARS

Eleven years of school is a big chunk out of anyone's life. They were overwhelmingly important for shaping me into an educated person. However, no amount of formal education could have prepared me for the world I entered at the completion of high school in 1939—a world that had gone berserk, defying all perceptions of normalcy and decency.

My education started with elementary classes, was followed by middle school, *Gimnazium*, and continued for two years of high school, *Lyceum*, preparing for a college admission.

I vaguely remember my first day at school. I blended into the group of youngsters with neither problems nor enthusiasm. The school where I was enrolled was a Category A, a government-approved community school for boys from all religious backgrounds, a majority of them Catholic. My attendance there came to an abrupt end when as a first grader, during the Passover holiday, my mother packed some *matzos* into my lunchbox. My classmates saw me eat the matzos and made fun of me. I told my mother about this and asked her not to put matzos in my lunchbox. The next day, I overheard Mother talking to my dad.

"Wladek, if Oles is ashamed of having matzos at school today, chances are he'll be ashamed of having Jewish parents tomorrow. We must transfer him to another school."

My father, as assimilated as he was, didn't protest, and a midterm transfer was arranged. The private school they chose was a member of the Association of Jewish Middle Schools of Poland under the leadership of Dr. Braude. One of the leaders of the Jewish community, Dr. Braude also was a member of the Polish Parliament for several terms. This school had the government's recognition as Category A. There were only five such Jewish schools in all of Poland:

three in Lodz, one in Krakow, and one in Kalisz. In Lodz, two were for boys, and one was for girls. In addition to the normal curriculum taught in Polish, we had to study six classes taught in Hebrew that were subject to separate matriculation exams. Upon graduation, the graduates were qualified for automatic acceptance without entry exams to any Polish university or to the University of Jerusalem in Palestine, which was under British mandate.

When I arrived at the private school, a Hebrew teacher was hired to help me catch up with the class. Those early years were routine, but fun. At first I rode a streetcar to get to school, but I tended to suffer from nausea in any enclosed vehicle. I preferred to stand at the platform, which provided a better flow of air through the open doors. Since I was so small, I often found myself squeezed by burly commuters. So I started walking to school, saving the fare and adding it to my weekly allowance for my favorite candy or American cowboy movies. My heroes were Tom Mix and Ken Maynard. There were two movie houses, "Czary" and "Corso," which showed American westerns regularly. At another movie theatre, the "Capitol," I saw my all-time favorite movie, *The Champ* with Wallace Berry, and the original version of *King Kong*.

I had a pretty good singing voice and became a member of our school's choir. My claim to fame occurred when the leading soprano had to retire because of the sudden, natural maturation of his voice on the eve of a prestigious Chanukah concert at the Philharmonic Hall. To my surprise, I was called at the last minute to fill in as the leading soloist, giving me my first experience with stage fright. But I relished my parents' surprise and pride listening to my successful solo rendition. It was one of many experiences during those eleven years that helped me learn, grow, and mold into a person.

* * *

One awful night in the mid-1930s, our Polish superintendent pounded violently on the door of our apartment to tell my father that his factory was on fire. Mother took me to the burned-out factory the next day. I hardly recognized my father. He was disheveled, his face was blackened by soot streaked with tears, and his eyes were reddened by smoke. He sat dejected in the cindered remains of his office. I listened to the firemen's description of his heroic efforts to save the factory. They had had to restrain him for his own safety. I looked at him lovingly, but I somehow could not see him as a hero. I saw a symbol of helplessness and defeat.

When the insurance money was collected, instead of using it to rebuild the plant first, my father rushed to pay off all of his debts. When he turned to his old friends, suppliers, and former creditors to ask for loans to help him rebuild his factory, they turned a cold shoulder, some ridiculing him for his honesty and naiveté. Disillusioned and depressed, he developed angina pectoris. He nonetheless started a smaller factory with a partner, an inexperienced young playboy whose wealthy father gave him the money for the factory to try to instill a sense of responsibility.

Although he continued to keep Ignac and me in our expensive private school, it was not without financial sacrifice. I became involved with a group of wealthy kids who lived in the fast lane, doing a lot of card gambling, cigarette smoking, heavy drinking, and playing hooky. I was humiliated when I failed to deliver my tuition to the school secretary because I had lost half of it in a card game with my schoolmates. I confronted my father and told him the truth, rather than inventing a lie about losing the money or having been robbed (not an unusual occurrence in those days). My father, who abhorred lies and was capable of becoming quite passionate and violent at displays of dishonesty, remained calm. After that, I resolved never to repeat my foolish mistake.

There were only two instances when he lost control and gave me a beating because of lying. The first was over a drink of water, strange as it may sound, when I was ten years old.

I was frequently sick as a child, often coming down with colds until I had my tonsils removed in my late teens. It was commonly believed then that any cold drink could trigger a strep throat.

I felt honored that my father usually chose me over my brother to go into the kitchen and get him a glass of cold water at our traditional midday meal. I would let the water run for a few minutes before filling the glass, and sometimes I could not resist having a couple of swallows before I served it to him. One day, he asked me if I'd drunk some of it. I denied it, of course, unaware of the few drops resting on my chin and the front of my shirt. The beating that followed cured me of my secret habit. That evening, when the tears dried from my eyes and my buttocks hurt less from the belt smites, my father spoke with me.

"Son, you do know why you made me punish you? It's not because you drank the cold water, which is bad for your health, but because you lied about it." This explanation renewed my respect for my father's values.

He gave me my second beating when I was fourteen and came home with a broken nose.

I loved boxing at the local sport club, where I trained under the watchful eye of the club's coach. I was motivated to change my image of a sickly youth. One afternoon, at my insistence, the coach allowed me to spar-box with one of the city's top contenders in the featherweight class. I was excited to be in the same ring with a real boxer and got carried away, becoming cocky and aggressive. A resulting angry counter-punch broke my nose.

My parents had no idea of this clandestine activity of mine. They assumed I was participating in some legitimate after-school activity. When I got home, I told my mother that some hooligans had attacked me and punched me in the nose. Calm as always, my mother applied cold compresses and placed a piece of raw meat as a remedy against swelling. When the family sat down to supper, my friend and boxing buddy telephoned to inquire about my injury. I was too slow to get to the phone before my father answered it. Inadvertently, my friend spilled the beans. My mother's attempts to intervene, and her arguments that I'd been punished enough for my folly, didn't prevent my father from putting a few welts on my behind. The lecture that followed reinforced the pitfalls of lying.

I was an average student, intelligent but not a hard worker. I got by. Although my school placed an emphasis on science, mathematics, physics, and chemistry, they were not my favorite subjects. I excelled in Polish literature, languages, history, and other liberal arts subjects. I was also very good at drawing; my charcoal portraits of famous people stood out at our semiannual art exhibition. My professor, Mr. Kahane, considered speaking to my parents about enrolling me in an art school. He changed his mind when he discovered that one day, on the pretext of a severe headache, I'd skipped his class to play soccer against a team from another school. My artistic career ended then and there. I didn't make it in soccer, either.

I did, however, do well in basketball, my favorite sport. Being short, I practiced outside shooting as much as I could. I developed a deadly aim and used my small size to my advantage, dribbling and eluding the reach of the taller and slower players. In 1937, our school reached the semifinals in the city's basketball championship tournament. We played the German Gimnazium for this coveted title on a neutral court. There was nothing neutral, however, about the audience. Clearly divided in support of either the German team or the Jewish team, the level of intensity was far greater than normal.

The cheering became wild. Every basket scored was met with a deafening roar as if the hordes of students were competing in a screaming contest. Coming from the depths of their young chests and released through hoarse throats, their voices molded into one mad cacophony, hitting the ceiling and descending onto a blanket of white-hot noise. The shrill sounds of the girls and the deeper voices of the boys spanned the entire musical gamut. It was quite a sight to see them all at the height of their excitement.

Unfortunately, we lost the game by four points. I found it interesting that many Polish kids rooted for us, the Jewish team. Despite our loss, I got a hug from my German friend Heinrich Bohnig and a kiss and warm embrace from his sister Isa. They were hoping the Germans would win, they admitted, but they still rooted for me whenever I had the ball.

I was courting Isa. Both sets of parents looked favorably at our teenage romance. Oscar Bohnig was one of my father's best distributors servicing the German community. He was a tall man, prematurely bald, with an open, friendly face. His black moustache fit neatly under his straight, generous nose, blending naturally with his ruddy complexion and green eyes. He carried his broad-framed body well, suggesting he might have once been an athlete.

His wife, Helga, was a heavy-set, matronly looking lady with gentle manners, and she projected warmth and friendliness. She also was an excellent cook. While some German and Polish dishes were similar, I especially enjoyed her *sauerbraten* and *schnitzels*. She and my mother liked each other, and our families spent a good deal of social time together.

Heinrich was a year younger than I. He inherited his mother's looks but managed to stay slim. He had dirty blond hair that spilled over his forehead, forcing him to constantly run his hand through it or tilt his head backwards to keep his hair out of his eyes. He had a habit of squinting, which made him look nervous.

We used to spend hours playing war games of every variation. As soon as a new game arrived in our neighborhood stationery and variety store, it immediately became part of our vast inventory. Another passion we shared was bicycle riding. We frequently took long trips together, racing and riding side-by-side. Our constant companionship annoyed my little brother, who felt left out.

Heinrich was aware of my attraction for his sister. He was jealous of the attention we gave each other, but he didn't interfere. He was even occasionally helpful in arranging for our privacy.

Isa was not a beauty. Her best feature was her long, blond hair falling loosely down to her hips. She was a great athlete and was built like one. Her body was firm but was full of female sensuality. On the rare occasions when we did have privacy, we explored each other's bodies, though we never crossed the line. Even at moments when we got carried away by passion, she managed to have her thighs deflect my caresses before they reached their target area. The more frustrated I became with the futility of my advances, the more hopeful I became at the promise she held for me. Alas, the brutal reality of life interfered with our relationship and put an end to our romance.

The Poles of German origin were known as the *Volksdeutsche*. Members of the younger set joined the singing societies and social clubs, which—with varying degrees of subtlety—served as recruitment centers for Hitler's expansionist plans. German minority organizations in Poland and other countries formed a so-called fifth column, which actively helped the Third Reich in conquering those nations. There hadn't yet been any official declarations of changing loyalties in Lodz, but a fifth column had been created beneath the surface. Young Polish Germans found themselves progressively more and more cultivated by agents of the Third Reich. While Oscar and my father continued their business relationship, the families ceased socializing with each other. Although we never spoke about it, I understood that both Heinrich and Isa had to—or chose to—join one of those societies. We occasionally spoke on the phone, but the intimacy was over.

My relationships with other gentile friends attending Polish schools remained cordial and unchanged. We met at sporting events or in one another's homes, clustered around the radio, listening to sport broadcasters, and rooting, of course, for the Polish national teams.

Our class averaged about thirty-five students. Some of them discontinued their studies or changed schools and would be replaced by other students, but we had a consistent core of about twenty-five students. Our faculty also remained the same, with the addition of a new teacher when our curriculum expanded to include a new subject. This created the sense of an extended family with close friendships. One group contained the top students, who bonded, studied, and played together even as they competed for scholastic recognition. Another group connected through their participation in sports activities. Another liked to hang out together just to have fun. There was some emphasis on religion, although the school was founded and supported by a secular segment of Jewish patrons. Religious holidays were observed, however, and the school was always closed on Saturdays. While we all came from well-to-do families, most of the kids belonged to Zionist organizations with socialist leanings.

My father supported the General Zionist Party, which aimed to build a capitalist system in Palestine through the use of investments and commerce. I favored the Revisionist Party, which endorsed the economic principles of the General Zionists but firmly believed in military training of its members as potential freedom fighters for a Jewish state. The Party didn't oppose peaceful means. But it had no faith in British generosity toward the Jews at the end of its Palestine mandate, knowing that Britain favored Arab interests. We believed the Arabs must be confronted by determination and strength.

The founder of the party Betar was Vladimir Jabotynski. His vision and aggressive policy appealed to me more than the passive approach of most of the other parties. He was constantly urging the Polish Jewry to immigrate to Palestine. He foresaw the danger looming on the horizon in Poland and predicted the physical extinction of Jews at the hands of Hitler. He was ridiculed as a prophet of doom and rejected by the unsuspecting, well-to-do Jewish community deeply rooted in the Polish environment, as well as by the Orthodox community waiting for the Messiah to lead the Jews to the Promised Land. Jabotynski's prophetic vision became a sad and devastating reality.

His deputy and successor was Menachem Begin, the future prime minister of Israel. Our opponents labeled us as rebels, fascists, and rabble-rousers. I found it prudent not to confess my political choice to my father. But, as usual whenever I attempted to withhold the truth from him, it caused me embarrassment and trouble. My brother Ignac found my Betar uniform hidden under my bed. He chose to show it to my father at dinnertime in order to get even with me for something I had done to him. This time, instead of punishing me, my father asked me to discuss, rationalize, and defend my choice. At the same time, he was disappointed that I kept my membership in Betar secret. This meant I didn't trust him to respect my views and convictions, he said. I argued my case for Betar with enthusiasm, and although he stuck to his own convictions, he respected my right to differ.

My circle of close friends changed only slightly over the course of my time in school. We did our homework together and read books voraciously. Our favorite authors, whose books were translated into Polish, were Jack London, Karl May, and James Fennimore Cooper and the stories of American conquest of the West. My favorite book was *An American Tragedy* by Theodore Dreiser. We frequented movies, played bridge, and created an amateur band using primitive instruments to play jazz tunes from American movies. Our favorite piece was "Alexander's Ragtime Band." We really had fun and enjoyed one another's company.

My Gymnazium classmates in 1935 with our teacher Mrs. Perelman. I'm front row, second left, with Ben Markowicz leaning on me

Ben Rosen and I used to spend hours together flirting on the phone with girls of our sister school. We skated with them in winter at the ice rink at a park called Helenowek, and we double-dated. It was all quite innocent, although Ben and I did lose our virginity. It happened to me just before my fifteenth birthday, when my family left for a picnic in the park and I stayed home with one of my frequent sore throats. Our Polish governess-housekeeper Kazia, who was thirty, brought non-alcoholic eggnog cough medicine into my room and sat down next to my bed while I drank. Kazia and I were very close. We spent time together playing cards, and I read poetry and novels to her and discussed my progress in school. She introduced me to several variations of solitaire, which helped me later in life in moments of solitude and reflection.

At one point, she left the room and returned with my freshly washed and ironed pajamas. She pointedly said, "I noticed you're having erotic dreams at night." She smiled at me knowingly, took off her dress, removed her brassiere, and slipped under the covers next to me.

The afternoon was set ablaze with our total abandon. She guided me skillfully into a new and exciting dimension of life, opening her voluptuous thirty-year-old body to my waves of passion over and over again. She set the pace of our lovemaking by controlling my youthful eagerness in order to maximize the experience for both of us. I wanted the afternoon to never end, and when she finally slipped out of bed, I felt dejected. Later, when I had rested and had time to reflect on the afternoon's events, an overwhelming feeling of gratitude, wonder, and happiness replaced my initial disappointment. The next night, I snuck behind the curtain of the alcove where she slept, ready to resume my newly discovered bliss. She gently refused, saying, "Yesterday was my gift to you for your fifteenth birthday tomorrow. I hope you'll remember and treasure it when you go on to find companions who will also share their bodies with you. Happy Birthday, my boy." My disappointment returned. Only much later did I understand the deeper meaning of her precious gift that broke the border between my childhood and adolescence.

I developed a close friendship with Moniek Szapowal, who also was a member of Betar. He lived only a few blocks from my home in a quiet neighborhood, across from the palace owned by the Poznanskis, one of the richest Jewish industrial families in Lodz. There were several of these palatial residencies owned by the top echelon of the wealthy German and Jewish manufacturing giants. When Moniek left for Palestine with his family, it came as a blow to me and created a void that was hard to fill. Their departure also made an impact on my parents.

The winds of danger blowing from the West put us on alert. Anticipation of war with Germany and the vicious Nazi anti-Semitic propaganda, which was effective in certain segments of the Polish population, filled us with uncertainty for our future. Our uneasiness was intensified by the emigration of my uncle Felix, who liquidated his thriving business in Bremen and left Germany for Palestine.

* * *

Leaving Poland became a priority for my mother. Her awareness of rising anti-Semitism and her concern for her sons' future made her urge my father to seek ways to emigrate. It was a very difficult decision. We felt patriotic and rooted in Polish culture. Polish was our primary language; Polish history, literature, theatre, and art were the basis of our intellectual lives. But although we had many reasons to stay, we also had a number of reasons to go. The death of my maternal grandfather relieved my mother from the responsibility of caring for him and providing a home for him. With the factory destroyed by fire and the small plant that replaced it too insignificant, there was little to hold us back.

Under pressure from my mother, my father went to Paris to consult with her youngest brother, Uncle Emile. He was quite wealthy by then and well-connected with the British consulate in Warsaw, where his firm also maintained an office. Father returned enthusiastic about the prospect of being granted visas under the quota assigned to capitalists who would build and manage industrial enterprises in Palestine. Uncle Emile would put up the required sum of English pounds as a guarantee. Although this was a loan, the papers would say that my uncle's payment to my father was an outright gift.

When the bureaucratic process had run its course, my uncle refused to sign the papers. Later, Mother found out that it was my uncle's wife, Lucy, who was responsible for her husband's refusal. The British consulate suggested to my father that he apply as a technical expert with a smaller sum of a collateral deposit and the machinery of his shop. With his technical knowledge, this would help start a factory. But by the time the snail-paced bureaucracy finalized the paperwork, my father had passed the allowed age limit for this category. Our attempt to leave Poland remained unfulfilled.

My father was not only extremely disappointed, but he also considered Uncle Emile's refusal a personal affront to his personal integrity. Never did it cross his mind not to repay the loan. Honesty was an integral part of his personality. Once, his playboy-partner asked him to sign a false statement so the partner could get money to cover his personal gambling debts. When my father refused, his partner pulled out a gun and threatened to drive him into bankruptcy. "I would rather be dead than bankrupt," my father yelled. He crushed a chair over the man's head. "You don't have the guts to pull the trigger. Get out of my sight!"

It was painful for all of us to see this once proud and courageous man lose interest in life and slowly capitulate to apathy and sickness. He became a man with a broken heart.

My mother, too, was crushed. She contacted her other brother in the United States, Uncle Maurice, to explore the possibility of moving to America. Since the Polish immigration quota had the longest waiting list, our chances to qualify were miniscule. Uncle Maurice had always communicated with my mother frequently, and his efforts now were directed toward securing a student visa for me. In the meantime, we continued our normal lives.

A close friendship with my classmate Haim Grynbaum lasted throughout our school days. Haim came from a well-to-do family. His three brothers and sister were quite a bit older than he, so the two of us spent a lot of time together. Haim was good-looking, with a swarthy complexion, smiling black eyes, and a crown of dark black hair that fell freely over his forehead. He used to tilt his head sideways in a rakish manner. He was only slightly taller than I, so we were always next to each other in our gym exercises or pre-military training at school, bringing up the rear.

We were both good at the pre-military training and quickly earned the required certificates for sharpshooting and excellence in sports. At first, the training was our only exposure to military exercises. The high status of our school exempted us from the compulsory military service—and Jews were generally unwelcome as officers anyway. Upon graduation, we were entitled to enter the Polish Officer's School instead.

Haim and I lived very close to each other and always walked to and from school together. We had another routine, too. We would get end pieces of salami and other end pieces that the finest delicatessen stores would give away. We would then find a Polish liquor merchant to cajole into selling us miniature bottles of vodka called *szczeniaczki* (puppies) despite our underage status. We would eat the meat and drink the vodka in one of the arched entrances of a nearby building. This clandestine and delightful activity was our only vice. We rarely smoked cigarettes, except for a puff now and then. It was mostly to show off when we walked the main drag, the *deptak*, on Piotrkowska Street, eyeing and flirting with pretty schoolgirls.

Haim Grynbaum, Sasha Rubashkin, and me in paramilitary training in Lodz, 1937, holding our Mauser rifles.

Another close friend, Benek Markowicz, was a fine basketball player on our school team. He lived near the school, and I often visited him after a game. We played hard, coached by our gym teacher Mr. Zajde, who inspired and occasionally disciplined us on and off the court. We didn't look forward to routine exercises in gym class, but we were enthusiastic about soccer and basketball. Benek's mother was very kind to me and encouraged our friendship. She always greeted us with glasses of cool lemonade when we came home exhausted and thirsty after a game or practice.

I also developed a close friendship with the Szladkowski brothers, Heniek and Abek. Heniek was my age, while Abek was Ignac's age. They attended a textile Gimnazium, which prepared them to enter the textile industry, the most sought-after profession in our town. Our families rented summer homes from Polish peasants in the same village. We kids had a wonderful time. Heniek was a short-distance runner and took part in our city's 100-meter championships with distinction. We all enjoyed cycling and became quite good at it. We competed against other kids in the village athletic festival, which was arranged by a group of sport-minded parents. After competing, we would meet at the swimming hole of the river that flowed through the outskirts of the village. Some of the local youngsters joined us "city boys" frolicking in the water, some of them in the nude, including local girls.

It was after one of these games that I walked home with our landlord's niece. Ania was no older than fifteen, of slim build, her body just beginning to reach womanhood and yet retaining the innocence of youth. She was in constant motion, leaping, hopping, and skipping, chatting incessantly, and always laughing. We found ourselves in a hedged-off part of a meadow when she suddenly stopped and kissed me full on the lips. I put my arms around her and drew her close. She wiggled out of the embrace, said "Later," and flew off like a bird to see to her evening chores, which included feeding the animals, milking the cows, and preparing supper for her family.

Later that evening, we met at the meadow. She beckoned me to a secluded spot and looked at me coquettishly, whispering, "You saw me naked at the river. Now I want to see you naked." As I stripped off my clothes, she removed her shirt and dropped her wraparound skirt on the grass. We explored each other with curiosity and wonder before our bodies joined in a tight embrace. The grass, cool under the outspread skirt, contrasted with the heat emanating from our bodies. The sweet smell of milk and the animals Ania exuded created an earthy fragrance that titillated my senses. I tried to remember the lessons I learned from Kazia, my sexual mentor. I discovered it wasn't necessary, since

Ania overwhelmed me with her passion. Her virgin body arched upward, and she emitted only a slight whimper.

The sky above us, lit by a bright moon, a million stars, and a chorus of crickets accompanying our lovemaking, made the evening as perfect and romantic as one could ever dream of. When Ania's breasts stopped heaving and our breaths returned to normal, we lay quietly, linked by embrace and overwhelmed by the enormity of our action. We slowly gathered our clothes, dressed quietly, and returned to our respective homes. We never repeated our encounter, and after the summer ended, we never saw each other again. For me, the experience had been a marvelous addition to growing up and was a memory to behold. I often wondered what fate had chosen for her, always wishing her well.

Some summers when we did not rent a country home, my mother would travel to Krynica, one of the health resorts in southern Poland located in the beautiful Carpathian Mountains, or she would go to Ciechocinek, north of Warsaw. Some of these spas were of international fame. My father would join her for short stays. My brother Ignac would go to summer camps organized and supervised by the school. I spent most summers with my mother's younger cousin and namesake, Mala Frydlender, in Kalisz, one of the oldest cities dating to the beginning of Poland's history located on the banks of the Prosna River. It served as a stopover on the old trading route that connected the Baltic Sea with the southern part of Poland and beyond.

The Skowrons were another family I visited. Herman was the cousin of my aunt Mania, the wife of Uncle Izydor. Herman's wife Natalia, whom we called Nadzia, was one of the most elegant women I had ever encountered. She had light brown hair, done in the latest style, the bluest eyes over the straightest nose, and generous but delicate lips, which made her oval-shaped face a portrait of beauty. She was quiet and always dressed in elegant and fashionable clothing, which nicely emphasized her modest bust, slim hips, and shapely legs. She was the essence of the woman I wished to marry when I grew up.

My secret desire made me very shy in her presence. I did not want her or anyone to discover my fantasy. Her older daughter Tola inherited her beauty and was the most popular girl at school parties. She was my brother's age. Nadzia's younger daughter Ada was extremely talented, and from early on she chose to focus on dance as her primary interest in life. She was also pretty in the adorable way little girls frequently are. She looked more like her father, with dark eyes and hair, and she had his swarthy complexion on her oval-shaped face.

Those summers away from home were extremely pleasant, full of fun, with a great deal of love and attention lavished upon me. I learned how to be a gracious guest. It helped me later in life, when I depended on the hospitality of others in strange circumstances and environments.

I had a relatively small number of teachers in my eleven years of school. In the early years, most of them were women. They were stern with us, living up to the task of forming our characters, or, as they preferred to say, "breaking us into becoming good human beings."

As we advanced, a male teacher became our educator—a combination guide, councilor, homeroom teacher, and den parent. An educator was solely responsible for us, involved in all problems facing the class and in an individual student's behavior and progress. For several years, Dr. Tauber filled that position. His subject was Latin, not one of my favorite subjects.

Mrs. Perelman, the wife of our school's director, taught geography. She carried herself with authority and made us work hard. I excelled when called upon to interpret the cosmos. I boasted about it at home, expecting the highest grade for my effort. Then, when the quarterly grades were posted, I received a failing grade. I insisted that my father confront the teacher and protest the injustice that had been inflicted upon me. Upon his return home, he relayed a message from Mrs. Perelman: "I consider your son an average student, bright but on the lazy side. His last performance convinced me that he can do more and earn better than the average grades he makes, and that's why I failed him." I got the message, which served as an incentive to end the year with the second-best grade in geography. Little did I know at the time that geography would become the basis of my future professional career.

Dr. Spektor taught social and political science. I enjoyed his classes, especially political science. The depth of his knowledge and the interesting way in which he delivered his lectures fascinated me. He enjoyed a wonderful rapport with the class. We got to know more about the United States and its Constitution, history, and political system. We probably knew more about America than the average American student did. He taught us about other countries and regions of the world with the same vigor and detail.

The Hebrew classes had two teachers. One, Mr. Luboszycki, taught Hebrew language, literature, and grammar. He was the oldest member of the faculty and a scholar in his field. To us, he was more like an amiable uncle than a demanding teacher. He was very generous in grading his students and would never fail any of us.

He did me a great favor. Everyone in our class had a Polish and Hebrew first name. Alexander was my only name, I didn't have a Hebrew name. It subjected me to ridicule until, during our Jewish history lesson, Mr. Luboszycki explained the origin of it. After Alexander the Great captured Jerusalem in 332

BC, he ordered his sculptured bust to be placed in the Great Temple, as was the conqueror's custom. The then-reigning Great Chaplain explained the Jewish concept of belief in one spiritual God, with no images allowed in the temple. In order to honor the benevolent conqueror, he offered to name every firstborn that year Alexander. My stature and popularity among my classmates increased after this explanation.

These were the mentors who shaped our minds and spirits in preparation for further study and adulthood. These were the shepherds who brought us, their flock, to the threshold of a new beginning on the hot June day of graduation. We shed our distinctive six-cornered caps and navy-blue blazers with sleeves proudly displaying maroon shields sporting our school No. 202, embroidered in silver thread. Thus we bid farewell to our adolescence. I could not foresee that when I separated from most of my classmates, it would be forever.

CHAPTER 3

1939

The summer of 1939 was full of nervous tension and the anticipation of bad things to come. Our apartment became crowded with the arrivals of Uncle Felix's wife's sister, Erna, and a cousin from Bremen, Germany, whom my parents provided with shelter and food. Ignac and I vacated our room and beds for them, sharing the large flat sofa in the living room as our new sleeping quarters. They were part of the newest group, thousands upon thousands of refugees created by Hitler's Nuremberg Laws directed against German Jews and other "non-Ayrans." To most of them, this development was a doubly humiliating experience. Proud of their history as loyal and patriotic citizens throughout many generations, considering themselves German first and foremost, they were devastated when they found themselves relegated to simply being Jews. To top it all, as refugees, they were now dependent on the hospitality of the Eastern Jews, whom they had somewhat looked down upon. The fact that they were received with compassion and kindness drove their humiliation even deeper.

* * *

The increasing sense of danger and fear of the unknown brought Ignac and me closer to each other. At family gatherings, we listened to the heated discussions about the imminent war and the potential danger from our own Polish compatriots. Some Poles were influenced by the Nazis' poisonous anti-Semitic propaganda and had adapted a more hostile attitude toward Jews. We anticipated a German invasion. We were hardly heartened by the pronouncement of Polish Marshal Edward Rydz-Smigly that Poles would fight with all their might—and, pointing to his tunic, that "we won't give even a button to the enemy."

Some of our extended family members thought we would be safer if we moved together to the countryside. Others felt we should all congregate in Lodz. But the idea of uprooting had little appeal to anyone. These discussions made Ignac and me more agitated, and for the first time we thought of our future with a sense of foreboding. We realized how much we loved and depended on each other. We promised that we would not separate no matter what happened.

Toward the end of August, the war frenzy became very real. Ditches were dug in open spaces between buildings as makeshift protection against expected bombing from the air. Each city block selected air spotters to warn the inhabitants of enemy air raids. We were moving inexorably toward war, which became a reality at dawn on September 1. It was the beginning of the War of all Wars.

The Polish infantry and the revered and acclaimed Polish cavalry were no match for the highly motorized German assault troops and air force. Fighting was sporadic, in some places heroic, but the Germans advanced quickly in their sudden attack and subsequent conquest of western Poland.

There was no fighting in Lodz. It was considered a German enclave. We watched with awe and fascination the orderly takeover by the motorized troops and units of the infantry whose uniforms were still unscathed by battle. Their heavy boots beating against the cobblestone streets emitted sounds of arrogance and conquest, accentuated by the singing voices of the marching troops reverberating against the gray walls of the city buildings.

On September 17, the Soviet army marched in to occupy the eastern part of the country. Once more, Poland became the prey of its powerful neighbors.

Curfew announcements and various proclamations appeared at news kiosks at street corners and on building walls. Our city, our lives, and our peace and sense of normalcy and security became a distant past. We were in the mighty clasp of an enemy, defeated, confused, and fearful. Jews became an early target of restrictions and harassment, dragged off the streets or from their apartments to perform heavy work furnishing and organizing the conquerors' newly requisitioned offices and apartments. Our apartment was located in a quiet section of the town, outside the prestigious center, and in that sense we considered ourselves fortunate. Yet a knock on the front door became a most dreaded sound. Gusta, our new housekeeper, would open the door so we boys would not be visible and become primary targets for forced labor.

Gusta had replaced Kazia, her cousin, who had returned to the village to marry. Gusta decided to stay on with us through the uncertainty. She really had no place to go and was loyal to our family, which over the years had treated her as one of our own.

It had been common for peasants from the countryside to sell their fresh produce to particular households, and we were lucky that ours was one of them. They knew and liked Gusta, and this made it easier for our family to face the hardship of getting food supplies. She would get freshly baked rye bread at the neighborhood bakery, where the owner was an old friend of hers. But one day, the local German unit requisitioned the owner's entire output, and Gusta came home empty-handed. As she shed her street clothes, there was a knock on the door. She opened it to face a German infantry soldier in his early forties. Frightened, acting on a reflex, she tried to slam the door shut, but she was a moment too late as he already had his foot in the door. Without a word, he handed her two loaves of freshly baked bread, turned around, and left. He must have followed Gusta from the bakery and decided to give her the bread for reasons known only to him. When she relayed this incident to the family, we were flabbergasted as well as grateful for this act of humanity in an inhumane world.

However, another knock on the door the following day shook that newly gained belief in humanity. This time, as the door opened, the figure of a Gestapo officer filled the space. He stepped into the hall, followed by a teenager wearing the brown shirt with a white, red, and black swastika armband on his sleeve. The youth directed the officer to the room I was in, pointed at me, and said in German, "That's him." When I looked up, I met the squinting eyes of Heinrich Bohnig, my playmate and friend, my old inseparable buddy. He had not changed much except for the look on his face projecting arrogance and cruelty. I was too shocked to react, to utter a word, before the Gestapo officer grabbed my arm and pushed me toward the front door of the apartment. I turned my neck to see Heinrich, only to earn the first blow to my head, delivered with authority by my Gestapo captor. We rounded the corner of the street and turned right, where we entered the building that used to serve as the city's minor-security prison for those awaiting trial. Before another Gestapo officer took charge of me, I managed to steal a glance at Heinrich. He was pointing to another name on a list he held in his hand. He looked up at me, swiped back his dirty blond hair by jerking his head in the familiar, endearing gesture I always remembered, squinted his eyes, and smiled at me with an expression that I still cannot understand and will never forget. Many times during the war, I hoped to come across him in combat so I could erase that smile from his face, in defiance of the promise I gave to my grandfather never to let hatred enter my heart.

The Gestapo sergeant supervising our workforce emphasized cruelty over efficiency. When I was unable to single-handedly move a large, heavy wardrobe, he resorted to fist and truncheon blows to my body, ignoring the fact that the piece could not fit through the door anyway. The beatings I sustained that day took just a few days to heal but were never forgotten.

The relief of my return home that evening was short-lived. Once I was "discovered," my services became routine, and various Gestapo officers would frequently pick me up and deliver me to my next place of forced labor. As unhappy as it made me, I was thankful that Ignac was spared this indignity and pain.

The one day that engraved itself in my memory was when I was taken to the new Gestapo headquarters located in the brand new building that my school had just built for itself. It was ironic to have the Gestapo select its headquarters in a Jewish school.

My escort brought me to the spacious entrance hall. There, to my surprise, I found my teachers—the familiar figures of Drs. Pines, Bretholz, and Berglas—crouching on their knees and scrubbing the floor. I didn't know whose perverted mind made them do this, but it left me with shame for their degradation as human beings, educators, role models, and community leaders. My task of emptying and refilling the buckets of dirty water for them added to my embarrassment. I muttered an apology to them and had to force back my tears. They looked at me with kindness and gratitude for this tiny expression of respect in the flowing sea of dirty slop. I managed not to cry that day, but as time passed I could not stop myself, and I would not force back the memory.

The first few days of November were filled with wild rumors. The November 11 holiday marking the anniversary of Poland's independence was rapidly approaching. The Germans started rounding up the youth, fearful of potential demonstrations. My father decided to send me to Warsaw to hide out with some distant relatives and avoid being taken away. He also contacted a professional smuggler to get me—as soon as feasible—across the new border between German-occupied and Russian-occupied Poland. I insisted on Ignac coming with me, but our father exercised his authority, forbidding us even to think about it. As a younger youth, Ignac was less exposed to the dangers than I was, and even though he was physically well-developed, his youthful appearance kept him out of Gestapo roundups for daily chores of hard labor.

We were crestfallen and disconsolate. All of a sudden we were to part, our protests notwithstanding. Our father, seeing our disappointment, promised that once I got settled he would try to have Ignac join me. His friend and distributor Mr. Melamud, from Lwow (which is now in the Russian zone), owed my father many favors and a substantial amount of money, and my father believed he would be able and willing to help. But our mother did not endorse this plan. We knew that she would never agree to let both of her sons go. In moments of tenderness, she would cuddle me, saying, "This war is forcing you into manhood, but you are still a baby, my very own little boy." It was reassuring to feel the unrestricted flow of her love, enveloping me into a blanket of warmth in a world that suddenly had turned cold and threatening.

It was cold and rainy that early morning of November 8, when, risking a curfew violation, we crept into the horse-drawn carriage waiting outside our building. A friendly coachman whom we had used for many years had agreed to share the risk. He shook the reins, starting us on a journey to the bus depot on Ogrodowa Street. There we were to meet my older maternal cousin Mietek Przedecki, a practicing attorney, to chaperone me on my trip to Warsaw and beyond.

The curfew was ending by the time we approached the terminal. To our surprise, hundreds of people had already arrived, eager to leave the city. It took us some time to find my cousin, who had managed to land a front spot at the boarding platform. We started bidding our good-byes as the first bus approached. Ignac embraced me briefly and yielded me to my mother. She held me to her chest and whispered into my ear all the things mothers normally do. "Be careful, don't take chances, listen to Mietek, and stay in touch, I love you, I'll miss you, and I'll watch over you, always." Not for a second did I doubt her assurances. I said "I love you, Mama" and kissed her. At that moment the bus door opened and the crowd surged forward. Someone stepped on my heel, pulling off my *galasha*. Mietek grabbed my hand and pulled me toward the door. I slipped my hand free and turned to my father. He looked forlorn, reached over to me, and kissed me with tears running down his face. His lips were trembling as they met mine. That was the last physical touch we exchanged and my last vivid memory of him. I never forgot that wordless parting from my father. The vibration of his kiss stays with me and will for the rest of my living days.

As the bus swallowed me into its crowded belly, I managed one last glimpse of my family standing in the soaking rain, shrunken with pain, tearful and reflective of the sacrifice the war imposed upon them. Their first-born son and brother was leaving in a world torn by conflict and filled with cruelty that would reach a level surpassing anything known to mankind.

I stood in the aisle of the jam-packed bus, watching the other passengers and trying to guess who they were and what they did prior to this journey. Somehow, the uncertainty of my own situation became less acute. At one point, I even chuckled remembering the loss of my right-foot galosh. I bent down, stripped off the left one, and threw it out of the partially open window.

All of a sudden, in Lowicz, the bus started slowing down until it came to a full stop. A motorcycle crew of two German Wehrmacht soldiers stood astride the road, motioning the driver to come forward. The automatic weapons trained at him made us feel panicky. The thought occurred to me that they might have seen an object thrown out of the bus and wanted to investigate it and punish us. Some bus riders started praying aloud, while others froze in terror of a possible execution. We all knew that the predominantly Jewish group on the bus would be the first target of a German assault. To our great surprise and relief, the soldiers didn't seem interested in the passengers. All they wanted was for the driver to siphon off some gas for their motorcycle, which had run out of its own.

As we left the outskirts of Lowicz, prayers of thanksgiving filled the bus and smiles appeared on some faces. When Warsaw came into sight, more smiles appeared, ending our journey on a happy note. What a good omen, I thought. The face and words of my mother—"I will watch over you"—flashed before me. I felt confident to face tomorrow.

My two-week stay in Warsaw was uneventful. I stayed with relatives of Aunt Mania. Most of the days and evenings were spent meeting with other relatives, discussing the uncertain future, trying to guess what would be happening, planning how to secure enough food, and researching our forthcoming trip. The city was teaming with activities, crowded by loads of refugees coming in daily from other towns and villages. I tried to avoid crowds and had little interest in the pulsating life of the city. I was missing my parents, but most of all my little brother Ignac. I became passive and remorseful, anticipating the journey to the East and the crossing of yet another border, another change in my young life.

CHAPTER 4

THE BORDER

One of my youthful fascinations was to listen to the conversations of adults, especially the stories of my parents and members of the family and friends whom they entertained. The stories included reminiscences about their life's experiences and those of their parents and grandparents, spanning over one hundred years of Poland's occupation by Prussia, Russia, and Austria until the modern State of Poland was born in 1918. Many of the stories dealt with the Russians, their habits, their good and bad characteristics, and their history. I developed a somewhat confusing perception of them as good-natured but extremely anti-Semitic.

I was told that Jews were widely persecuted in Russia, denied basic human rights, and were subjected to outbreaks of violence during pogroms under the Czarist rule. After the 1917 revolution, when Russia became the Soviet Union, anti-Semitism was officially suppressed. Yet there remained an undercurrent of resentment against Jews in powerful state positions. Throughout history, in every economic downturn, Russian nationalism soared, and Jews became the scapegoats and subject to violent hatred.

Other stories described the proverbial Russian fondness for music, song, and dance. This stood in contrast to some Russians' slave-like dependence on vodka that brought a malaise of drunkenness, causing them to be moody and romantic. They spoke of the bitterness of oppression, first by the Czars and followed by communist rulers. The severe climate under which most of Russians lived added to the strain of hard living conditions. Severe cold caused them to be lazy, unreliable, and, in order to survive, devious and cunning.

It was no wonder that listening to all these descriptions, anecdotes, and stories, I had developed a negative image of the Russians as suspicious and hostile to strangers with an attitude of antagonism and a contrarian trait bordering on cruelty. Now, after eighteen years of blissful innocence of a sheltered life under the protective wings of my family, I would be compelled to put this image to a test.

As 1939 ended, the time to leave Warsaw came upon us. My parents secured the services of professional smugglers. Mietek and I started on a clandestine journey to the small village near Belzec, on the German side of the new border, which divided the German- and Russian-occupied parts of Poland. We traveled by day, sometimes by night—always disguised in peasant clothing—and used local trains, hired lorries, and peasant horse-driven hay carts, offering bribes all along the way to our destination. At Belzec, the local Polish peasants profited by smuggling groups of people across the border under the cover of night with varied degrees of success. Our group's attempt to avoid the German patrols ended successfully.

On the Russian side of the border, Red Army border guards apprehended us. They led us to a small village, where they herded us into a large barn with other refugees to await the dawn of a new day.

Although there were some Poles and Ukrainians among us, most of the refugees were Jews trying to escape the Nazi menace to find safe shelter and establish a new temporary existence until Poland became free again. Most of the non-Jews were returning soldiers of the Polish Army whose homes were in the eastern part of Poland. The barn filled up to more than two hundred people, including entire families. It buzzed with all kinds of gossip and speculation about our immediate fate. The prevailing hope was that we would be directed to various parts in the Soviet zone. Mietek rehearsed with me the information that he said I must remember and stick to if I were questioned. As a lawyer, he coached me as he would a client: I had to remember the name and address of my father's friend in Lwow, who would provide me with living quarters; details regarding his occupation; and certain information about my family and myself. He urged me not to disclose my father's background as a capitalist factory owner. I was to assume the identity of someone coming from a working proletarian family. Thus equipped, I would be prepared to qualify for what Mietek saw as my way to safety and freedom from German persecution.

The morning arrived. Soldiers of the border unit of the Red Army brought in a long, plain wooden table and three chairs, positioning them at the barn's huge double door. Soon, a lieutenant and two second lieutenants entered the barn and sat in the chairs prepared for them, facing the anxious and hopeful mass. They motioned to the people to approach the table in three single lines, each facing one of the officers. Their smiles made them seem friendly at first, but I saw no smiles in their eyes. The lieutenant sitting in the middle spoke Russian only. His comrade to the left must have been Jewish, as he spoke Yiddish in addition to Russian and German, while the one on the right spoke Polish and Ukrainian. There was a lot of shuffling in the lines once the respective knowledge of the various languages of the interrogators became obvious to us. We could hear and follow the questioning process. "What's your name?" "Where are you from?" "Why did you cross the border?" " How much money do you have?" "Where would you live?"

Vast majority of answers were predictably identical. "We are Jewish and are afraid of the Germans." "We admire the Soviet Union." "We will be productive workers." "We don't carry much money, but we will live with friends until we get established." And so on.

Patterns started developing. I looked around and noticed that most of those interviewed were sent outside the barn to an area heavily guarded by a platoon of soldiers. Two of the soldiers held fierce German shepherds on tight leashes as they walked the perimeter of the assembly area. A few were directed to another area with only two soldiers, who were relaxed and chatting with some of the refugees. Back in the barn, I watched the officers carefully and decided to make my way toward the Polish-speaking second lieutenant. There was something about the other two that made me uneasy. Their smiles seemed insincere, and the way they avoided eye contact with those appearing before them filled me with trepidation and suspicion. I started listening intently to the questions and answers and the subsequent assignment to the respective groups. I was looking for hints and nuances that would possibly guide me when my turn for questioning arrived. My intuition told me I had better avoid falling into the larger of the two groups outside. I shared my observation with Mietek. He scoffed at me and insisted we proceed according to the routine we rehearsed.

We edged forward, and there I was facing the Polish-speaking officer, the red star with a golden hammer and sickle adorning his olive-green cap, resting slightly askew on his head, giving him a boyish look. I was surprised how young he was, no more than one or two years my senior. He looked up at me and started asking the expected questions about my name and age, which I answered unemotionally. For a split of a second, I glanced sideways to see Mietek being waved on to join the larger group outside. I couldn't explain what made me feel that way, but suddenly I knew with unshakable certainty that I would never see him again.

I looked my interviewer straight in the eye and reversed my rehearsed routine. "I was caught at the border trying to leave the Soviet Union to join my family in Lodz," I said.

Surprised, he asked me, "Aren't you Jewish?"

"Yes, I am," I answered.

"Don't you know the Nazis don't like Jews? Aren't you afraid?"

"It doesn't matter. I'm missing my family, they are missing me, and we would like to be together," I answered stubbornly, all the time thinking of the chance I was taking in being caught in a lie.

"Then why did you leave them in the first place, and what were you doing on this side of the border? Don't you like the Soviet Union?" he asked, his head cocked to the side, his eyes narrowed with suspicion.

"I studied at the University of Lwow, staying with my father's friend," I rattled on.

"What did you study?"

"Medicine."

"That's a very useful choice. Doctors are always in demand. You should go back to study."

"But I miss my family and don't like being alone."

"Maybe you don't like us Russians, heh? In the Soviet Union, you will never be alone. We are one big, friendly family. Don't play clever with me. You are going back where you came from," he said angrily, and with a wave of his hand he dismissed me. The fear of overplaying my gambit disappeared when he turned to the next person in line without giving me a second look. I was escorted to the smaller group, and a few hours later, sitting in a horse-driven hay wagon, I was on my way to Rawa Ruska, from where I continued to Lwow. My intuition had paid off. I had remembered my relatives' stories and gambled on the "contrarian" part of the Russian character. I thanked my father for all those wonderful times he had let me sit in on his adult conversations and storytelling sessions. I felt elated that I had negotiated what I thought would be my way to safety, even though I had relied on lying, which defied my father's teachings. I did not yet realize that I had even negotiated my ticket for survival and had traded the loss of my youth and innocence. I was on my own; I crossed the border leaving behind the protective wings of my parents. All I had left were their images, love, prayers, and hope.

Seeing Mietek in the large group, which had been forced back to the no-man's-land between the borders, and eventually to the German side, tormented me for a very long time. After the war, I learned of his internment in the death camp of Auschwitz (Oswiecim), where he perished. Many years later, when I visited the Auschwitz-Birkenau Camp, passing through the arched portals with the overhead sign containing the cynical words "Arbeit Macht Frei" ("Work Makes You Free"), the enormity of the Nazi crimes hit me. I realized there was no limit to man's inhumanity to man. To think that in that camp alone, a million and a half defenseless people, mostly Jews, were systematically murdered after being stripped of their dignity, clothing, luggage, jewelry, shoes, and spectacles, with their hair and gold fillings from their teeth systematically collected, is beyond the scope of human imagination.

CHAPTER 5

INNOCENCE AND FREEDOM LOST

"So you are Wladek's son." Those were the first words I heard from my father's distributor and friend upon my arrival in Lwow. Somehow, for reasons not clear to me, I took an immediate dislike to this small, shriveled man, with a balding head, narrow eyes, and thin lips.

His lips parted in a warm smile, however, conveying a sense of welcome and kindness. He was widowed and lived alone in the very center of the city. At that time his apartment was a bit crowded, as my older cousin Bolek, son of Uncle Moryc, and Salek, husband of cousin Hela, were both staying there. I was given a folding army cot to sleep on, to which I adjusted without a problem. Each day, Mr. Malamud would give us an assortment of silk stockings from my father's supply to be sold at the city bazaar, which was located behind the beautiful Catholic Church adjacent to City Hall. Every day, huge crowds milled about, looking for all kinds of merchandise. The Russians, both men and women, were eager to buy anything, since they had been deprived for so many years of even the simplest clothing, not to mention certain food and household items.

Silk stockings were the hottest items and brought in a decent income, which I had to pass on to my host against my room and board, retaining a small commission. I immediately spent it all on chocolates and cookies, for which I had developed an irresistible craving. The value of money as a means of survival, a source of wealth, or as a status symbol had not yet penetrated my psyche. That was still a part of my innocence lingering from a protected life. My contact with Bolek and Salek was almost non-existent, as they used their free time to play cards with our host. I felt lonely, in a strange city with no friends, no school to go to, and no family to communicate with, except for messages delivered by strangers, with my mother's loving words written on her thin, scented stationery. It made me feel that much more lonely and unhappy. I abandoned my career as a salesman and took a job as a so-called black laborer, or menial worker, removing rubble from bombed-out buildings. Somehow, physical work became my preference, and for a while I enjoyed it very much. It made me feel more of a man, working with rough and tough individuals of various backgrounds and denominations as well as different political persuasions. I felt that I was joining the real world, most certainly different from my old one. I was invited to partake in the short lunch breaks with my co-workers, who treated me to vodkas as an inseparable part of the lunch. I was growing up.

In December, my cousin Romek and his two friends Sewek and Mietek arrived from Warsaw, and we decided to stick together. We found an abandoned basement in one of the damaged buildings I was working on, and, miracle of miracles, it had a heat-supplying boiler. We got hold of some discarded mattresses and blankets and set up our own "residence." We got a job loading and unloading freight cars at the railroad station. Each day's load was a surprise: coal, potatoes, hay, cabbage, machinery, and even weapons. We played a game trying to guess the load of the day with the winner getting an extra piece of cake from a local bakery, which we had adopted as our headquarters. We became acquainted with some old Polish railroad men, who convinced us to move to a suburb called Lewandowka, where most of the widows of deceased rail employees welcomed tenants who could help with finances and some household chores.

Romek and Mietek made their home with an old Jewish widow, Mrs. Fein. Sewek and I settled with a neighboring Ukrainian family of two, Mrs. Borodaykiewicz and her son Vladymir, who soon befriended me.

Vladymir was an amateur boxer, not of great renown or talent, but he liked me. I became his "coach" without any pretense of knowing the finer points of boxing. With my motivation, he maintained his mental stamina and a positive attitude, despite his losses. He boxed every Friday night.

One night he fought a Jewish opponent. I rooted for Vladymir, my protégé. The fight ended in a draw. After the fight, recognizing my loyalty to him over a fellow Jew, he invited me for a drink. Embracing me, he said, "You are a fine fellow and a true friend. I love you."

His mother set aside her disapproval of Jews in light of the growing friendship between us. She volunteered to do my laundry, by hand of course, and even managed to hug me, pulling my head into the enormous expanse of her breasts. She was missing most of her front teeth, which—to my relief—made her refrain from kissing. She and Mrs. Fein provided us with a haven, although the lives of our foursome would soon change.

But momentarily, we settled into a routine. In the early morning, we walked across open fields to the railroad depot for our work assignments. In the spring, summer, and fall, the ground had been cultivated to grow vegetables in small plots owned by the local residents. As winter took hold, the fields were covered by deep blankets of snow as far as one could see. We would trudge through the snow, sometimes playfully throwing snowballs at each other, tripping one another, becoming kids again. We also took the opportunity to relieve ourselves in the deep snow, hidden by its depth, in order to avoid the smelly outhouses in the backyards of our homes. The snow helped us to keep clean, since washing or bathing without running water created too much of a problem in our respective houses. The sensation of the cold air and snow on our private parts lent itself to all kinds of jokes.

In January 1940, the Soviet authorities in Lwow, under the auspices of NKVD—the forerunner to the KGB, the notorious all-powerful Soviet secret police—had ordered young men and women of Polish origin to report to offices set up as registration centers for resettlement to the various regions of the Soviet Union. Those who had high school or technical school education were especially "encouraged." Promises were made for continued education, good jobs, and, eventually, the "super prize," Soviet citizenship. The alternative was an uncertain status as an "undesirable element," with no job guarantees and with a not-so-thinly veiled threat of forceful resettlement or prison.

Roman registered. He had graduated from a mechanical school together with Sewek and Mietek. He settled in a small town, Bogorodsk, in the Gorky region, a city on the Oka-Volga Rivers, where he was assigned as a mechanical engineer at a regional repair center for heavy agricultural farm equipment. He soon became the man in charge. I received one letter with his address, which I committed to memory and which proved to be a godsend to me later on. I did not trust the recruiters, and, given my negative predisposition to the communist regime, I remained unmotivated by their promises. I also did not want to increase the distance from my old home, hoping someday to be reunited with my family. I took my chances by refusing to sign the application to relocate. I became lonely again and moved back to Lwow to rejoin my cousins. It was a fortunate decision, because the NKVD raided my previous residence looking to arrest me.

After five months, the time had come for all three of us to move north to a small village buried in the wilderness forest of Bialowierza, where our companions were the famous bisons. These powerful animals had always attracted world-famous hunters, including royalty and Germany's Air Marshal Herman Goering. My cousins, Bolek and Salek, continued playing cards all day, and again I was left to myself. Since we tried to be inconspicuous, I could not make any friends among the Polish peasantry. I wandered into the woods by myself, picking berries and mushrooms, whittling sticks that became bows and arrows for target shooting.

I started some serious thinking about my future. The idea that I might never rejoin my family kept creeping into my mind. As much as I tried to push it away, it was coming back to haunt me. At the same time, I realized that my dependence on the family had come to an end, and that from now on I had to take care of myself. This realization crystallized into a decision to leave my cousins and our aimless existence in the small village hut. I left with a peasant in his horse-driven wagon loaded with produce to be sold at the market in the city of Bialystok. Refugees would gather at the market, and to my surprise, I encountered two of my schoolmates from Lodz who helped me to get some odd jobs and provided me with the much-needed social companionship I was starved for. A smuggler allowed me to communicate with my parents, who had moved to Warsaw with Ignac. My father was ill and could not work or provide for Mother and Ignac, who had been trying to make ends meet. Their only source of real income was the money my father's old German friend Oscar Bohnig was sending him after taking over his factory. Alas, this source dried out when Bohnig liquidated the factory and moved to Germany with the factory's entire machinery and inventory.

Through my intermediary, I received my mother's message that my uncle Maurice in New York was in the final stages of getting permission for me to immigrate to the United States as a student. I was supposed to report to the American Consulate in Riga, Latvia, to obtain my visa. My mother sent me a letter from him, written in German, confirming this information and urging me to get to Riga.

In ten days, a team of border smugglers, arranged for by my parents, contacted me in Bialystok. I knew what a sacrifice it must have been, considering the condition my parents were in. It made me sad and humbled. The two Polish smugglers were in their early twenties, handsome, vivacious, well-spoken, and intelligent. I took an immediate liking to them, joining them in night-clubbing and having a good time while they recruited people who wanted to cross the border to Lithuania. From there, I hoped to reach the American consulate in Riga.

As the time for us to get ready approached, Kazik, the leader of the group, handed me five U.S. ten-dollar bills. "This is from your mother. And this is from me," he said, presenting me with a loaded revolver. When I asked why

I would need a weapon, he shrugged his shoulders and said with a charming smile, "Take it to America and give it to a cowboy. They love them there." I did not appreciate the joke, but at the same time I felt good that this dashing fellow had treated me as an adult.

On a dark, moonless night, our group of twenty-five started out on our way to the border. I was shocked to see that our group included a young woman with an infant in her backpack, its little head sticking out to allow it to breathe. I questioned Kazik about the risk to which he was exposing us all. He assured me that the baby was drugged and that the mother took a vow to choke it rather than endanger us. I persisted; he turned hostile, saying, "You have an option to turn back." Puzzled and hurt, I filed in with the group. These were the last words Kazik and I exchanged.

My first physical contact with a "Russian bear" was actually with a German shepherd, teeth bared, inches from my throat, as I laid on my back in the wet grass under the dark sky on that warm June night, yards away from the wire border fence. The weight of his body, with his front paws planted on my chest, immobilized me. Even if I could have moved, I didn't attempt to, realizing the futility of such an attempt. The people in my group had dispersed, and I never saw any of them or Kazik again. Shots ring out nearby, but I didn't bother to pay attention to what was happening around me. I knew I had to get rid of the gun and the dollar bills to avoid being accused of the crime of possession of arms and foreign currency. The voice of the dog's master distracted the dog's attention for a split second, when I got rid of the incriminating evidence with one toss. The border guard, with his rifle pointed at me, came into my view. He collared his dog and summoned another soldier, who tied my wrists behind my back and ordered me to stay put. I noticed that the same type of rope was used on their rifles instead of the usual leather straps. I was surprised that my mind focused on this relatively unimportant detail in the serious situation I faced. I remembered my previous successful border crossing after a difficult cross-examination and wondered if I'd be able to be as verbally adept a second time.

The officer who frisked me took my wallet containing Russian money, my watch, my little pocketknife, the copy of my school certificate, and the letter from my uncle in America written in German.

My first questioning by an officer of the NKVD took place at the break of day in a tiny room in the local village school. After the first session, I was placed in a barn in a small group separated from others. I hoped that Lady Luck had smiled at me again, but this hope disappeared when I found out that our group was classified as enemies of the State. We spent almost three weeks in the barn in the village of Szepetowka before we were transferred to the old city prison in

Bialystok. As the heavy iron gates closed behind me with a clank, I realized that my innocence and freedom were left behind. I was on my own without being able to control my will, my actions, and my destiny.

Was I prepared for it? The question lay heavily on my mind, despite my natural instinct to let the chips fall where they may, and despite my belief that my luck would prevail. I tried to chase away the dark thoughts, looking for a scenario that would override my anxiety. This time, I found none.

Poland in 1939

CHAPTER 6

THE GERMAN SPY

Cell number three was built to accommodate twenty-four inmates. When I entered it in the company of another prisoner, the count of the prisoners in the cell rose to eighty-six. I stood transfixed at the scene before my disbelieving eyes. The cell contained two rows of iron beds along its long walls. Facing the cell's entrance were two small heavily barred windows inches below the ceiling, providing the only daylight. Between them, a wooden pine table that two inmates used as a bed completed the cell's furniture, except for the tall metal can to the left of the heavy door that served as a toilet. Prisoners were often two to a bed, which consisted of metal frames with twisted wire net. For mattresses, some prisoners had an assortment of rags and straw-filled sacks. The bare cement floor was filled with bodies, heads against the row of beds, legs stretched into the center of the room, almost flush against the feet of prisoners from the opposite side, leaving a passage barely a foot wide. I could not figure out how those lucky enough to have the beds were able to use the toilet-can without stepping on the heads of those stretched out on the floor. I soon found out that this was the main cause of frequent quarrels and fights.

There was no room for me to move away from the toilet can, and all of a sudden I realized that I was standing on the exact spot that was to become my new home. As I absorbed this thought, the stench that filled my nostrils and the July heat made me dizzy. I started to perspire heavily and reached up to wipe my face when I realized that my own tears had caused the wetness. I started sobbing, my entire body trembling and shaking uncontrollably.

I felt an arm around my shoulder, and through my tear-filled eyes I looked into the face of the stranger with whom I was pushed into the cell. His aqua-blue eyes were set above an upturned nose, and his broad-boned Slavic face was surrounded by a thick, light-blond crown of wavy hair. He appeared to me as the image of an angel. I regained partial control of myself and muttered a thank-you to my compassionate stranger. His heavily Lithuanian-accented Polish words sounded like music.

"My name is Vitus. I'll take care of you. I'll be your neighbor on the floor. What's your name?"

"My name is Olek," I responded weakly.

He kicked the closest body lying on the floor, causing it to move a few inches, and indicated for me to lie down. He took the last spot next to the toilet-can. A wave of happiness overcame me. Many times since that experience I have pondered over the definition of happiness. How does one recognize it when one reaches it? Is happiness a dream, a figment of one's imagination, an abstract state without a form or a frame?

I still remember that moment that I shared with Vitus in the stench of cell number three as a moment of pure happiness. A spontaneous act of compassion for a stranger in his moment of pain and need still symbolizes the deepest meaning of happiness for me.

My brief happy moment soon gave way to reality at six the next morning. Every morning and evening at this hour, we were led by two guards in groups of twenty through a long corridor, lined up with numbered cell doors, to what the prison officials sarcastically called a "sanitary facility." It consisted of a long, narrow, tiled room with a row of ten open holes serving as toilets, over which one had to stand or squat to relieve oneself. On the wall facing the toilets was the washing facility, made up of ten faucets supplying cold and lukewarm water over a sink, running the entire length of the wall. The sink also was used as a urinal in an emergency.

Once our sanitary needs were completed, it was time for our meal. For breakfast, a chunk of dark bread and a watery substance, which in color and taste was vaguely related to coffee, was poured into the mess-tins that our captors had issued to us upon our arrival at the prison. Our meals were brought into the cell by outside veteran prisoners and distributed by our cellmate Jan Olszewski, who to everyone's knowledge was an informer for the prison authorities. He was in his early thirties, ugly, owlish looking, stooped over like the hunchback of Notre Dame, his eyes always shifting, never to meet your own. Lunch and supper procedures were the same, except for the difference in food. Usually it was limited to a portion of barley or *kasha* (buckwheat groats) or thin cabbage soup with a chunk of inedible fat gristle or a leather-like chunk of beef floating in it. Every other day, we were split into groups of twenty and led to the prison yard for a thirty-minute walking exercise.

Lacking any free floor space, nobody could move around the cell, and most of the time we would sit talking across the space with other cellmates. They came from every level of society and ethnic group: Lithuanians, Latvians, Ukrainians, Poles, and Jews from all of these countries. A small group of intellectuals mixed with peasants, blue-collar workers, and members of the underworld's hardened criminals. The reasons for their imprisonment were likewise varied, ranging from petty crimes to murder, political infractions to treason; all were considered criminals and enemies of the State. Some knew what they were accused of; others, including I, were still waiting for a first interrogation. Still others, after being sentenced, left us with warnings of the beatings and torture they had been subjected to. The composition of our cell kept changing as we made room for newcomers who replaced those who left the cell to serve out their sentences. Thus I soon progressed away from my spot near the smelly can.

My relationship with Vitus Kurdus, my benefactor and protector, remained warm and steadfast. He deferred to my higher intellectual status, while I recognized his raw strength and total lack of fear. Very often at night, we conversed in whispers, trying to block out the noises of snoring, farting, and cries of pain and anguish permeating the stale air, which kept us awake. I told Vitus about my family, my school, and unfulfilled plans for my studies. He told me of his being an orphan, never knowing his parents. Brought up by a religiously tyrannical grandfather, he fled his home in a village south of Vilnius (Wilno in Polish) at the age of fifteen, to join a gang of thieves, steadily advancing to become the leader. A challenge by another gang member led to a fight in which he stabbed his opponent to death.

He felt no remorse for his deed, but he abhorred violence. His reaction was simply a case of survival of the fittest. His sense of power brought out in him a compassion for the weak and the desire to use his power to protect them. We established a bond of understanding and friendship. He told me stories of his gang experiences in return for stories from famous writers I had read. One of the prisoners, lawyer Simon Trachtman, overheard me and suggested that I share the stories with my inmates to fill the boring hours of the day. I was too shy and insecure to consider the invitation, but yielded when Vitus, proud of our relationship, urged me to do it. I selected Pearl Buck's *The Good Earth*. Each day I would sit on the table recounting the book's story and became the storyteller of cell number three. I hated sitting on that table, which was full of mean, biting bed bugs, but enjoyed the attention it accorded me.

I found out soon enough that Olszewski not only reported my activity to the authorities, but also put his own spin on it. Distorting the context of Pearl

Buck's story, he described me as an agitator, denouncing the exploitation of peasants by the ruling class, with allusion to the Soviet Union's policy of collectivization of small farmers' private property.

I was brought into an interrogation room the size of my prison cell, built to accommodate twenty-four inmates. The interrogator was seated at a desk, flanked by two high bar stools. A chair for me faced him; large portraits of Marx, Lenin, and Stalin dominated the pale green walls behind me, looking down on him. Were they there to watch his performance? I noticed rusty smudges on the wall, and a fleeting thought about their origin gave me a pang of fear.

His khaki military tunic had one star confirming that he held the high rank of major, which surprised me. He greeted me with a smile and invited me to sit down. A sergeant and a corporal positioned themselves behind me, their pose relaxed and unthreatening.

After the formalities of confirming my identity were over, the major assumed a stern look and surprised me by saying, "You are an intelligent young fellow. Why would you want to throw your life away?"

"Pardon me, Major," I replied, "but I don't understand what you mean. The last thing I want is to throw my life away."

"Then why are you engaging in illegal activities against the Soviet Union? Why are you spreading anti-Soviet propaganda in your cell? Why are you spying for the Germans?"

I was dumbfounded by his accusations. They appeared to be so ridiculous, almost comical, causing me to smile and chuckle. A vicious blow to my head delivered by the corporal wiped the smile off my face. I tried to regain my composure, but my head was swimming, my eyes filled with tears, and I became tongue-tied. I managed to mutter, "Major, I'm Jewish. I left German-occupied Poland to avoid persecution. How could I ever be spying for them?"

"You fucking, lying son of a bitch," he screamed, coming from behind his desk to confront me head on, his features distorted with disgust and hostility. He screamed again, "Then why have you tried to cross the border to Germany? Why did you get German instructions to go to Latvia? Why are you provoking your cellmates against the Soviet Union? You are an enemy of the State! You are a German spy!"

He shoved my uncle Maurice's letter from America in my face, the letter the Russian border guard had confiscated when I was caught trying to reach Lithuania, while another blow to my head from behind made me lose my balance. As I struggled to regain it, a blow delivered by a truncheon to my right kidney stunned me, making me lose my breath. I felt a warm wetness along my right leg as I lost control of my bladder. Momentarily, a sense of shame overwhelmed me, and embarrassment overshadowed the pain in my back, which began turning numb.

Slowly my head cleared, and I started to explain that my uncle Maurice, knowing I didn't understand English, wrote to me in German, having forgotten his Polish long ago. Before I could go on, the major turned around, sat at his desk, and raised his hand to stop me from talking. He produced a document and asked me to sign it.

"What is it I'm being asked to sign?" I asked innocently.

"A confession that you are a German spy."

"I'm sorry. I will not sign it. It's not true."

His lips turned into a crooked smile when he said, "You don't have the slightest idea how *sorry* you will be."

My first interrogation was over. As I was escorted to my cell I wondered, did he really believe the accusation he hurled at me? Was he a prisoner of a sick, indoctrinated system carrying out a function he was not in power to change? Or was he genuinely convinced by the communist doctrine that made him see others and me as a threat to his own beliefs?

The answer became obvious in the weeks that followed. Every session I had with the various officers of the NKVD followed the same line. In Russian and Polish, they resorted to threats, followed by coaxing and enticing me to confess. "If you sign, you will be sentenced to one year in a light labor camp, after which the State will help you to study medicine. You are young and smart, and we need people like you in our country. Your stubborn refusal will result in a sentence of ten years in a hard labor camp, without any benefits afterward—that is, if you happen to survive the Siberian winters and the rigors of the gulag. There is no reason for you not to sign."

"But there is a reason," I would point out each time. "The accusation is false. I'm innocent of the charges. How can I confess to something I haven't done or admit to being someone I'm not?" When coaxing failed, beating resumed. When I was visibly tired, I was offered a rest on the tall bar stool. As I would start climbing it, the sergeant would jerk it from under me, causing me to crash to the floor. Kicks to my ribs would be followed by his burst of laughter. This mental and physical torture became my daily existence. This went on for days stretching into weeks, turning my body into a painful sack of skin and bones. At night, exhaustion lulled me into sleep, but pain ravaging my body would awaken me again. Then came a period when I was completely ignored, which was part of the war of nerves, as it kept me on edge. Each time prisoners were led to their hearings, my heart would stop beating. Would I be called next? What was going to happen to me? This mental torture ended each night when

I would be taken to a solitary cell. As soon as I fell asleep, pounding on the steel door awakened me. Whenever my need to sleep became strong enough to overcome this harassment, the sentry watching me through the peephole would enter my cell to awaken and beat me.

When I rejoined Vitus, who hated the Russians with a passion, he kept my spirits up, praising me for my perseverance and courage in resisting the pressure to sign a false confession. His support ended in September when he failed to return from questioning. Through the grapevine, we found out that he had attacked the investigating officer and was shot dead. We never knew how true this rumor was, but I felt sadness and a deep personal loss. I realized how precious human contact between total strangers could become.

When my torturous sessions resumed, there was a step-up of pressure. Several times, I was placed into a wooden booth resembling a broom closet. I had to stand upright; its narrowness did not allow me to slacken my knees, which after a long while became extremely painful, causing me to pass out. I never had a sense of time, since there were no clocks anywhere. This became yet another form of torture.

After several months, one day I was led into the cellar, where I was stripped of the clothes I'd arrived in and shoved into a dark cave, its floor and walls made of rough cement. One of the guards splashed a bucket of ice-cold water on the floor. The only position I could assume in the small space of the cave was to lie on the rough, wet, and cold cement. I could not move without scraping my skin and bleeding. I didn't know how long I was kept in that hole, having lost the sense of time as my shivering body and mind froze into oblivion.

I had no recollection of when and who took me out of the cave. My next memory was being fully dressed and brought upstairs to face a panel of three officers, presided over by the major, who was my initial interrogator. They constituted the famous *troika*, or threesome, who passed judgments and sentences, acting respectively as a prosecutor, so-called defender, and judge. I knew that a life-changing decision was imminent. In a somber manner, I was once more asked to sign a confession. My frozen body, numb from my most recent torture, yearned for the end of the punishments inflicted upon it. My mind, however, seemed to disassociate itself from my physical being. In flashes of memory, I saw the image of my father defying the barrel of a gun pointed at him by his young playboy partner; I sensed the tight grip of my grandfather's hand on mine, defying the group of hooligans; and felt the protective warm embrace of my mother. I became focused on defying my tormentors to a point of obsession beyond any reason. I could not explain it then, nor can I explain it now. All I know is that my life had changed in that very room, at that very moment, when I heard myself telling my prosecutors, *I will not sign.*

Thus, after five months of my life in the Bialystok prison, I was sentenced as a German spy to ten years of hard labor in one of the archipelago of gulags somewhere in the vastness of the Soviet Union.

Strangely enough, the nature and severity of the sentence became insignificant compared to the elation I felt for standing up for the truth, for defying a powerful, cruel system and its henchmen. The reality that I was to spend the next ten years of my life in a hard labor camp had not penetrated my consciousness. I felt a sense of victory in a battle, where all the odds were stacked against me.

The thought of my parents nagged at me. I yearned for their love and approval and their expression of pride in me. Unfortunately, this was never to happen. I had lost contact with them forever.

Four decades later, browsing through the photo albums and old correspondence of my uncle Maurice, I found postcards my mother mailed to him in New York. Heavily censored by the Nazis, with whole sentences obliterated by black ink, her persistent question and plea were, "Where is my son, please help me to find Oles. Dear brother, I pray for his safety. You are the only one who can help."

Her love and concern, as well as her prayers, must have been heard, but I'm sure they were responsible for helping me endure and survive my suffering in the gulag.

Translation of one of my mother's postcards to my Uncle Maurice in New York City. Written November 9, 1940, in Warsaw. She wrote in German, because by the time Uncle Maurice had settled in America after his world travels, he had used German more, and his Polish had become rusty. Note that in order to protect the sender's identity, on the front of the postcard, at the bottom left, the name of the sender is a fictitious name. The street address, Nowolipie Street in Warsaw, also might have been fictitious. The country indicated is "Deutschland."

"Dear Ones,
I received your postcard of October 9 on the 4th of November and am answering it immediately. I have informed you already that I received your money only once since the beginning of the war. At the same time, I have written several times about how you could send packages. Have you yet contacted the firm B. Richter Riga (Latvia). This firm receives packages for resending when you transfer money to them. I note we may give up thinking about our trip; maybe it's possible on the basis of our application, which could be sent over to us, and pending numbers, for all of us to become American citizens. Inquire about it would be for us a tremendous thing. Why doesn't Elek write anything to Dodek, who recently had to change his apartment in the Jewish Quarter, he lives now on Sienna Street 28. The office is still in the old place, but it will likewise change. There was a letter from S. Glogowski who writes that he is making ready for a trip to Brazil. I did not receive any news regarding my Oles, these worries about my child make me crazy. I will not be able to survive this. Maybe he has turned to you from somewhere so as not to worry [us]. We are sending you all kisses.

Your Mala"

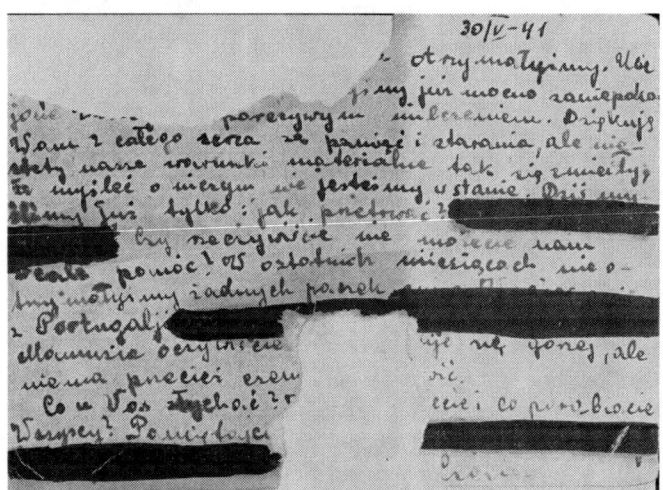

My cousin Cesia's May 30, 1941, postcard to Uncle Maurice in New York City, written in Polish; again, a fictitious sender's name. Censors blacked out some areas and probably caused the two torn areas.

"… we received.… we are greatly concerned … at prolonged silence. Thank you from the bottom of my heart for your thoughts and efforts, but unfortunately our financial conditions are changed to a point where we are unable to think about anything. Today we only think: how to survive? … Can you not really help us at all? In recent months we have not received any packages.… from Portugal … Mother of course.… feels worse, but there is.… What is happening with you? How are you all? Remember.…

Cesia

On November 8, 1940, one year to the day I left my home, family, and country, the heavy prison gates opened for my transfer to a temporary assembly point in the city of Baranowicze. From there I would start my journey to a yet-unknown destination to serve out my ten-year sentence.

My memory turned back to Lodz and the words of the striking worker hurled at my mother: "Don't you know better than to walk the border of freedom and oppression?"

The challenge of crossing that border between my present oppression and freedom began to dominate every fiber of my consciousness.

CHAPTER 7

THE GATES OF HELL

The cattle train rolled for five days and nights through the immensity of Russia. Live bodies of strangers connected by the same fate, traveling to the same destination, packed the boxcar. A small barred window above showed a patch of blue sky by day and the star-studded firmament at night. The hissing of the locomotive was the only outside sound, spelling a dreadful message of no return. Inside, the voices of many languages filled the air, permeated with the odors of unwashed bodies. Quarrels erupted, frequent and senseless. We were all hungry, crammed in and easily irritated. Each time the train would stop, one fellow would be hoisted on the shoulders of his friend, and, peeking through the small window, he would hurl names at us, some familiar, others we never heard of. Minsk, Moscow, Gorky, Ivanov Voznesensky, Jaroslavl, Vologda, Korgopol. We were moving north toward the city of Archangelsk, or possibly beyond it, to the subpolar vastness and the end of humanity. Nobody really cared.

Throughout the five sleepless nights, lying on the bare floor of the moving boxcar, I relived the action-packed year with all its horrors. I shuddered. The floor couldn't isolate me from the cold whistling wind under the moving train. I had no warm clothes to protect me, still wearing the light summer suit I had worn when apprehended at the border. Fortunately I had acquired from Vitus a sleeveless sweater and a pair of long johns, which were my only protection against the might of the Russian winter.

On the morning of the sixth day, a sudden jolt brought the train to an abrupt halt in a remote obscure corner of the world. Our journey had come to an end. Its finality shuttered all hopes, if there were still any alive. The snow-sprinkled sign spelled the name OSINOVKA. The guards unbolted sliding doors, and we were ordered out. Guards with stern, unfriendly faces, in their heavy winter hats and long coats, pointed their weapons at us as we jumped off the train, blinded by the brilliant whiteness of the snow. We were pushed and forced into a formation of two abreast, creating a long column. With guards on both sides of the column, we started to march toward the camp. The march was a long one, with many of us staggering in the knee-deep snow. My gait became unsteady, my feet wet in the loafers I wore, my toes numb. A white blanket of snow covered the ditches and depressions some of us kept stumbling into, only to feel a rifle butt on our backs and a barking command to keep moving. Finally, the large rectangular camp came into view. It was enclosed by a solid wooden fence topped with barbed wires and guard towers positioned at four corners. We moved faster to enter the double wooden gates. Passing through, I caught sight of a thermometer hanging from a wooden post reading minus 33 degrees Celsius (minus 27 Fahrenheit). We stood in the assembly area, in quiet sadness, our minds and bodies surrendered without a fight. One of the marchers muttered loud enough for me to hear, "Welcome brothers, we just passed through the Gates of Hell."

The camp commander, Colonel Stulov, came out to meet us. He was short and burly, his body wrapped in a thick winter uniform topped by a large fur hat. A grotesque, thick red nose of a drunkard and a pair of gray-blue eyes devoid of any warmth dominated his ruddy face. He pointed to one of the barracks and said, "You are very lucky that a crew of your fellow inmates created this barrack for you. Your first job will be to repay this favor by constructing another barrack for future arrivals. You will be given the tools tomorrow."

How lucky indeed, I thought, while stamping my feet in place and beating my arms against my back to keep myself from freezing. After a few remarks about the importance of discipline, obedience, and adherence to the rules of the camp, he turned us over to one of the older prisoners, who ordered us to form groups of twenty-four each. He then assigned other older prisoners to take each group to the *magazin*, as the supply room was termed, where we would exchange our clothing for attire more suitable for the weather conditions and working patterns we were to assume. I wasn't fortunate to have an early pick of the clothes, as my unit had been the one before last of the entire trainload. I wound up with a quilted short coat and padded trousers patched in places, torn in other places, worn out and thin. So was my quilted cap with earflaps and a pair of mittens. I did pick some warm underwear, but when it came to the footwear, I struck out completely. Unlike others, who were given *valenki*, knee-high felt boots ideal for winter, I wound up with makeshift slippers made of old rubber tires bound to the foot by strings, with an assortment of rags to wrap around my feet and ankles. I must have reflected my disappointment when I looked around to see the averting glances of my fellow inmates. The smiling face of Vitus flashed on the screen of my subconscious, and a whispered plea escaped my lips, "Where are you? I need you to protect me." There was no answer. With sadness, I surrendered my old civilian clothes to join the gray mass of humans who were to become my new family.

We followed our leader to the recently constructed barrack, our new home. It was built of round logs with straw stuffed at the joints and a pointed slanted roof made of rough lumber. A chimney spitting out black smoke was the only possible welcoming sight to our frozen eyes.

Inside we were greeted by rows of two-tiered bunks. The walls and floors were made of matched wooden logs. Every six feet, a vertical supporting beam with cut-out notches was the imitation of a stepladder for those occupying the upper bunks.

Opposite the entrance door was the only window, frosted over, allowing a bleak streak of light to penetrate the glum darkness of the barrack. A huge barrel was placed next to the window. It contained drinking water, colored green from the extract of pine needles to protect us from scurvy. A ladle and a tin cup were hanging on long chains from the edge of the barrel. I never thought I would be drinking such a concoction. As time passed, I actually acquired a taste for it.

The other round object, not far removed from "the well," as we learned to call our drinking station, stood the bucket to accommodate our needs between trips to the latrines. The bucket was located outdoors by the barbed-wire fence within full view of the guard in the tower above. In the center of the barrack's long wall, a limestone oven served as the only source of heat. It became our gathering center for social exchange, conversations, and disputes, a source of light in addition to the one created by low-voltage lamps hanging from the rafters—and, I soon found out, was the most important place for delousing.

There was a lot of pushing, shoving, and verbal abuse once we entered the barrack. The fiercest competition was to be close to the stove. I settled on the upper bunk about two-thirds into the barrack.

Directly below me, a fellow by the name of Kozlowski put down his bundle. We had noticed each other during our train journey but had had only a couple of brief conversations. I noticed that he was lame, his left leg dragging precariously. I offered to help him set up his bunk. He accepted, and soon we were calling each other by our first names. He was Tadek, short for Thaddeus. His manners were those of a cultured person, and as we shared our backgrounds, we found a lot in common. He was a few years my senior, from a family of wealthy merchants, who as capitalists were shot in the early days of the Soviet takeover of eastern Poland. He managed to escape their fate only to be sentenced to ten years of hard labor. Ironically, his sister was married to a rabid communist who was put in charge of his in-laws' business. It proved to be a blessing, as she was somehow able to keep Tadek supplied with parcels of food and clothing. This, in turn, allowed him to gain favors with the squad leaders, who had the power to excuse him from daily outdoor work, assigning him instead to light chores within the barrack.

The rest of us were not so lucky. After erecting a new barrack for the next transport of prisoners, we were divided into squads and assigned to work in the dense woods. Thus I started on my new career as a lumberjack.

Not far from the thermometer at the entrance gates was another post with a heavy metal bar hanging from it. The day would begin with *reveille*, an iron stake mercilessly pounded against the bar at five o'clock in the morning. Darkness and fatigue made us feel that it was the middle of the night. It took us a long while to shake off the stupor of deep sleep, yet we awoke to the painful reality of facing another day of tortuous labor. The trip to the latrine or the bucket, if it wasn't overflowing, was the first function of the day. We did not waste any time on changing clothes, because what we worked in was the clothing we slept in. Our next function was the eagerly awaited trip to the camp kitchen. A line would form in front of a large window-like opening through which "breakfast," to last us until the evening meal, was dished out. The vision of the cook's ladle filling our tin cans, accompanied by *paika*, the daily five-hundred gram ration of black bread, made us momentarily oblivious to the bitter cold that filled our lungs and bit through our clothes to our very bones. We wouldn't even dare to steal a look at the thermometer, all our senses concentrating on the food we were about to receive. I kept remembering my grandfather's blessing before we sat down to a meal, offering thanks to God. The irony of it would hit me with a wave of nostalgia and self-pity. The sight of steam rising from kettles containing hot oatmeal intensified the cold within us. Most of us quickly turned around and raced back to the barrack with our ration, seeking shelter from the wind and cold. Some unloaded their misery and frustration by cursing the cooks, accusing them of cheating on their portions of bread. "You son of a bitch, you gave him a larger piece than me. You will rot in hell for that." A shrug of the shoulders was the reply of the accused. As I witnessed this scene, a silent voice within me said, *You poor bastard, you threaten him with hell. Isn't where we all are?* And another voice within me answered my own question:

Yes, indeed, but I never imagined that Hell could be so cold.

CHAPTER 8

MY DAYS IN HELL

Day after day, we filed out of the gate in a long column, two abreast, surrounded by guards with fixed bayonets on their rifles. The leading guard barked out the marching orders, which became our morning greetings.

"Keep in line. Pull in tight. Keep a steady pace. A step to the left or right will be considered an attempt to escape, and you will be shot without warning!"

We hated the sound of his voice and the message it carried. With each passing day, we were longing for the moment in time when this tirade would stop haunting us. We often talked about it after the day's labor and tried to figure how long we would have to endure this routine. Most of the members of our brigade, including my squad, were *decadniks*, sentenced to ten years. They counted the days until the completion of the sentence and subsequent freedom. The count started with three thousand, six hundred and fifty-two days. Some counted the weeks, five hundred and twenty, and others kept score by months, one hundred and twenty, taking solace in the lower numbers, as if their suffering would be shorter. Keeping score was very difficult, since we had no access to calendars, hardly knowing what day of the week it was. Fortunately, there were a few in our group who assumed the task of "living calendars" and kept track of the passing time.

Suffering would most certainly be the mildest term to describe our daily life in the camp, which the Soviet rulers called *Ispravitelnoy Trudovoy Lager*, Corrective Labor Camp.

We marched through deep snow until we reached the railroad tracks about a third of a mile from the camp. We continued our march on the tracks, which proved a tiresome and dangerous task.

We were ordered to lengthen our steps in order to land on the railroad ties placed one meter apart. This was a tricky exercise since the ties were covered with frozen snow and ice that caused us to stumble and slip, break the ranks, and bump into or try to hold onto one another.

"You stinking cattle, fall in line or we will shoot you dead," sounded off the rear guard, pointing his rifle at the swaying and weaving marchers.

"They fed you too much. Your bellies are full of shit. Stop pushing and straighten up your fucking backs before we bury you in the snow."

This flow of verbal abuse, accompanied by kicking and striking of the prisoners, wouldn't end until we veered off into a clearing, where we were to set up for the day's labor.

The guards took positions along the perimeter of the work sites, a couple of them warming up by the roaring campfire, rotating every so often. Our brigade's assignment was to fell trees, strip them clean of branches, saw them into logs of various lengths, and haul them to an area along the railroad tracks, where we would pile them into stacks. At the end of the working day, the stacks would be measured by the commander of the brigade and reported to camp management. We were supposed to produce our quota of cubic meters. I reflected on the irony of my situation, remembering my late, beloved grandfather, the forester. I felt some kinship with him now that I was gaining experience in what had been his profession, and this buoyed me somewhat and even helped me retain a sense of humor in my deplorable situation.

The commanders were merciless in imposing a certain pace to our work so they could earn praise for a quota fulfilled. They would be rewarded for reaching or surpassing the goal. No rewards were ever passed on to us.

As we started to work, the air filled with sounds of axes, hatchets, iron wedges, sledgehammers, handsaws to fell the trees, long saws to cut the logs, and shovels to clear the snow from around the bottom of the tree trunks. We would load ourselves up at the tool shed at the gate of the camp and drop the tools back off there upon our return.

In the weeks and months of my imprisonment, I worked with every tool, performed every function of a lumberjack, carried on my shoulders weight surpassing my own. While I had no way to choose, I tried to end up with branch-stripping detail. It gave me a sense of satisfaction to see the huge tree trunks cleaned of their branches, assuming a straight and powerful form of a fallen giant. Having been born a Virgo, under the sixth sign of the Zodiac, it was innate in me to bring order to chaos and to do any job cleanly and perfectly. It suited my personality to have things organized and tidied. Under the circumstances, this became my only little reward. The brigade commander soon discovered my preference, and when he was in a bad mood he would purposefully assign me to other labor. I learned how to fell trees by making a deep cut with an axe on the side the tree was to fall, then using the saw inches above the level of the cut on the reverse side, until the creaking noise called for me to loudly sound the warning to those around. The thunder of the falling trees used to pierce the frozen stillness as we advanced deeper and deeper into the virgin forest.

On other occasions, I was assigned a partner to saw the cleaned tree trunks into logs. I hated to work in tandem with others, as they always picked on me. I was too fast or too slow, too eager for my partner, or too slow for the overseer. The cursing was relentless, and the meanness and cruelty of men was in vivid contrast to the beauty of the surrounding nature. My body became scarred from misjudged strokes of the axe, scratched by the branches of the falling trees, and bloodied by the teeth of the saw. I was in constant pain, my back hurting from crouching and bending. It hurt especially at night, as I lay on the bare logs serving as my bed. I broke out in a heavy rash, and my continual scratching of it caused open boils oozing pus. My knees and ankles were swollen from the constant immersion in the snow. I especially suffered at night, as I lay on the bare logs serving as my bed, with throbbing pain everywhere competing with my fatigue. The pain made me lose a lot of sleep, robbing me of my only precious luxury.

At noon, we were allowed a half-hour smoke break. The guards would vacate their spots at the fire, and the prisoners would assemble around it smoking their cigarettes, if you could call them that. They were usually made of the cheapest kind of tobacco rolled in small strips of newspaper. Sometimes we suspected the source to be dried animal dung. It didn't make any difference to the smokers as they inhaled the smoke and washed it down with *kipyatok*, hot water, in lieu of lunch. I envied those who were able to save a part of their bread ratio for a lunch *al fresco*.

I had no source of tobacco supply, relying on some friendly soul to let me have a drag. Unlike others, I did not enjoy getting too close to the fire. I did not want my frozen clothing to warm up and refreeze after the break. I had learned to exist in my frozen shell. The *perekur*, as the Russians called the smoking break, produced the only opportunity for the prisoners to engage in conversation. This conversation usually turned into the prisoners chiding and picking on one another, always enriched with the prolific variety of profanity.

No wonder I preferred to distance myself from it. I dreaded the afternoons, when the tree trunks were sawed into logs of various sizes or whole tree trunks were transferred to the railroad tracks and piled into stacks. Teams of two carried the heavy loads. The cruel commanders would often assign me tall partners. Being shorter, I carried the heavier burden of the task as the tail man of the twosome. The exhaustion and ache at the end of the day became a routine highlighted by the tedious, long march back to the camp for a head count and a report of the day's accomplishments by the commanders of the brigades.

The camp commander took a sadistic pleasure in keeping us lined up in the cold of the evening, strutting up and down our ranks, making comments about our worthlessness interwoven with heavy, vulgar cursing. He enjoyed making fun of the different ethnic and religious origins of the prisoners. He often berated the political prisoners, lauding the system of prisons and camps as too good for us, the "worthless scum" of traitors and counterrevolutionaries. This litany of verbal abuse, on top of the brutally exhausting slave labor of the day, was meant to break whatever spirit was still left in us. It was an effective, destructive weapon of physical and mental punishment.

Yet the punishment that affected me most was hunger. The daily ration of bread became the focus of my existence. I couldn't resist devouring it as soon as I laid my hands on the black chunk of doughy substance filled with scales, husks, shells, and other unidentified impurities. I envied those who had the strong will to ration and pace themselves to have the bread last throughout the day. I dreaded the nights, when I could not control the twisting and cramping in my stomach demanding nourishment. I observed some of my camp-mates dividing their daily portion so they could chew on it during the night. Once I tried to imitate them by wrapping half of my portion in a rag, which I fastened around my neck. A sharp pain on the right side of my head woke me up shortly after I fell asleep. My bread was gone, and my right ear was bleeding from rat bites.

The realization of losing my precious portion of bread intensified my frustration and anger. I forced a restless sleep that was filled with dreams. I saw myself bent over in agonizing pain, crying my heart out in a fit of pity over the condition of my life. I saw myself through the eyes of a third person that had curiosity and sympathy for my suffering. That person kept asking, "Why, for God's sake, why?"

When I woke up, my face was wet from tears I had shed while dreaming. The pains were miraculously gone, and I felt at peace with myself. I was actually happy to be alive, with my body and mind suspended in a state of utmost tranquility. The thought of the rats stealing my bread struck me as funny, and a small chuckle escaped my breath. I decided then and there against rationing bread, a decision I adhered to for the rest of my gulag days.

Unfortunately, my habit of devouring bread at once turned into an addiction in my later life. Even today, dining in restaurants, I empty the bread basket clean before I have a chance to study the menu and select my food.

My fellow inmate Tadek, who spent most of his day doing chores in the barrack, would help me occasionally with a small portion of bread or soup he would not eat. He and another inmate, Jakob Kaminski, were supplied with sporadic food packages from their families, giving them a kind of privilege. Jakob, a clever operator of unknown profession in his late forties, worked out a deal with the camp's command, *natchalstvo*, to qualify as a "patient." This entitled him to a hospital diet in exchange for the cigarettes and candy from his packages. The hospital kitchen food was distributed from a dispensary, checked against a posted list of patients. The food consisted of such delicacies as soft wheat rolls, a thick milky barley soup, fish, and even chunks of boiled beef or lamb. One evening, Jakob, feeling unwell, asked me to fetch his dinner for him. I lined up in the queue, and when I mentioned his name, the cook looked at me suspiciously before he dished out the food. I explained that inmate Kaminski was too sick to personally claim his food. Jakob invited me to share it with him. I expressed my gratitude, savoring these long-forgotten tastes and textures. I was not prepared for the excruciating hunger pangs that attacked me a short while later. My stomach was screaming for more food with an urgency I couldn't subdue.

My actions following Jakob's kind gesture were even more startling, even to me. Whenever I spotted him enjoying his newly received food packages, I would sneak out to claim his food from the dispensary and gobble it up on the way back to the barrack. One evening, Jakob caught me in my deceitful practice. It didn't occur to me until that moment that what I was doing was essentially stealing. Jakob forgave me, but I learned yet another life's lesson about the need and despair that drives the underprivileged into committing petty larceny. As much as society must disapprove it, it must also show compassion and understanding for the underlying causes of these transgressions.

Along with the losing fight against hunger, our leisure time was devoted to a losing battle against lice infestation. Every evening, we took turns removing our shirts and underwear in front of the roaring fire in the limestone stove, exposing the lice to heat until they burst. We tried to eliminate the surviving ones by zeroing in on these blood-sucking creatures and smothering them with our thumbnails, pressing one against the other. Yet we could never eliminate all of them. This ritual became the social event of the day. The conversation flowed, touching every subject imaginable. It ranged from cursing, using the foulest terms in a host of languages, to serious political discussions, some displaying boiling hostility and accusations, some dealing with reminiscences of a better life in the not-so-distant past, others expressing the faint hope for survival and a better future.

The cast of characters was as diverse and interesting as the topics of conversations. Polish Jews, some Poles, Lithuanians, Ukrainians, and Byelorussians populated our barrack. In this mix, we shared a geographical and ethnic commonality that greatly reduced the cultural differences. This is not to say that we were a completely homogeneous group. We were at odds with our diverse religious beliefs and our native countries' historical backgrounds. What united us, however, was our strong antagonism to the communist dictatorship of the Soviet Union. We represented every spectrum of society, from the "criminals," referring to murderers and thieves, to the "politicals," those accused of anti-government or anti-communist views, to those who, like myself, were accused of some drummed-up charges of espionage, speculation, or capitalism.

Unlike others, our barrack was fortunate not to be dominated by the Russian underworld and its hardened criminals. These were among the cruelest, deprived of any humanity and feelings. The stories we heard about them from inmates of other barracks were horrifying. Even the camp authorities were in awe of them and treated them with a fear-inspired respect.

We heard of some inmates who committed suicide to avoid being subjected to the physical, sexual, and mental abuse in other barracks. On occasion, driven by desperation, someone would attempt an escape from the camp. None succeeded. The severity of the terrain, and the fear and hostility of the scarce local population, if one could succeed in reaching it, proved too much even for the fittest and bravest. The camp's well-trained dogs would flush out the runaway and tear him apart. The sadistic camp commander Colonel Stulov would assemble the entire camp population to view the torn body on public display and to demonstrate his absolute power. Such a show was meant to underline the hopelessness of our situation, make us forget our past, and make us resigned to having no future and accepting the reality of our present existence. It would turn us from intelligent human beings into unthinking, unfeeling creatures.

So there we were, in small groups in front of the burning logs in the hot stove, killing the blood-sucking lice, exchanging stories and reasons for our being sent into this God-forsaken hell on ice.

Osip, a good-looking Ukrainian in his forties, had beat up his fourteen-year-old daughter when she came home pregnant. She took revenge on her father by denouncing him as a counter-revolutionary who maligned the name of Stalin and the communist party. He swore that when he completed his ten-year sentence, he would kill his daughter.

"Osip, don't be stupid. If you do that, you will find yourself right back here for the rest of your stinking life," said Misha, known by the name "Mishka the Thief."

Osip shrugged his shoulders. With a voice filled with sarcasm, he replied, "Look at the wiseguy giving free advice. The day you will get out of this shithole, you will go back to stealing, so fuck off."

"You are both crazy. When I get out of here, I'll become a model Soviet citizen praising the system and trying to put as many parasites as I can into this paradise, especially those squealing rats who got me in here." Dimitry Ivanovich Zharkov's deep baritone added strength to his statement. He was one of the few Russians in our barrack. In his late thirties, as foreman of a steel mill, he was punished by his party boss superior for not reaching the production quota, which would have earned his boss a dacha in the countryside and other perks and privileges.

Once, a fellow inmate asked me what crime had earned my ten-year sentence. I did not respond, heeding the warning of Tadek Kozlowski: "Never tell the Russian screwballs that you were accused as a German spy. The Russians will tear you to pieces, because under all their hostility and their tough talk against the Soviet system, their government, police, and the NKVD, they are at heart Russian patriots loving their Motherland, in spite of the corrupt regime, which rules them and placed them here. In their minds, you would become an enemy of their Motherland. Tell them of your being Jewish from a bourgeois family, or any other reason you can invent for being here."

He was so right in describing the love and loyalty of the Russians for their country as the source that sustained them. Rejected and condemned, they would not be robbed of their Russian soul and their ties to the Russian soil.

These and similar conversations and exchanges provided an outlet from the daily fatigue and frustrations, giving some inmates a reason to endure, think of the future, and build up their determination to survive.

I found out that those who dwelt in the past were the ones who were fading fast. I resolved to block out my memories and concentrate on the task of daily survival. I could not tolerate, however, those who counted the hours, days, or weeks of suffering separating them from the day of deliverance. Although I could not figure out how and when, I nevertheless felt that I wouldn't perish in this frozen hell of God-forsaken northern tundra. Even later, when spring arrived and we exchanged laboring in deep snow for a no-less-exhausting labor in the deep water of the thaw that the ground couldn't absorb; when the ferocious mosquitoes, almost matching butterflies in size, ate us alive, crawling up our trousers, sleeves and under collars, my faith in survival did not abandon me. It carried me through the onslaught of malaria that spread throughout the camp, claiming many lives. I was thankful for this stroke of good luck. Hailing from a home that was not particularly religious, I wasn't fond of mumbling words of prayer that I did not understand or feel. I nevertheless found a way to communicate with God in the simplicity of a silent prayer. It was more like an expression of wishful, hopeful thinking, which, if one were to analyze it, is the essence of prayers.

They must have worked on a hot and muggy day in August 1941, two months after Nazi Germany broke its unholy alliance with Stalin by unexpectedly invading the Soviet Union, that we heard the following short announcement from Stulov at the morning reveille: "All Polish prisoners will be released to comply with the order of our great leader, Stalin. Processing will start tomorrow." Stulov turned around abruptly and marched off to his command headquarters barrack.

The announcement stunned everyone. It took a while for us to absorb the significance of this development. Jubilation on the part of the Poles matched the envy of those who were about to resume the daily slave-labor routine. That evening, as we returned to our barrack, someone shouted, "They are not all Poles. There's a bunch of fucking Jews among them. They should rot in hell like the rest of us!"

The following day, the processing began. Our names were called one by one.

"Are you a Polack?" asked my interviewer, a non-commissioned officer of the camp's commandant's office.

"I'm a Polish citizen of Jewish faith," I replied.

"I don't understand. Polish citizen means you are a Polack. Yes?"

I nodded in agreement.

"We have heard on the Moscow radio that all Polacks are being amnestied to help us fight the Nazis. I think you should be grateful to Stalin for being granted this opportunity. So you are free, you lucky son of a bitch," he said amiably.

I had a hard time suppressing the impulse to dispute my "stroke of luck" and gratitude to Stalin.

Each of us was given a temporary identity card as an official release from the camp of Osinovka. It was hardly a document one would want to use as a recommendation anywhere, but it would keep us legitimate in a country where every citizen had to be in possession of an identity document. We learned that our release was the result of an agreement reached between Stalin and General Sikorski, the head of the Polish government in exile based in London. We were freed to join the Polish Army, which was yet to be formed in the Soviet Union in order to fight Nazi Germany. We were to assemble in a transition camp from which we would be officially released.

That night, I hardly got any sleep. The Jewish group of the prisoners stayed alert, as non-Polish inmates threatened us, "You will not get out of here alive." Their rage was understandable. There is no greater envy and deeper hatred than that of a prisoner toward a liberated fellow prisoner.

I spent the night reviewing my gulag days. As if in a movie, newsreel images kept appearing in flashes, fading out to make room for new ones. I saw the frozen naked dead bodies of the caught runaway prisoners, bearing bullet wounds, their flesh mangled by the vicious German shepherds displayed for all of us to see and fear.

I saw myself in my unsuccessful attempt to be hospitalized, when the axe I aimed at my knee tripped over a tree branch, causing only heavy bleeding. Instead of an intended hospital stay, I was penalized by spending twenty-four hours incarcerated in a tiny unheated shed near the watchtower, with no food, no light, and no place to rest my body. To keep from freezing, I used every callisthenic exercise I have ever known. I paid no attention to the constant teasing of the guard posted outside. I tried to concentrate on the positive, anticipating the days ahead, imagining that I no longer suffered hunger, was no longer being bitten by bread-stealing rats, no longer enduring hours of hard labor which endlessly sapped all my strength. Not that I had the slightest idea of what the future had in store for me. It was all wishful thinking and hoping.

I walked out through the Gates of Hell to board the morning freight train to take me to the last stop on my way to freedom, my ten-year sentence reduced to six thousand, five hundred twenty-eight hours, equaling two hundred seventy-two days, equaling thirty-nine weeks.

Soviet Union and Poland

CHAPTER 9

JOURNEY TO BOGORODSK

After fifty-one days at the Ostrovnoy transit camp, fifty miles from Osinovka, we were subjected to additional processing, a checking of everybody's identities. I was finally released as a free man to the snow and freeze of the Russian November, emaciated, with one loaf of bread as my whole supply of food and a "farewell gift" of thirty rubles. I was trying to figure out the rationale behind the amount of thirty rubles, which could hardly buy anything, since the country practically operated on a barter system. Obviously, I had nothing to barter except my misery. I performed all kinds of equations, but the solution always came out the same: it equaled to less than one *kopeck* (penny) for each day of my gulag detention. This shockingly ridiculous discovery helped me later appreciate the relative value of one's efforts and the compensation received as a reward.

Now, my body covered by my torn gulag rags as my only clothes and protection from the elements, I wandered for two weeks headed south to the only address I knew in the vastness of the Soviet Union, that of my cousin Roman. He had written to me a long time ago, before my imprisonment, and I hoped that he still lived there.

In my journey to reach him, I experienced a whole gamut of human emotions, from kindness and sympathy, compassion and charity, to contempt, hatred, and rejection. I humbled myself by begging for food from strangers on trains; I cajoled drivers of heavy trucks to get a lift between towns and villages. I lived through two weeks of a most torturous journey fighting hunger and the elements on open platforms of freight trains and trucks, occasionally sleeping on the floor of small railroad stations, living on the crumbs of food handouts, and boiling hot *kipyatok* as my only nourishment. There was something magical about this drink. It almost had the restorative powers of a medicinal remedy, being able to soothe one's hunger pangs, quench one's thirst, warm one's body, and bring an inner peace as if an elixir of life. And yet, come to think of it, it was only plain boiling hot water.

On train trips, every stop was welcomed as the human load spilled from the cars, clutching their tin cans and running toward the locomotive to gather the precious nectar the engine released, turning its vapor into hot liquid. It didn't matter that it carried the metallic taste of the often-rusty pipes. It was the immediate comfort it provided that uplifted one's soul and brought temporary relief to one's body. I couldn't help but be amazed at the relativity of value in certain circumstances.

I forgot how to live not being cold and hungry. Once, a peasant woman and the three children she was feeding shared their meager meal with me. Another woman, a railroad station supervisor, took me home, where she fed me, washed and mended my clothes, and tended to my ulcerated body. Her compassion overwhelmed me, and I broke down in tears thanking her for her kindness. Sadly, trying to control her own tears, she said, "I hope someone would take care of my husband Igor and my son, Misha, when they return from their Siberian gulag."

Then there were those who spat at me, seeing me as a subhuman creature, a symbol of their own fears, trying to fend off the image of their own uncertain future under a regime that robbed innocent citizens of their freedom without cause or reason. They took out their hatred for the system on me, rather than on those invisible powers, which filled them with fear.

And then there were those who, like myself, tried to find a secure spot on a train on their own journeys. Not welcomed inside the passenger cars, I managed to squeeze myself into a niche of a platform directly above the buffers between the cars. With luck, I was able to ride at the tail platform rather than the front one that faced the direction the train was headed. I was thus less exposed to the chill and wind.

It was there that another vagabond challenged me, a bulky square man with Asian features who appeared to be from one of the Central Asian Republics of the Soviet Union. He came at me brandishing a dagger to take away my "luxurious" hideout. As he lunged at me, I managed to kick his shin with all the might I could muster, upsetting his balance. He hung a moment, holding on to the buffers, looking at me bewildered, with his eyes wide open, before the fast-moving ground under him claimed his body. My body shaking, I managed to control my anger and guilt by uttering a prayer for his soul and mine. My mind stood arrested, separated from its ability to think.

Numbed by the incident, I could not focus on anything positive or creative. In a daze, I started to count the telephone poles as the train moved through the Russian countryside. I even tried to count the little swirling white flakes of the falling snow and the bright stars in the sky when the clouds disappeared and a clear winter sky spread its wings over the whiteness of the earth. I lost the perception of time until the moment when an orange-colored thread on the canvas of the dark night sky slowly turned into bright sun, and a sign of the small railroad station spelled out the name BOGORODSK. My heartbeat turned into heavy pounding as I descended the train's steps and planted my feet on the snowy surface, which I hoped and believed would become the base of my return to the human race. I entered the station's men's room, which to no surprise consisted of an open lavatory and a dripping faucet over a sink that had seen better times. I had no other facilities to clean myself up with for the anxiously anticipated reunion with my cousin Roman.

I ventured into the small town asking for directions. The expressions on the faces of people I approached were enough to give me a picture of myself without having to look into a mirror. I knew exactly what they thought, and how right they were! When I reached Number Five Kladbishtchanskaya Street, nobody answered my knock on the door of the semiattached green wooden house. I sat down on a tree stump in front of the Mitin residence. I was there for a very long time, until the sun receded behind the horizon, bowing to the advancing darkness of the evening.

I recognized the slightly stooped figure of my cousin as he rounded the corner heading directly for the house. He passed me over as some apparition. He reappeared after a moment with a loaf of bread, which, without a word, he handed to me.

I faced him and said, "Roman, don't you recognize me?" Stunned, he peered at me and stammered, "Olek? Are you my cousin Olek?"

After an emotional reunion, he and the Mitins invited me to use a bed, a home, and a peaceful place filled with warmth to thaw out the icicles of the freezing hell I had miraculously survived and escaped.

Roman worked as the chief mechanical engineer for an overhaul and repair center of agricultural machinery servicing four regions surrounding Bogorodsk. I found out years later that without joining the communist party, he was promoted to the position of chief engineer, which gave him some privileges. The one he treasured most was his own car.

Roman lodged at the house owned by Ivan Mitin, a handsome, tall, trim, highly educated and intelligent man who worked as the chief engineer at the electrical plant of the city. Serious, and a little reserved at first, after a few weeks he became more open and interested in my experiences. He absorbed my story with no comment, showing no emotion and without revealing his own views. I understood that it was difficult and outright dangerous for him to acknowledge the injustices inflicted upon me and countless others. He limited himself to expressions of sympathy for my suffering. His wife Marina, a pretty woman in her late twenties, full of energy, was a nurse working in the town's hospital nearby. She showed a great deal more involvement with me, tending to my sores and relieving my constant itching by supplying me with a variety of salves and medical drugs. She took care of my laundry and equipped me with clothing suited for the severe climate that allowed me to blend with the rest of humanity. She was the one who fashioned my bedroom out of the small entrance hall, cleaning out of a number of snow removal tools and other household items to make room for a cot. It had little privacy, but it was incomparably superior to my gulag accommodations. She made me feel welcome and happy.

The Mitins' house in Bogorodsk, where I found shelter with my cousin Roman.

Roman and his grandson Vladyslav, named after my father, whom I visited in Bogorodsk in 1999.

I felt embarrassed whenever she ordered me to remove all my clothes so she could medicate the sores on my body. My embarrassment reached a peak when, responding to the soft touch of her hands, I felt a growing erection I could not control. She smiled and waved a finger at me, saying, "Now, be a good boy and be thankful for the miracle of nature, for the gift of life and the desires that sustain us. Here is a cold towel, which will take care of your problem for now."

It did indeed, but that night I dreamt of a different outcome dealing with my erection. I saw Marina's face bending over mine, whispering endearments as she lowered her naked body to join mine. In the next moment, her face faded to be replaced by Ania's, my young summer love, to again switch to the face of Kazia, who first initiated me. As a massive orgasm shook my body, the image of an Asian face flashed before my mind's eye, joining me in the explosion. It was the face of the assailant on the train to Bogorodsk, his narrow eyes mocking me and his lips curling in a menacing expression. The scream he emitted as his body hit the ground woke me up. I realized that it was me who was crying out in the darkness. I lay awake the rest of the night, puzzled by the dream and pondering its meaning. The correlation between sex and death intrigued me and had occasionally recurred in my dreams. I remember the explanation offered later by my physician friend, Dr. Julian Przyrowski, that it is not uncommon for men experiencing a potent orgasm to exclaim, "I wish I could die now!" It expresses the moment of ultimate pleasure life offers and the wish to retain it as the last memory of life. I was happy when the morning greeted me with the aroma and sound of sizzling bacon.

I started gaining weight, felt stronger, and became restless over my immediate future. Since there was a shortage of manpower, with most men fighting the war, I was eagerly hired by the leather factory manager, Roman and Ivan's friend. The factory produced a variety of leather goods for the army consisting of belts, officer pouches for maps and documents, knapsacks, straps for rifles, and similar articles. I couldn't help laughing as I remembered the guards who stopped me at the border crossing, their rifles held by heavy ropes, and the irony of my present job cutting leather straps to hold rifles. The cutting was done on thick oak boards. Every so often, the boards were taken to the carpentry shop on the main floor to be planed smooth.

The foreman of the carpentry shop, Stanislav, took a liking to me, and in three weeks he had me transferred to work beside him. His parents were of Polish origin, and we spent hours talking about life in Poland while I became an expert with the plane. I told him a story from my school days, when I skipped an art class by faking an injury in order to play soccer. We became good friends.

He asked me how long I intended to stay in Bogorodsk. The question did not surprise me. My life had settled into a pleasant routine, and I felt good about offering to share my earnings with the Mitins and to assume various domestic chores, relieving Ivan and Marina. But as time passed, I was becoming restless and uncomfortable living in the Soviet Union, where I hadn't wanted to go in the first place and which had actually led to my imprisonment. In the gulag, my whole being was focused only on survival; here I began to feel an odd combination of boredom and anxiety. Temporarily safe and certainly revitalized to some degree, I was working at a repetitive job that was hardly stimulating, and I had no social life. Still apart from the loved ones I had left behind, I began to miss them again ever so much more, and not knowing their fate intensified my anxiety. I started making inquiries about recruiting centers for the Polish Army. Roman was adamantly against this. "Why do you stick to the Poles? Didn't you suffer enough humiliation from them? Do you want to risk your life for *them*? Do you really think *they* want you?" It was hard for me to explain to him that

I didn't want to live under communist rule and that I found it very difficult to renounce my cultural background and the prospect of reunification with my family. He shrugged his shoulders and said, "Do you really believe they are alive?" In turn I shrugged my shoulders and replied,

"Roman, I'm sure they consider me dead or lost forever, yet I'm alive. Why can't I hope that they are? Besides, I would be fighting a common enemy, which your adopted country fights. What's wrong with that?" To this he had no reply, as he had been excused from military service by holding a job essential to the war effort. Ivan, who had lost three fingers on his right hand as a result of an accident on the job, and who also was considered essential to the war effort on the home front, listened to our discussions without comment.

One evening, while Roman attended a meeting, I asked Ivan for his opinion. He was flattered at being asked.

"You must do what your conscience dictates. You were spared from your sentence to help the war effort. I know your basic motivation won't be fighting for the Soviet Union, and maybe not even for Poland, but against an enemy that is set to destroy all of us. You are welcome to stay with us as long as you wish, but at the same time I want you to know that we will offer you our blessings if you decide to leave." I was touched by his response and thanked him for his honesty.

However, my tranquil life at the Mitins' home changed abruptly. Every day before she left for work, Marina would put a cast-iron pot filled with potatoes, chunks of lard, and pork rinds (greaves) in the heated oven, which would slowly cook them for our dinner that night. While at work, I fantasized about the pot and its contents. My work schedule placed me at home before Roman and the Mitins returned from work. My obsession, most probably caused by starvation in the gulag, made my body crave fat, and I was driven to every so often picking out of the pot a few of the crunchy rinds and devouring them. It was clandestine, and I suffered a nagging feeling of guilt for the impropriety of my action.

One evening, my transgression was discovered, and it led to our parting. Roman was crushed by this turn of events, ashamed of my behavior, understandingly reluctant to intervene on my behalf. The Mitins, while sympathetic and understanding of my failure to control my craving, were hurt and lost the confidence they had entrusted in me. As a matter of principle, Mitin asked me to find another place to live. I offered my sincere apologies, remembering a similar situation in the gulag with my inmate Kaminski, and wondered if the depravation I suffered there might become a permanent condition of want for the rest of my life.

I found temporary lodging for a couple of weeks with the family of my factory friend Stanislav. I contacted the Polish Mission recruiting service in Alma Ata and was able to be included in the transport of volunteers for the newly forming Polish Army in Uzbekistan. After a tearful good-bye with Roman, Stanislav, and the Mitins, accentuated by hugs and kisses, wishes, and blessings, I left on a clear day in February 1942 for another journey into the future.

CHAPTER 10

"LIFE IS WHAT HAPPENS TO YOU WHILE YOU'RE BUSY MAKING OTHER PLANS"

The puffing sound of the locomotive and the heat of the wet steam filled my nostrils, arousing all my senses. Another railroad journey began after I completed the registration procedure at the Polish Mission in Gorky and joined the huge group of Polish citizens and nationals freed from gulags and villages to which they had been exiled to perform hard labor.

Throughout the one-month-long journey, I kept dreaming of the day when, donning a Polish soldier's uniform, I would join the fighting forces. This would help me leave Russia, ending the tragic period of my life there, a nightmare to be gotten rid of forever. I was eager to contribute to the advance of Nazi Germany's defeat and to reunite with my family. I shared this feeling with the hundreds of volunteers in our transport and especially with six new companions, with whom I shared a corner of the boxcar, where we bedded down on the bare boards at one end as the train chugged through the endlessness of the Soviet Union.

All originally from Poland, the oldest was Grisha Diament, from a small town near the city of Lublin; Zygmunt Bargad from the town of Rowne; Pawel Hopengarten, whom we called Pinio, and Bolek Szlinger, both from Warsaw; Misha Horowitz from Boryslaw; and Szymek Rosenbaum from a small town in eastern Poland. We bonded in the daily routine of our journey, caring for one another, sharing the rations of food, and combining our wits to make our lives better by acquiring extra food. We agreed to stick together.

From the clutches of winter, with its wall of snow-covered pines and the leafless white-skinned birches at the journey's start, to the sandy immensity of the Central Asian Republics, we reached the village of Lugovaya in Uzbekistan, the recruiting center of the Polish Army under the command of General Wladyslaw Anders. We arrived a short time before the liquidation of the center and the departure of the 100,000 men and families from the Soviet Union. They would travel via the Caspian Sea to Iran, Palestine—then under the British mandate—and on to England to fight alongside the British.

As we filed out of the train, the sight of the tented army compound, spread in a valley several hundred feet down from the railroad tracks, with the red and white Polish flag fluttering against the impeccable blue sky, filled our hearts with joy and pride. I believe that one measures one's life in memorable moments, and I felt that this moment would stay with me forever. I saw my dreams fulfilled!

What followed not only shattered my dreams, but also changed the course of my life. It left me with a memory I would never be able to erase from the deepest recesses of my mind. A smartly uniformed Polish captain by the name of Chmura greeted us. We lined up and answered his command to "Attennnnntion." With his arms locked behind his back, he inspected the "troops" and turned to face us from a low wooden platform. He called on all men of Roman Catholic faith to take three steps forward and stand "at ease." Then he called for those volunteers of other Christian denominations to take two steps forward and assume the at-ease position. I noticed that a small number of Jews stepped forward as well. I wondered why, but not for long. He then called on all those of Mosaic faith to take two steps backward. Planting himself in front of the Jewish volunteers and pointing to a compass held in his hand, he intoned:

"The world is divided into four main directions—north, south, east, and west. Choose any one of these and get the fuck out of here."

His unblinking eyes soaked in our shock and disbelief. We looked at his face, a face twisted by a vicious grimace of hatred and the smirk of superior power. He barked out the command "Dissssmissed," executed a smart "about-face," and walked away to address the other, chosen recruits.

I thought of my cousin's Roman's question, "Do you really think they want you?" It became a fulfilled prophecy. Stunned, we dispersed into small groups debating the enormity of what had just transpired. A few more aggressive members of the rejected group boldly approached Capt. Chmura, demanding to speak to the camp's commanding officer. He answered that he was carrying the

Command's irrevocable orders. When asked whether his message conveyed the exact "language" of the order, he just shrugged his shoulders without a reply. His arrogance and display of absolute power incensed some in our group so much that we had to restrain them from physically attacking him. Three members of the Catholic group stepped back with unconcealed expressions of disgust and shame to join the file of Jews. They were the only ones of the Christian denominations to stand with us, even though we had all shared the ordeal of the long trip, as well as camaraderie and hope as future brothers in arms. It made the small group of three a token of human conscience, emphasizing the most painful lesson about the evil of indifference in the face of bigotry.

We stood confused, robbed of purpose with no means or place to go. Someone suggested we ask the Soviet military headquarters, located behind the railroad station depot, for help. A friendly-looking Red Army major by the name of Stolarov received our delegation. After hearing us out, he explained that the Soviets had no jurisdiction over the Polish Army and suggested that we approach the Polish civilian authorities in Tashkent, the Republic's capital, or in Alma Ata, the capital of the neighboring Republic of Kazakhstan. Since the train that brought us to Lugovaya was scheduled to leave soon for Alma Ata to pick up and carry freshly recruited Russian troops to the front lines, he explained, we might as well travel to Alma Ata. He generously arranged to provide us with supplies of food for the trip and bid us good luck.

Bonded by the cruelty of our rejection and humiliation, with our desire to join the fight against Germany ruined and our hopes to leave the Soviet Union choked by the noose of prejudice, we found ourselves suspended in a vacuum, with our immediate future curled into the shape of a giant question mark.

We split into smaller groups of strangers, creating makeshift family units to face the unknown tomorrows. In my group, we were seven youths from different parts of prewar Poland of varied social, economic, and educational backgrounds hoping to pool together our wits and determination to survive and to rebound our damaged psyches, which had encountered heartbreak. We managed to restore our spirits and desire to pursue our common goal, departure from the Soviet Union.

We arrived in Alma Ata, and our immediate problem was to find a supply of food. We hung around the Alma Ata train depot watching departing uniformed and civilian groups as they loaded provisions obtained from the quartermaster's headquarters located behind a wooden fence in an open field several hundred meters from the railroad tracks. We realized that this was the only source of food supply, and we had to invent a way to qualify for it. I suggested that we get our supply under the pretense that we represented a unit of conscripts departing for the front. This caused a heated discussion among us. Misha called the idea too dangerous. If caught in our deception, we could face a court-martial, or possibly a firing squad, since we were civilian imposters. Zygmunt called it courageous but stupid. Bolek pointed out that courage was based on stupidity. Pinio, the calmest of the group, said, "Let's consider the practical part of Olek's idea, evaluating how and who would dare to do it." It was at that moment that I assumed the role of a hero by volunteering for the dangerous, potentially suicidal mission. I exchanged clothing with Pinio, putting on his military greycoat and cap with a red star affixed to it. Accompanied by Szymek, who also wore the Russian military tunic, we marched off in the direction of the compound. We memorized the identifying number of the military unit numbering one hundred twenty recruits we had overheard at the depot. While the rest of the group waited in the open field, the two of us were admitted to see the officer in charge. As coolly as I could manage, I addressed the quartermaster carrying the rank of captain. I spoke in military fashion and rattled off the number of our unit, two digits higher than the one we had memorized. I was grateful for my command of the Russian language that I'd gained in the schools of hard knocks, in Lwow, the prison, and the gulag.

The Captain checked his list and looked back at us. "I don't have you on my list. You must be a new unit. Where did you come from?" I didn't sense any suspicion. Encouraged, I reported, "We were formed in Lugovaya, in Uzbekistan, by Major Stolarov. We are sixty men strong."

"Ahhh, Major Stolarov, a good man. We can give you supplies for only three days. We will deliver it to your transport. Which track is your train on?"

"Track number three, Comrade Captain," I snapped out in answer, "but my men are waiting outside, and we wouldn't need any help from your staff to haul the provisions."

"That's very good. We are short of men. Here, take this order to Sergeant Klemov outside my office. He will release the supply to you." He rubber-stamped a piece of paper and handed it to me. "Good luck in your fight for the Motherland." We saluted, executed a perfect "about-face," and were out of the room to face our next hurdle.

Sergeant Klemov couldn't have been more accommodating. Apparently the bureaucracy of the military, as well as the communist system, bowed with respect to troops destined to fight on the battlefields. This preserved the cushy safety of those in the support services far away from the real action. His staff placed sacks of supplies at the gates of the compound. I waved to our gang to come over. They hesitated until Szymek and I were left alone. We could not believe our luck, each of us bending under the weight of the sacks filled with supplies. We stopped a Kazakh peasant with an empty mule driven-cart, which we loaded with our loot. We asked him if he knew of some available quarters where we could stay overnight. A generous supply of food from our supply did the trick.

He led us to a home of a Kazakh woman whose husband had been recruited by the Red Army and sent to the front to fight the war. She provided us with temporary shelter. Her house consisted of one large room, bare of furniture except for one low table and flat pillows serving as substitutes for chairs. As was the custom, her bedroom was the top of the huge clay stove with an inside oven, the hearth of the home used for cooking and baking and as the only source of heat. Two built-in steps hoisted her to her bed in a niche on top of the stove under the low ceiling, where her embroidered quilt bedding was neatly spread.

Her husband's sister, Karina, young, tall, and slender with a delicately chiseled face, betraying a mix of Russian and Tartar ancestry, occupied the only bed tucked into a corner by the window. It was guarded by a mosquito net and surrounded by a white embroidered curtain for privacy. All of us slept on the dirt floor, using our long coats for bedding. By day we explored the city, trading food for clothes, cooking and eating utensils, and personal items we thought we might need. At night, exhausted after the day's wanderings, each of us slept embraced by his personal sweet memories of the past and a variety of visions of the unknown future.

I found it impossible to shut out of my mind the image of Karina behind the curtain in her bed next to me. The teasing fragrance of her, magnified by my erotic hunger and the vision of her body behind the wall of white muslin, bolstered my courage to climb over the invisible fence of propriety separating us. She responded to my hunger with a passion of her own, surprising by its intensity and depth. We lost ourselves in each other, rising and floating in total abandonment, in a world that excluded everything and everyone, except our long-suppressed need to touch, to feel, to love. We spoke little, and when we did, we called each other by every term of endearment, of which the Russian language is so richly endowed.

For five long nights I lived to love, experiencing the thrill of discovery, exploring the unending riches of the female body and its capacity to take and give the ultimate pleasure beyond one's wildest imagination. I wanted it to last forever.

To my deep regret, on the sixth day, our group decided to move on. We expressed our gratitude for the hospitality and left a handsome supply of food for our hostesses. As we parted, Karina looked at me for a long time, embraced me, and whispered in my ear:

"Sashenka, I will bear you a son and will name him Aleksandr. May God be with you and protect you."

I was too emotional to find an immediate reply before she disappeared from the house and from my life. We gathered our belongings and set out into the great unknown.

We were aware that the United States had been attacked by the Japanese at Pearl Harbor and had declared war against the Axis powers, making Americans allies of the Soviet Union. The Russians believed hopefully that a "second front" would soon become a reality, easing the pressure on Russia in its fight against Germany. We knew about Leningrad being under siege by Hitler's armies with his order that "Leningrad must be wiped from the face of the earth." We also heard tales of the "glorious victories" of the Red Army, which everybody discounted as pure propaganda. However, none of this affected our situation directly.

The proverb "Necessity is the mother of all invention" was never more timely or applied more accurately than it was in our present predicament. Walking east for five days, through villages and small towns, we were heading toward the Chinese border. We hoped, in time, to cross it on our path of escape to freedom.

CHAPTER 11

EVGENEVKA

Our wanderings ended when we came across the village of Evgenevka, nestled at the foot of the mountain chain called Tien Shan, translated as "Mountains of Heaven." This culminated in Victory Peak, about 25,000 feet high. We were enthusiastically welcomed at the *kolkhoz*, the collective farm, called Voroshilov. All young able-bodied men of the village had gone to war. Our group of seven was a godsend, representing a healthy, all-male working force in the almost exclusively female-populated kolkhoz.

The village spread out along its only unpaved dirt road running parallel to the county road, which had brought us all the way from Alma Ata. Two wooden buildings facing this road were the administration headquarters and the kolkhoz manager, a benign, middle-aged Ukrainian, Semyon Osipovich Tarasenko. He was the one who, despite inquisitive questioning by Irina Zhurova, his communist party-appointed deputy, welcomed us with open arms. He had been forcibly transplanted from his native Ukraine by Stalin's henchman Nikita Khrushchev, who earned the title of "the butcher of Ukraine" for his cruelty in breaking up the resistance of the peasants to collectivization of their privately owned lands. Semyon found immediate kinship with us, a group of Poles, similarly forced by war to abandon their native land. He accommodated us, over the protests of Zhurova, in one of two large rooms of the free-standing building serving as the village's assembly and recreation hall, located between the administration building and the only street of the village. It was built of wood, unlike the majority of lime and dirt houses of the village. He helped us build a wooden platform, on which we placed straw-filled sacks in lieu of mattresses. A wooden table with two benches completed our furniture. A wide window of the room, protected by a roofed porch, faced the formidable Talgar and Komsomol mountain peaks covered with eternal snow. Beyond them lay China.

We settled in our temporary home, warmly accepted by the population of the village as a group of friendly Polacks. We decided not to disclose our Jewish background. Each of us was assigned or chose work, performing various chores such as tilling the land, tending to livestock, building mud houses, forging iron at the local smithy, harvesting crops, and all other farm-related work. Pinio, only a few years older then I and the most mature, acted as our confident leader. He easily adapted to the circumstances and used his street smarts to our advantage. Thus he became an expert watchmaker, a master fix-it man, and a barber popular with the older men. Szymek, the most docile of our group, become my best friend. He made sure I ate well, helped me mend my clothing, and was always available when I needed advice and support. He was the most religious of the group, but he didn't impose religion on any of us. I knew he didn't approve of my sexual activities with the ladies I befriended, but he wouldn't criticize or reprimand me for it. He spoke little of his past, and we didn't press him. We gathered it was not too exciting. He had worked in his father's dry-goods store in the small town of Polehynk, populated equally by Jews and Ukrainians; his speaking pattern very much reflected his Ukrainian background.

Bolek was the very opposite. Second oldest, my senior by seven years, tall and dark-haired, he was full of nervous energy and had symptoms of bulimia. He never told us the origin of it, but we surmised that it was a reaction to his term in the gulag, which earned him our sympathy. His hawk-like long nose, matched by his jerky movements, made him appear as a bird of prey, yet he was liked by the ladies and availed himself of their company. He and Szymek took upon themselves the cooking chores for our group, serving up potato dumplings, thick soups, lamb, and available vegetables, all cooked in a pot over the hearth.

Misha became the official blacksmith of the kolkhoz. Thin, slightly bent, and seldom smiling, he was distanced from most of us except Pinio. His involvement with one of the young widows of the village took up most of his evenings, estranging him from the rest of us. The other loner among us, Herman, whom we called by his diminutive name Grisha, went through the routine of our daily chores without making much connection with any of us. He suffered from an unfocused eye alignment that made him appear constantly quizzical and made those in his company slightly uncomfortable. He was, however, the most focused on our goal of escaping the Soviet Union, which he kept reminding us of at the meetings that we held to discuss the problems of our little collective.

And it was a true collective. We shared everything: clothes, wages, and food supplies received for our daily work. Our allotment consisted of bread, flour, a limited amount of lard, and a variety of vegetables grown in the village. The allocation was made in accordance with the quota we had to fulfill by working a certain number of hours. Women whose husbands were away in active service had a steady stream of chores for us: gardening, chopping wood, digging holes, repairing fences—and they also paid us in extra food that we shared. I can still taste their apple and plum cakes.

Zygmunt, of my height and build but broader in the shoulders and with a more rounded face adorned by a thin moustache, commanded most attention in our close family. Like myself, he was *Gimnazium*-educated. He would always think and talk about his past and his family, particularly his mother. His emotional ties to her prevented him from getting involved with the local females. One of them, Vera, fell in love with him and didn't keep it a secret. He would meet and spend long hours with her, but he would not get sexually involved, even though, of all of us, he was physically the best endowed. We used to prompt him to consummate his relationship with Vera, a beautiful, blue-eyed blond with long hair framing her face and a Rubenesque figure. He made it clear that he would never choose a woman without his mother's approval; we felt he suffered from an Oedipus complex.

I welcomed the opportunities offered by the male-deprived, ravenous village females. My first liaison, which lasted several weeks, was with Anna, a society lady from Leningrad, the wife of an army general. She had left Leningrad at his insistence to live with his sister in Evgenevka. Our dates were clandestine in an orchard removed from her house. She was a fragile, tender, and gentle partner, easily satisfied, hungry for affection more than sex. When we paused to relax, we would talk about the books we read and recite poems, she in Russian, I in Polish, of which she had a fair command since she had a Polish mother. Our liaison ended when her husband, seriously wounded, returned from the front to a hospital in Moscow, where she joined him.

It didn't take long for me to become involved with Tatiana, a young widow who kept me busy in her vegetable garden and her bed. Our lovemaking drained my energies, and it was probably my youthful stamina that allowed me to be fit for work the following morning after our long nights. She insisted I move in with her and her three-year-old daughter, who had become attached to me. Knowing that Evgenevka was only a stopover on my quest to leave Russia, I declined. Gradually we limited our relationship, which brought me closer to my buddies. I enjoyed this new balance of spending more time with them.

In the evenings, we would all gather on our porch singing old romantic ballads and folk and military Polish songs, which were answered by beautiful Russian folk songs sung by young women marching up and down the country road playing accordions. One could hear, late into the night, the voices and sounds baring the souls of the people united in revealing their passions, their longing for the past, and their hopes for the future. Occasionally we would join their procession, flirting with the women and singing along.

On one such evening, I met Marisa Kotchtova, a teacher from Alma Ata, who came to her native village to help with the July harvest. I became instantly attracted to her. I asked if she would like to meet with me the next evening. We did meet, and while sitting on the lawn in front of her house, we shared the stories of our lives, our hopes, and frustrations, all the time under the watchful eyes of her teenage brother, known as the village's *zhulik*, a knife-yielding hooligan. It was not until working brigades were formed to go to the remote fields belonging to the *kolkhoz* to harvest the wheat and trash it in the huge "combiners," machines set up for the duration of the harvest, that we became lovers. We stayed together for two weeks, working side by side during the day and burying ourselves in the freshly erected straw stacks in marathon sessions of lovemaking. The fragrances of nature mixed with those of our bodies increased our excitement to the highest pitch. It became almost painful for our bodies to disengage from one another. I realized that I had fallen in love with her and slowly approached the subject of sharing our lives. She was flattered by my proposal but said she was not ready. After the harvest, we managed to continue to have privacy when we met. Marisa was very clever, knew everyone in the village, and was able to arrange rendezvous in her neighbors' homes when they traveled to Alma Ata and other neighboring small towns to sell their part of produce the *kolkhoz* allowed them after they produced the required quota for the collective. We spent long hours in the little saunas these homes were equipped with, lost to the world and reality. Reality hit me in September when the school year resumed; Marisa went back to Alma Ata, and I learned from her brother Igor that all along she was married to a high party official and I should not attempt to contact her again. I detected a note of threat, as well as regret, when he turned around after his warning and waved at me.

The shock of the news and the breakup of the relationship was devastating. She was intelligent, sensuous, and earthy, and I found comfort in her presence. For the rest of my stay in the village, I abstained from any contact with women, concentrating on work. My bad moods turned me into an unpleasant companion to my friends. They sympathized with me, but they were glad my romance had ended. I looked for solitude, and with the approach of winter I volunteered to work on a sheep base about twelve kilometers from the kolkhoz.

The sheep compound was fenced; a small hut with a wood-burning stove and a stable where the Kazakh shepherds kept their horses were the only structures. We all slept on mats spread over the dirt floor, drew water from a nearby stream, and, when it froze, used melted snow to drink and wash. Our biological functions were performed in the great outdoors. As far as one would cast an eye, there was only the vast expanse of the steppe with patches of tall brush breaking the monotony of nothingness. There was plenty of feed for the sheep, despite the winter. The problem was the wolves, which feasted on the stray ones, especially the young lambs. Losses of livestock were routinely reported by the kolkhoz to the regional communist party office in the town of Issyk. Late in the year, this resulted in a visit by a party delegation to verify the reports. We all knew that the true reason was to get a few sheep for their Christmas and New Year's celebrations. Of course, in return, the delegation approved and endorsed the claimed losses. After a supple lunch of lamb roasted over an open fire, accompanied by rounds of ice-cold vodkas, the delegation was ready to return home. Alas, their truck wouldn't start. A broken part of the engine needed to be replaced. With no telephone available, someone had to reach the kolkhoz manager to get help.

By a twist of irony, I, who never rode a horse, was selected for the chore. What ensued would be another experience forever ingrained in my memory. When I explained that I had no experience with horses, I was told, "Don't you worry. Ninotchka knows her way to our base. Just relax, trust her, and let her get you there." I was helped to mount the mare by the young Kazakh and wondered why he smiled at me, shaking his head sideways. I was too tense to respond to the delegates waving at me encouragingly. It took some time before my body adjusted to the pace and sway of Ninotchka. We traveled through the hard surface of frozen ground, avoiding the many icy patches. At one point, when the mare lowered her head to drink from an unfrozen stream, I almost catapulted over her head. I was not prepared for her sudden movement. As darkness set in, she became restless. I soon discovered the source of her anxiety when I noticed the shining spots reflecting the eyes of a pack of wolves and heard the unmistakable sound of their distinct howling. My heart and stomach left my body, and a feeling of unavoidable doom entered my half-conscious mind. The semicircle of the pack narrowed as Ninotchka broke into a trot. Unused to this new motion, I almost fell off her back. The feeling of helplessness, intensified by the freezing night air, overwhelmed me, when I suddenly spotted the lights of our hut. I was stiff and lifeless when I was lowered from Ninotchka's back and rolled in the snow to avoid frostbite before being taken into a warm room. The sight of people and the welcomed warmth emanating from the red-hot stove was the last thing I remembered before fainting. Acclaimed as a hero, my thoughts turned to my mother and the conviction that she was watching over me. I was filled with a sense of longing and gratitude. I visited Ninotchka the next morning, offering her some cubes of sugar and placing a thank-you kiss on her nose. She understood and responded with a snort and a friendly kick. I made a silent resolution that she would remain my first and last horse I would ever ride.

Before the winter's end, I rejoined my gang and was grateful when they received me with open arms. We continued to work hard and productively, never forgetting our plan to escape. We realized that without local help, we wouldn't succeed. We befriended some of the older villagers and among them a young fellow, the nephew of the manager Tarasenko, Boris Stephanovich Tabakov. He had escaped mobilization to the Red Army by being lame, his left leg shorter than the right one.

He became quite fond of us, and we reciprocated. He loved to spend time listening to our stories about the good life we led in Poland before the war. He was envious of our exposure to the West, our youthful adventures and romances during the summers spent in vacation resorts, the pranks we played in school, and the hopes we had for our future careers, until the war interrupted it all. In turn, he was the one to introduce us to some of the Kazakh members of the community, most of whom used to tend cattle, drive mules to performing many chores, and cultivate the tobacco plants, the main source of income for the kolkhoz. We befriended some of them, visited with their families, and learned their customs and social behavior. Sitting on cushions placed on the dirt floor, we shared meals with them, conversing with those who spoke and understood Russian.

We were surprised by a comment during one such visit when we were discussing the rapid advance of the German army. The host, speaking with an air of authority, blamed the Jews for the Russian defeats. Asked whether he had encountered any Jews and why he thought they were to blame, he answered, "I never met or saw a Jew, but everybody knows they are evil and cause all our troubles." Maintaining our identity as Poles, we didn't get drawn into a discussion of his views, but marveled at this display of prejudice as proof that ignorance is a fertile ground for spreading distortion even in the most remote places.

Boris became very close to us. We practically adopted him as our eighth member of the family. Eventually we confided in him about our dream to escape and return to the lives and the country we left behind. We learned to trust him, seeing his genuine interest and longing for a better life and freedom. He volunteered to scout the mountains for an escape route to China under the condition that he would join our group in the escape. We readily agreed. Scouting was easy for him, since he regularly wandered into the mountains collecting dry wood for the collective's winter needs. He often stopped to chat with the border patrol troops and made friends with some of them, supplying them with tobacco and home-distilled alcohol. He kept extending his reconnaissance ever so much further, keeping us informed of his progress. One day he reported that a new troop made up of soldiers wounded on the front had replaced his old friends. It upset him, but he sounded confident, believing that the day we were all waiting for was fast approaching. One week later, he came back all flushed and excited, telling us that he had gotten the closest yet to our potential border crossing.

We were left in total shock and disbelief when his bullet-ridden body was brought one late evening to the village. His funeral buried our hopes of escape and left us depressed, mourning the loss of a friend whose life and dreams ended so tragically. We bid him farewell at the small cemetery, where he was laid to rest, and the Soviet border guards perfidiously eulogized him as a victim of a marauding Mongolian gang. We found out that the Soviet guards had shot him when one of the guards disclosed it in a drunken moment. The cruel, real cause of his death hung on us as a heavy burden and a sacred secret that the seven of us were left to carry.

We lost our enthusiasm and interest in our work and the people around us. We started finding fault with the management, which despite its approval of our presence and efforts were not responsive to our needs. We had worn out our shoes and asked for replacements to continue working, but to no avail. At our meeting, I proposed we call a strike. No shoes, no work. The very idea of a strike was anathema to the Soviet system. Nobody dared to exercise this human right under the rule of the communist party. It was considered counterrevolutionary activity with an automatic banishment to a gulag.

Gulags under the communist system were crowded with Russian citizens whose so-called crimes might have been much less significant than a strike. An innocent critical remark about the Party or Stalin made to a neighbor, a friend, or a family member who would choose to report it to authorities was enough to send one to the Siberian freeze. How well I knew it from all the tales I had heard during my own internment in prison, as well as my experiences in the gulag of Osinovka.

Our discussion became quite heated until I took the floor. To my own surprise, I heard myself ask, "Do you remember the day in Alma Ata when we risked our lives to obtain food? Let's take the risk now. And if our demand is refused, let's threaten to report it as discrimination to the Polish Mission in Alma Ata." We realized that the Mission had no authority or power, and it was naïve to expect it to intercede, but our failed plans to escape to China and the ensuing frustration made the decision easier. When we confronted Irina Zhurova with our case, she coldly suggested that if we considered the Polish Mission as an authority, we should ask it to supply us with shoes. The idea took root and became the catalyst for our immediate future. We found out from the Polish representative that a second Polish army was being formed under the command of General Zygmunt Berling. According to the accounts of some of the soldiers of the First Polish Army, who boarded the last boat at the banks of the Caspian Sea, then-Colonel Berling stayed ashore and bid his farewell to the troops. Asked why he was not joining them, he replied:

"Well, someone must stay behind to take care of all those Poles left behind in the Soviet Union." Thus, thanks to his resolve, a new opportunity opened up for the vast number of Poles spread over the Soviet Union to join World War II as members of the fighting forces.

It was from the head of the Mission that we learned for the first time about Hitler's rule of terror in Poland, about the ghettos where Jews were gathered, and about where they were sent next, the concentration camps that later became death camps to millions. It made us that much more eager to take part in the war and the battle against the barbarian German enemy, ruled by Hitler and his Nazi gang.

After a tearful farewell, with handshakes, hugs, thanks, and blessings from the grateful villagers who had become our friends and a part of our lives, we started our second journey to enlist into the Polish Army.

As the seven of us left Evgenevka, we promised each other that if we survived the war, we would visit the grave of our Russian friend, Boris, and offer our respects and gratitude for his ultimate sacrifice to achieve our common dream.

As we passed through Alma Ata, we revisited the friendly Kazakh hostess who had provided us with the shelter when we were in need of a place to stay. She was mourning her husband's death at the front line of the Great Patriotic War. We offered our heartfelt condolences and assured her of our future efforts to avenge her husband's sacrifice. I inquired about Karina's whereabouts. She had no idea where she lived. She had recently received the only postcard from her, with no return address, in which Karina informed her of the birth of a baby boy named Aleksandr. In the many years and the many visits to come, none of my efforts to locate Karina succeeded, leaving me with the heavy burden of an unfulfilled part of my life as a father of a son.

Our group of seven parted ways as we drew assignments to different units and lost contact with one another. Only Zygmunt and I were assigned to the same artillery unit. I never found out how many, or if any, of the group survived the war to fulfill the promise to revisit Boris's grave.

It was over thirty years before I found the opportunity to return to Evgenevka to honor my pledge. The Kazakh manager of the kolkhoz, Chokan Suleyev, treated me as a guest of honor. I joined him and his family for an early festive dinner and was given a tour of the village. Gone were the grazing meadows, the fertile fields of golden wheat, and the proud stalks of corn. The entire collective was turned into one giant vineyard.

When the time came to fulfill the purpose of my trip, I asked to be taken to the grave of Boris Tabakov. My host's eyes narrowed furtively. "There is no grave of Boris Tabakov. He died a hero's death at the front during the war fighting the Nazis." He led me to the center of the village square, dominated by a granite monument. Suleyev pointed to the inscription on the stone's smooth polished face.

> "TO OUR BELOVED HEROES WHO GAVE
> THEIR LIVES IN DEFENSE OF THE FATHERLAND
> AGAINST THE EVIL FORCES OF FASCISM"
> June 22, 1941–September 2, 1945.

The list was in alphabetical order, and Boris' name appeared on the bottom row. I must have looked incredulous and stupid with my mouth open and my eyes riveted to the inscription. I bowed my head, praying for Boris' soul in silence. I looked up at the villagers who were gathered around the monument, curious of the identity of an unexpected American visitor. I caught sight of a woman who looked at me through the narrow slit of her eyes. I tried to juggle my memory to identify her. She spoke to me first.

"Your name is Sasha. I remember you. I'm Gala Vereshtchagina, a friend of Marisa. She died last year. It is nice of you to pay respects to Boris. I too remember the cause of his death." She turned and slowly walked away, giving me no chance to speak with her. I understood her message.

In the car heading for Alma Ata, my mind wouldn't rest. I was unable to absorb the perfidy of the system that made mockery of human tragedy to whitewash its own inhumanity.

CHAPTER 12

IN THE ARMY

The train became my home again. Day after day, its rhythmic clatter accompanied me, lulling me to sleep only to awaken me again to the monotonous, endless repetition. Again, names of places I never heard of flashed before my eyes. Nobody, including me, knew or cared what our destination would be. I was finally traveling with a purpose toward a goal that had proven so elusive in my previous efforts. I would be joining the Polish Army to fight evil forces, which had uprooted me, separated me from my loved ones, and caused me to suffer.

This spirit prevailed among the entire contingent of the young volunteers. I recognized quite a number of them from our previous ignominious encounter at Lugovaya. We settled into our routine, interrupted by stopovers in exotic places. As soon as the train would come to a halt, we would try to find out how much time we had to hurry to the nearby villages to talk with the local people, trade with them, and look for souvenirs. It felt good for a change to have the familiar snow cover replaced by the hot sand of the desert. Occasionally our stops would coincide with the local or regional market day. We would watch with interest how the various ethnic groups intermingled: Russians, Ukrainians, Tartars, Uzbeks, Tajiks, and Turkish tribes, all wearing their national dress and providing kaleidoscopic images of the composition of the Soviet Union. Although we were not in the market to buy cows, sheep, or other living creatures, it was interesting to watch the trading among these culturally different groups.

Finally, the word spread that we were headed for Stalingrad. It was barely three months since the Germans surrendered after a five-month battle that had no equal in the annals of wars. The Germans were thought to be invincible until they tried to take Stalingrad in August 1942. The five-month assault cost more than a million lives and left 90 percent of the city in rubble. The house-to-house, room-to-room fighting earned a chapter in history, with examples of heroism, sacrifices, tenacity, and ingenuity in hand-to-hand combat. The stubborn ferocity of the valiant defenders brought about Germany's first real defeat in the war. The surrender of General von Paulus marked its turnaround, compared only to Napoleon's surrender to the Russian winter and his retreat from Moscow in 1812.

We stopped at Stalingrad for three days. Every day we were escorted to see the damage and to absorb the picture of destruction. We voluntarily helped remove some of the debris created by collapsed buildings. We were told how under continual bombardment from the air and artillery, the workers, side by side with the soldiers, repaired tanks and guns and continued to manufacture arms and munitions. We were brought here as living witnesses to the martyrdom of the people of this city, their courage and self-denial, the glorious victory of the Red Army, and, of course, the "greatness" of the leader of the Soviet Union: Josif Vissarianovich Djugashvilli, known as the man of steel, Stalin. It was effectively planned propaganda to stimulate us, the future soldiers, in our mission to defeat Hitler's Germany.

From Stalingrad, we headed north until we reached Novosybirsk, known as the new town of Siberia. Here, the Polish authorities established an assembly center for other trainloads of volunteers and recruits. Our group was temporarily transported to a coal-mining village near Kamerovo. We hardly had time to explore Novosibirsk. An industrial region in Western Siberia, the city developed rapidly from a population of three thousand in 1893 to become the fifth-largest city in the Soviet Union. While waiting for the arrival of the expected contingent of men, we were assigned to work in the local coal mine. I kept wondering how many more professions or trades I would have to learn before becoming a soldier.

To my surprise, I enjoyed my new assignment. Being lowered underground in a primitive manually operated lift, finding myself surrounded by blackness, the only light provided by hand-carried lanterns and a few sparsely located low-voltage lamps, and energy supplied by huge outside generators, I felt transplanted into a new mysterious world. My job was to load the chunks of coal onto little rail cars that then traveled to an assembly area, were loaded into lifts, and pulled to the surface. We were outfitted with special attire. It was all a new experience, complete with a sense of risk and a sampling of what mining was all about.

After the day's labors, we would all head for the *banya*, the communal bath. Men and women together were enveloped by the steamy warmth, soaped each other's backs, and then swatted each other with the willow twigs bunched together to invigorate circulation and to rub their backs clean of the black soot. Strangely, the sight of naked bodies of both genders was not erotic. Nobody made provocative moves or off-color remarks. Yet the moment we would get dressed, our imaginations would take over, and our normal sexual fantasies surfaced. This transition amazed me each time we left the banya.

The first night, most of us were lodged in a large barn-like wooden building. We all slept on straw-filled mattresses laid on the floor alongside the walls. I was squeezed between a Russian man in his fifties and a young Russian woman whom I noticed in the baths and remembered for her well-proportioned body. The barn filled with noises of sleeping bodies. The occasional cough, the breaking of wind, snoring, and mumblings chased away my sleep, despite the fatigue. As I contemplated what the next day would bring, I felt something crawling up my upper thigh. With a sudden motion I trapped the invader, to discover that it was the hand of my female neighbor. Before I fully realized what was happening, her body was pressing against me, and its motions turned the night into an endless blissful fantasy. I marveled at how she managed not to arouse our neighbors on the left and right. I whispered to ask her name, which she answered with a "Shhhh." The first pink smudge of the rising sun appeared when I finally fell asleep. My benefactress of the night's delight was gone when I woke up. My eyes searched for her the whole day in vain, and my hopes to see her again at the bath did not materialize. Still today, it remains one of the little surprises and quirks life plays on you. I do not regret this one.

Members of our group were assigned living quarters with the local residents. My hostess, Katya, was a woman in her late thirties. She must have been a beauty when she was younger, and she still maintained her good looks despite the lines that creased her face showing the traces of lost time and a hard life. She considered herself a widow, since her husband was declared lost in action at the very beginning of the war. Her inquiries about his whereabouts produced no additional information. She lived with her cousin, whose husband perished in the war. Julek Bader, one of those rejected at Lugovaya, became my roommate. This arrangement lasted only the first day. By the second night, we were intimate with the ladies, I with Katya and Julek with her cousin Galina. For the short time that we spent in Kamerovo, we expended more physical energy in endless lovemaking than either of us thought capable of.

Katya was insatiable. Every late afternoon, upon returning from work, I was assaulted by her needs. I would surface from her hungry embraces for a quick dinner, which she prepared, and then returned to satisfying her demands. I felt she knew that this might be her last opportunity to love and be loved, and she wouldn't let go of it. When I asked for respite, trying to get some sleep and rest, she would taunt me by saying, "You dig for dry, cold, and dusty coal all day. Enjoy now digging in something warm, wet, and friendly." She endeared herself to me with her simplicity, honesty, and sincerity, and for sharing her body and soul with me. She made me appreciate the plight of many women of this time, separated from their husbands and lovers, driven to loneliness, longing, and hopelessness by the war. It was much harder for us to part than I would have imagined. Her face quivered when I was about to leave. Her breasts, pressed tightly against my chest, transmitted a feeling that her very heart was pressing against mine. I held her in my arms while she whispered in my ear her blessings for my safety. "Stay alive, Sashenka. May God reunite you with your loved family. I will pray for you. Good-bye, my fierce lover." I was deeply touched and grateful that I had come to know her. Somehow, I had the feeling that I was saying good-bye not only to her but also to Russia itself. Later on, the more I thought about that moment, the more I became convinced that this had indeed been my farewell to Russia.

At the recruiting center in Gorky, we registered and shed our civilian clothes for new military uniforms of the Polish army. Moscow was our first stop on our journey west. The snow mixed with rain marred the silhouette of the Kremlin as we marched through the streets. We were surprised at the wooden peasant houses standing in the shadows of drab brick housing complexes for the workers, clashing with the majestic classic palaces and monuments to Moscow's founder Prince Yuri Dolgoruky; Russia's great poets, writers and composers; and the famous Bolshoi Ballet. Our marching column reached Red Square, where we paraded past the reviewing stand in front of Lenin's Mausoleum before a group of high-ranking Soviet military leaders. This was our first visit to the Soviet capital, and for most of us it was the last one. We could not believe it when we heard the order to line up to enter the Kremlin, where we were led to the impressive St. George's Hall, which was decorated entirely in white. This hall, the largest in the Kremlin, 61 meters long and with eighteen twisted columns, is named after the Order of St. George, the highest military distinction under the Tsars. On marble plaques on the walls were carved the names of the Russian regiments and knights of the Order under Nicholas I.

As I was moving in a single line, admiring in total reverence the awesome display of history, there was some commotion at the entrance to the hall. I turned my head and stopped, riveted to the floor. I looked directly at the living statue of Stalin. He walked slowly, moving his head left and right to absorb everyone in the two rows of soldiers. His right arm was raised, bent at the elbow, and his hand moved imperceptibly in a combination of a salute and a blessing motion. His face had a fatherly, benevolent look conveying serenity and kindness. I could not believe that this was the same man whose orders were responsible for millions of innocent people being deprived of their freedom, rotting in jails and gulags, being tortured to admit to crimes they had not committed, and dying ignominious deaths. Zygmunt nudged me, whispering, "Olek, it is Him. It really is Him." I shared his astonishment, but at the same time noticed that Stalin was not a tall person. Seeing his monuments displayed in every city, town, and village, where he appeared tall and majestic, I expected him to be a towering figure. He wore the familiar tunic and trousers with a sharp crease and finely polished shoes, but he fell short of the image his portraits and monuments had projected. We felt let down. Still, I could sense power radiating from him. I stood confused, not knowing whether to feel proud and humbled by his very presence on the eve of the Polish unit's departure for the front, or resentful and angry, remembering my gulag experiences. The commonality of purpose we all shared, to defeat Germany, brought clarity to my mind, surpassing all differences and antagonisms.

It took another journey by train from Moscow before we reached the village of Dratchonina and the camp that would become our training center. Traveling together, Julek and I had the time to relive the short Kamerovo interludes with the ladies, who had made it unforgettable. We joked that we had become cousins through the relationship with our hospitable hostesses. We promised to stay in touch and try to get together after the war. The interesting aspect of these promises was that we so casually took for granted the uncertainty of survival.

Our camp was located in a dense pine forest. Each company was lodged in a *zemlanka*, a hut, dug and half-buried in the ground and covered by a camouflaged roof. These barracks provided natural warmth supplemented by the heat from a wood-burning stove. The bunks were made of rough boards covered by straw mattresses and pillows draped by flax bed linens and a warm, woolen blanket. A narrow table ran the entire length of the barrack, with benches on both sides. It was used at meals and during artillery theory training sessions held after field exercises. At the entrance, a small desk-like table and a straight chair served as my "office." A window an inch above ground level provided some light in addition to the light from a ceiling lamp. Across an open stretch from our hut stood the 122mm and 152mm howitzer guns on which we trained. Our battery commander, Karol Jarosz, was a pre-war cadet in a Polish officer school. He now carried the rank of lieutenant. Pleasant to the enlisted personnel and curious about everyone's background, he appointed me as the battery scribe. My work was to produce a daily schedule, keep track of supplies, and report about the sick and hospitalized. Generally speaking, I was performing the battery's secretarial staff function. These duties took time from my field training with the heavy guns, but I made sure not to miss the reconnaissance training sessions.

Our regiment was composed of two *dyvizyons*, the artillery equivalent to the infantry's battalions. Each dyvizyon was made up of three batteries. My duty called for filing daily reports with the regiment's chief scribe by the name of Julian Feingold. Initially he treated me with an air of superiority, but as time went by he gained respect for my performance and became a friend. He confided in me about his desire to draw and paint and made me pose for a charcoal-drawn portrait. He was quite talented and gained recognition in the United States after the war. In turn, I confided in him about my writing poetry, and occasionally he would invite me to recite it to him. My friend Zygmunt Bargad completed our threesome.

From Dratchonina, we were transferred to a number of other training camps in Khlebovo, Sielce, Divovo, and Potchynok-Polany. We trained hard and learned quickly to operate the heavy howitzer guns and radio and telephone equipment, as well as army discipline. We went through live ammunition-training exercises and became real soldiers. On February 18, 1944, a midnight alarm sounded to abandon camp. Our march to the front to join the fighting began. News reached us of the gallant battle of Lenino, where the First Polish Division distinguished itself in a bloody battle. It suffered many losses, but established a reputation of courage, bravery, and perseverance as Polish fighters.

We arrived at the outskirts of Smolensk, an ancient Russian city that in the course of history was ruled by Slavic tribes, Lithuanians, and Poles until it was reclaimed by Russia. Conquered by the Germans in the beginning of their onslaught on Russia, it was the most recent site of heavy fighting before the German retreat.

I was summoned to report to Feingold, by now promoted to the rank of sergeant. Bargad and another soldier, Czeslaw Zimnoch, were with him when I arrived. In a cold, officious manner, Sergeant Feingold ordered us to pack our personal items and be ready in an hour to be taken to the brigade headquarters.

"What happened? Why us? What did we do wrong?" We questioned him anxiously. He held our gaze, and slowly his features softened when he said, "You have been picked to leave for the Artillery Officers Academy." Our joyful surprise was topped by the news that it was Julian's recommendation that singled us out for this assignment, honor, and challenge. After an exchange of hugs and wishes for good luck, we were off to a new adventure. When I looked back, Julian was standing in the doorway waving at us, a Cheshire-cat smile beaming from his face. We kept walking away and waving until his figure became a blur and finally disappeared from our sight.

The first month of our schooling was at Kostroma, a city on the Volga River north of Moscow. It consisted of marching drills, hard physical exercises on obstacle courses, and a variety of basic functions that we, as future leaders, would train and expect our troops to perform. The next three and a half months we spent in Ryazan, another river city south of Moscow. Here we started focusing on the finer points of military education and leadership. The discipline increased, and inspection of our sleeping quarters and frequent night alarms and marches became the routine. Courses on armaments covered all caliber guns, from the light field artillery to the heavy 122mm and 152mm howitzers. In addition, we learned the use of automatic weapons as well as handguns. It was here that we heard of the American landing in Normandy on June 6, "D-day," the long-awaited opening of the second front in Europe. The Russians were elated at the news, while criticizing the long time it took the Western Allies to start the offensive against Germany. Needless to say, to us, the Polish cadets, the news was a harbinger of a successful outcome of a war in which we had yet to participate.

From Ryazan, we headed for the final three months of our schooling to the Polish city of Chelmno, recently liberated from the German occupation. On our way, our train made a two-hour stop in the town of Rovne. It was the birthplace and home of Zygmunt. He asked me to accompany him to visit his old home. We ran from the station the entire distance, arriving there breathless. The one-story house bathed in the July sun looked pretty, with plants and flowers surrounding it. The front door was wide open, and when we peeked in a woman noticed us and waved to invite us in. Zygmunt recognized her immediately as the old caretaker his parents employed before the war. I moved discretely away to allow them privacy, but Zygmunt motioned for me to stay. We quickly learned that his entire family had perished in a German death camp. The tragic news made us suddenly immune to the beauty of the surroundings. I put my arm around Zygmunt's shoulders as he broke out sobbing. The caretaker left the room and soon reappeared with a small package, which she handed to Zygmunt.

"Your mother left it for you. She was sure you would return and wanted me to pass it on to you." The package contained his mother's favorite amber broche, and a pair of *tefilim*, or phylacteries (small leather cases containing strips of vellum, inscribed with certain Hebrew verses of the Law and worn on the forehead and left arm by male Jews during Morning Prayer). This gift from the grave threw Zygmunt into a spasm of weeping. He regained control of himself, and after a quick farewell, we ran back to the train that took us to Chelmno.

We briefly celebrated the occasion of our return to Poland before we hunkered down to tackle the theories of warfare. This was the most interesting and rewarding part of our education, since many of the aspects we studied would apply to civilian life as well. It was mind-broadening to learn strategy, tactics, use of manpower, and resources. My favorite teacher was Major Seredov. Decorated early in the war with the Gold Star as a Hero of the Soviet Union, he managed to overcome serious head injuries that had resulted in a brain operation. His scar ran diagonally across his forehead, giving him a sinister look. Yet he was the mildest, kindest, and most patient teacher, tolerant with the slow learners, but demanding attention and total involvement in our studies. The wisdom and philosophy he would dispatch held us in awe. He, like most of our instructors, was bilingual, having mastered the Polish language or hailing from homes where Polish was the second language. When he found out I was writing poetry, he encouraged me to continue.

"Poetry is the mirror of one's soul," he used to say. "Poetry is seeing, hearing, and feeling. It is an acknowledgment of being alive."

I respected Seredov and tried to earn his approval. I studied hard and was pleased by his praise when I graduated among the top twenty cadets.

General Berling attended the graduation and the ceremony of installing us as officers. His sword touched my shoulders while he pronounced my rank of second lieutenant. A single star was pinned on each of my epaulets by Captain Kubsz.

At the age of twenty-three, I became an officer, a potential leader of men. The thought struck me that my life was one giant paradox. I still felt like an orphaned teenager, torn away from his loved ones, his home, and his safe environment, stopped in his natural progression of life and normal growth into adulthood. On the other hand, I was an adult hardened by suffering and depravation of the basic elements of human development, thrown into a hostile world filled with cruelty, injustice, and pain, which I effectively conquered in order to survive and to lead others along the way. And then, of course, the question kept creeping into my mind: *Survived for what?*

The now-freely circulating news of the German atrocities in Poland, the concentration and death camps, the heroic acts by individuals and communities of the persecuted, the Warsaw ghetto uprising and the annihilation of its brave fighters, startled me and filled me with anxiety. Zygmunt's recent experience intensified the question. *Survived for what?*

I remembered the time in the gulag when I willed myself not to dwell on my past in order to concentrate on the task of survival. Now that I succeeded and was heading closer to my old home, I couldn't help wonder what I would find there, who would be there to welcome me, and whom I would be able to embrace, hold close to my heart, and fill the gap of separation with words of gratitude and love. I knew it would still take time before Warsaw and Lodz, my hometown, were liberated, and my reunion with the past could occur. So, again, I decided to push these thoughts aside and concentrate on the present. The proverbial *live one day at a time* became my reality.

Zygmunt and I got an unpleasant surprise when our assignments were announced: we were separated into different units. We parted with an embrace and good wishes. He handed me a small package with the words, "May this keep you safe and sound." It was one of the tefilim that he was given in Rovno. I was moved by his thoughtfulness and friendship. To this day, I treasure this talisman from a friend whose fate is unknown to me.

The Second Artillery Division started forming in late August 1944. The 7th Brigade contained three regiments. I was assigned to the 44th Regiment. We were located in the village of Adampol in a former estate of Polish nobility, the Zamojski family's. Surrounding us was a dense forest. When I arrived, the training grounds and the living quarters were all cleaned up and ready. The uniforms for the recruits, who hailed predominantly from the region of Lublin, started arriving, and the normal training routine and exercises began. I took command of the regiment's reconnaissance platoon, which was divided into observation and communication sections. My specialization and training came in handy, and I quickly adapted to my duties and tasks. My soldiers seemed to sense it and responded with interest and a serious attitude toward their training.

The fact that I wasn't a Russian was an additional positive factor in our mutual relationship. The Russian and Polish officers found their relationship awkward at first. Most of the Russians were front-line experienced veterans, while the Poles were mostly new graduates of the officer schools. At the same time, the known mutual dislike between Poles and Russians created an undercurrent of distrust. Yet these differences and nuances receded into the background when we all started working and playing together. Each evening, some of the Russian officers would sneak out to the village, where the local peasants would sell them their moonshine vodka and some willing females would offer their company. The officers were led by First Lieutenant Sergey Mironov, commander of the second battery, a good officer respected by his soldiers, notorious for his drinking and womanizing. He and I enjoyed a friendly working relationship but were not socially close. I stayed away from these forays. They held no attraction for me. I felt mellow and found fulfillment in composing poetry and keeping a diary while taking small sips of vodka.

Each morning and every evening, the Polish troops assembled in the cleared grounds in front of the barracks, singing a Polish hymn with religious undertones, thanking God for safeguarding Poland. After a while, the Russian officers would join us in this ritual to the amazement and satisfaction of the Poles. This love-hate relationship would not change throughout the entire campaign. It would become the glue to hold us together.

On January 17, 1945, Warsaw was liberated. That evening, a spontaneous celebration took place around a huge outdoor fire. As the flames lifted to the sky, an automatic gun salvo blasted into the stillness of the night, honoring the momentous occasion. Lodz was taken from the retreating Germans two days later, and a personal celebration, fraught with anxiety and misgivings, took place in my heart.

Our troops were ready and eager for the order to march west toward the battle lines.

CHAPTER 13

A VISIT TO REMEMBER

The long column of trucks on caterpillars moved slowly through the snow-covered road, dragging the heavy cannons. The strong, cold January wind blowing from the east kept up its monotonous whistling tune. Every once in a while, its whistle changed to a whimper, then burst into a sudden roar, only to change back into a quiet whine to finally assume the original whistling sound. The truck's laboring engines blended with the sound of the wind, disturbing the deep silence of the countryside.

The caterpillars, biting hungrily into the hard and dirty surface of the road, kept kicking up chunks of snow and ice against the powerful guns. They followed obediently, guided to their next unknown destination.

I had finally joined the war for real. The Officer's School became a faint memory, the training grounds in the thick woods of the artillery camp south of the city of Lublin left for other units to come. We were on the move, marching west. It was just one week since Warsaw's liberation; her gaping wounds cried out for vengeance for the bloodshed and the destruction inflicted upon her during the recent brave uprising against the German occupiers. Our hearts filled with the burning desire to be part of the punishing blow that would finally bring the barbarian enemy to its knees.

We had just left Lublin, passing the Nazi death camp Majdanek. The neat rows of empty barracks gave no hint of the atrocities committed against thousands upon thousands of innocent, defenseless human beings. To most of us this was a revelation, since in the news-controlled environment of the Soviet Union, we were made aware only of the German persecution of the Russian people. Little, if anything, was mentioned about the wide range of atrocities committed against Jews, Poles, Gypsies, and other groups, which the Hitler-appointed executioners had methodically exterminated with proverbial German efficiency and inventiveness. I did not know then that Majdanek was the grave of my only, beloved young brother, Ignac.

After a stopover in the city of Radom, our units left for Lodz, my hometown. My feelings were a mixture of anxiety and curiosity, apprehension and excitement, dread and hope. We stopped outside Kochanowek, which housed a well-known insane asylum. Very often, while playing our youthful games, we used the term "you belong in Kochanowek," implying one's dumbness and detachment from reality.

As soon as we established camp, I approached my superior officer for permission to leave for the city to visit my old home and to look for traces and information about my family.

He looked at me incredulously, saying, "Lieutenant, it is late in the evening, snowing up a storm, and you have no transportation. How the hell do you expect to accomplish this?"

"Just tell me when we are scheduled to march on, and I will be back in time," I said.

"I received no orders and have no idea when they will come. If I permit you to go, and you don't return in time, I'll have to declare you as absent without permission. You know the consequences. I cannot give you my permission." I looked at the captain, my pleading eyes saying the things my pride wouldn't let me. A moment passed. It seemed an eternity to me. He shrugged his shoulders and turned away, and with a wave of his arm, he expressed both his frustration and approval.

I entered the darkness of the night, lit by the white streaks of the swirling snowflakes. There was not a living soul on the road outside the tall red brick wall of the compound. I started walking, my boots crunching the snow-covered surface, not knowing how and when I would reach the city. The headlights of a truck, which appeared behind me, proved to be a gift from heaven. It carried supplies for the city's garrison. The driver seemed as eager for my company as I was for his kind consent to give me a lift. We tried to chat, but my mind was racing.

What would I find? Would I meet someone to connect me with my past? How would I react seeing my old home?

These and more were the thoughts piercing my resolve. For a moment, I thought of turning back. The moment passed.

Two hours later, at midnight, almost six years since I had left home, I stood in front of the apartment building where, thanks to my father's painful decision to save my life, I had bid good-bye to my adolescence to become a teenage orphan.

I pounded repeatedly on the heavy building door and pressed the doorbell, which was frozen in place; at last a young woman dressed in a heavy overcoat answered the door. When I asked to speak to Mr. Sobierajski, the janitor whom I remembered, she said that he had died the year before. I explained who I was, referred to the apartment I had lived in, and explained the urgency and purpose of my visit at such an inopportune time of the night. I asked to see the list of present tenants on the chance that I might find a familiar one. The heavy gate opened, and I was invited to the apartment of the old janitor's granddaughter, Janina. She was kind and understanding, spoke educated Polish, and was sympathetic of my predicament.

I took a quick look at the list she handed me. The name Markowicz jumped out, hitting me like lightening. My school friend Ben had survived and had just moved into his old flat! I thanked Janina profusely, apologizing for my intrusion. She offered a smile, saying she was glad to be of help to the son of her grandfather's friend. I must have shown a sense of confusion at the term "friend," because she immediately followed with an explanation.

Every Christmas and New Year's holidays, as was the custom, her grandfather visited all tenants and offered holiday greetings. The custom called for the tenants to respond by tipping him.

"Your father was the only one in this building who would invite my grandfather in to share a drink with him, offer him good wishes accompanied by a cash bonus, while your mother would present him with a freshly baked sponge cake. My grandpa always considered your father a gentleman and a friend. I'm glad I can be of help to you."

Filled with pride and humility, I embraced Janina and bolted to the front staircase, taking two and three steps at the time, climbing to the third floor. I rang repeatedly for more than five minutes, but there was no answer. I was beyond myself and decided to camp on the staircase until morning, when I suddenly sensed a movement behind the apartment's door. I looked through the peephole and to my surprise discovered an eye looking at me. I called out Ben's name and identified myself, including the description of our last get-together, to convince the person at the other side of the door.

I heard the chain being removed, and the door opened. Ben was standing in a cautious crouch, pointing a gun at me. I broke into a smile and raised my arms in a sign of surrender, while calling out Ben's name and repeating, "It's me, Ben, your old buddy Olek." Ben passed the gun to a woman standing behind him and opened his arms in a welcoming gesture. We embraced each other, holding the embrace for a long time.

We settled into wooden chairs in his sparsely furnished dining room. He introduced his wife, and she served us hot tea and biscuits. We appraised each other, noticing how much we had changed. He found me looking strong and masculine, enhanced by the officer's uniform I was wearing. "You lost your baby fat," he said, laughing. I found him more mature and manly than the young Ben I had played basketball with. There was a settled sadness in his expression, making him look older than his age. The knee-high boots with britches and the military-like tunic completed this new image of my old friend.

When I asked him what prompted him to face me with a pointed gun, he became sad and introspective. "There is a lot to be said about the way some of our Polish compatriots look at us now. Instead of sharing our joy of survival, some have become a new threat to us. Hitler's 'Juden frei Deutchland' [Germany free of Jews] virus has taken root among some. There are those who even say they regret Hitler didn't finish us all off.

No one slept that night as we shared stories from the time we parted at the outbreak of the war to the present. Ben's parents had been deported from the Warsaw ghetto into one of the death camps. He had participated in the heroic Warsaw ghetto uprising, escaping through the sewers to join a Jewish partisan unit. It was there that he had met his wife.

While in the ghetto, he had maintained close contact with my parents, who lived in the adjacent building. After they'd left Lodz to find what appeared to be refuge in Warsaw, my father's German friend, who took over our factory, supported them for a period of time. After dismantling the factory and transporting the machinery to Germany, the friend left Lodz too, and his support ceased. My father died of heart failure shortly thereafter. My brother Ignac, at the age of sixteen, was rounded up randomly on the street by the Gestapo and sent to the Nazi death camp Majdanek. The loss of the last of the family took a toll on my mother and led to her starvation, as she could not fend for herself. I sat transfixed and devastated listening to Ben, unable to conjure up the picture of my mother, the steadfast, strong woman with a heart filled with love and compassion, succumbing to death by hunger.

My shock was too intense for me to force a cry to relieve the pain. For the rest of my life, the image of my family hung in the air like the moon, out of reach but never out of sight, the pain dwelling in my heart and their images in my psyche.

* * *

As the morning approached, I was ready for the last chore of my trip, the visit to my old apartment. Then Ben was to give me a ride on his motorcycle to rejoin my unit.

A lady in her early thirties answered the bell on its second ring. Seeing a uniformed officer, she opened the door, admitted me into the familiar narrow entrance hall, and looked at me inquisitively. I identified myself, explaining that for sentimental reasons I wished to visit the apartment I had lived in before the war.

"Lieutenant, you must be mistaken. Before the war, Jews lived here," she said with obvious disdain.

"I know. I lived here," I replied, my eyes riveted on hers.

"So lieutenant is a Jew?" The half-question, half-statement oozed with contempt as she continued. "Let me tell you that I moved here legally, I have documents to prove it, and my brother is a high-ranking officer in the U.B." This was the abbreviation for the name of the security police. "I'm going to call him right now!" In her excitement, she raised her voice to a shrill. "I want you to give—"

I stopped her in the midst of her tirade, and as politely and calmly as I could, I repeated the sentimental nature of my visit, since my unit was moving to join the fight against *her* German enemy. I explained that I would be leaving for the front as soon as I left her apartment.

"Madam, this may sound ironic, but the truth is that I'm on a mission to make sure that *you* may continue to live in this place in peace, not having to worry about being under the German occupation again. Enjoy your apartment," I said, without trying to hide my contempt.

Struck by my words, she let me see the apartment. My sentiment and curiosity were gone by now. She had sounded like Ben describing the attitude of some Poles toward the returning Jews. I hardly felt anything when I saw some of the pieces of furniture that were part of my happy past. The place had become cold and alien.

As I bid good-bye to the hostess, I wondered whether this feeling of alienation and indifference would apply to the country as well, to the Poland I was so proud to call my own, to the Poland that was my home and my Motherland.

Would I ever want to return to Lodz should I survive the war? What happened to the rest of my large family circle? Would I find any of them if I returned? I found no answer to a sudden rush of questions and wondered if I ever would.

114 BREAKING BORDERS

Poland, 1945

CHAPTER 14

THE BATTLES

1
The Northern Front

Much later, I came upon a Turkish proverb that aptly described my mood at that moment of my life: *Man is harder than iron, stronger than stone, and more fragile than a rose.* I realized how true and accurate these words were.

With my thoughts filled with confusion, my heart mourning for my parents and the fate of my brother, and the stinging contemptuous words, "So lieutenant is a Jew?" still ringing in my ears, I rejoined my unit to continue the march westward.

Burying the past, living in the present, and planning for the future make up the continuity of life. One cannot achieve continuity by dwelling in the past and trying to revive it. The purpose and the art of survival are in maintaining this continuity.

But as we pushed on toward the old German border, I felt fragile, puzzled, and hurt. At the same time, I felt a surge of anger, strength, and determination to fight for a future I couldn't perceive, plan, or define. There were too many questions and feelings, which created a giant mosaic of uncertain possibilities. I needed time to sort them out, but there was no time.

Our 2nd Division of the Polish Army, attached to the command of Soviet Marshal Zhukov of the 1st Byelorussian Front, crossed into Germany to engage in what proved to be two of the fiercest battles we faced. After crossing the border, the spirit of our troops soared. Now that Poland was freed from German invasion and occupation, the battle was finally carried to their own soil. We kept congratulating one another, embracing, hugging, and kissing. The custom of men kissing men was an accepted Russian custom. One of my fellow Polish officers, Antoni Lis, looked at the scene with disgust and turned to me. "God damn these imposters wearing the Polish uniforms, calling us comrades, when they really despise us and think of us as their inferiors," he said. "I hate seeing them defile the Polish eagle adorning our traditional distinguished military four-cornered caps, wearing them on their stupid *Moskal*[2] heads."

I wasn't surprised at his outburst. I too had an uncomfortable feeling about the composition of our army. The Russian contingent of officers was there because there were not enough Polish officers to command units, which had been formed, trained, and equipped in the vastness of the Soviet Union. This 2nd Polish Army was an army of exiles, prisoners, and "graduates" of Siberian labor camps, torn from their Polish homes and thrown eastward in 1939. Molded into fighting units, they were considered inferiors by their Russian officers and instructors. In turn, the Poles never considered themselves comrades of the Russians. Oh, sure, we had great fun together drinking, singing, dancing, and carrying on, but at the bottom of our souls rested a layer of pain and silent hatred. The Russians sensed it. They too would prefer to wear Russian uniforms and quit pretending and posing as Polish warriors. The deep-seated resentment was rooted in the history of Poland and Russia from the time of the tsars to the communist-ruled Soviet Union.

Yet we were now fighting a common enemy to achieve a victory over evil and oppression. The picture of my recent visit to Lodz flashed through my mind again, with the contemptuous words of the occupant of my old apartment ringing in my years. I realized that bigotry and intolerance were blinding, obscuring every reality.

I recalled the words of my beloved grandfather facing the youthful hooligans in Lodz. I put my hand on Antoni's shoulder, turned him to face the west, and said, "This is the direction to which our anger must flow now. We cannot afford to have hate spread and divide our ranks. Prejudice will only make us bitter, unhappy, and weaken our resolve to fight. We should not become beholden to it or victimized by it. The war will end soon. We will have a lifetime to sort things out."

"You are right. We cannot fight both enemies at once. Let's get this one over with first," he replied, pointing toward Germany.

In the early spring of 1945, on the Eastern front, the German Army defended an area between the rivers Oder and Elbe, including Moravia, Czechoslovakia, Western Austria, Italy, and the south and southwest parts of Germany. Toward Berlin, the distance between the Americans and British driving eastward and

---

2   An offensive term for *Russian*

Russians driving westward was about 120 miles. Along the old German-Polish border, three fronts of the Red Army faced the Germans.

Completing the war's final battlefields lineup were the 1st Belorussian Front, under the command of Marshal Zhukov; the 2nd Division of the Polish Army; the 1st Ukrainian Front, toward the lower Oder River, under Marshal Konev; and the 2nd Belorussian Front under Marshal Rokossowski.

All three of these Russian military leaders figured prominently as heroes in the annals of World War II history. Marshall Zhukov, along with American, British, and French representatives, accepted Germany's official surrender at the fall of Berlin. He went on to serve as head of the Defense Ministry of the Soviet Union and became a powerful figure in its government.

Despite the overwhelming forces facing the Germans from the east and west, as well as poor strategic and economic conditions, Hitler's policy was not to give in to defeat. His High Command tried to retain its positions at any price, and if forced to retreat, it was ordered to level the land. The order to defend the country to the last soldier was so strict that death penalties were instantly carried out, including against German civilians who would dare to hoist the white flag of surrender. To defend Berlin from the Russians, a substantial number of German troops were transferred and thrown into battle on the Eastern Front, making it possible for the American 1st and 9th Armies to advance more easily.

Near the village of Chlebowo, south of the city of Szczecin, we pitched our tents at the edge of a clearing before a thickly wooded area that provided heavy camouflage. I posted our guards and disposed of the rest of my cold barley dinner, drank some water from the flask, and stretched out on a blanket to catch some sleep. I ignored the not-so-distant thunder of heavy artillery gunfire coming from the direction of the front line we were about to join the next day. But sleep wouldn't come. I lit a small candle and started writing a letter. I had this overwhelming desire to share the moment with someone. There was no one close to write to, so I started composing a love letter to Katya, still close to me as a lover whose starvation for male company had turned my short Siberian interlude into a sex marathon. I chuckled at the memory of being exhausted, when I had pleaded for some rest and sleep, and her answering with a broad smile, "You dig for dry, cold, and dusty coal all day. Enjoy now digging in something warm, wet, and friendly." The memory was sweet and welcome. I hoped that my words of love, passion, and gratitude would eventually reach Katya and lighten her mood. Yet I needed this pretense of a contact with another person even more.

I wrote about everything that had happened since we had parted and about the battle I would be facing soon. I actually looked forward to it with a sense of curiosity mixed with doubt about my ability to participate in real combat.

I had never hunted animals, never carried a gun except at target-shooting exercises at school. Now, equipped with a Russian-made automatic gun, I was to face other human beings in order to kill or be killed. Yet in all these images, I never saw myself dying. It was almost uncanny that the only real fear I felt was of becoming incapacitated. The memory of my maternal grandfather in a wheelchair stood out to feed that fear. The last flicker of my candle plunged my tent and my consciousness into the restful darkness of the night.

It was two days later, two mornings that seemed like eternity, when the first sparkle of sun penetrated the thick crown of the forest reaching the damaged camouflaged roof of the observation-point bunker. There was silence. I lay there, at the bottom of the bunker, my eyes closed, my fingers clawing into the rich enemy soil. Slowly, consciousness returned, and my nerves and muscles lost their knots and my body filled with a sense of life. With it came a new wave of alertness. Something must have gone wrong, something *was* wrong, that sound of moaning and the occasional burst of artillery fire colliding with the eerie silence. In a flash of a second I was up, and with one quick sweep of my head I saw everything. The unmistakable look of death in the wide-open eyes of Sergeant Paluch, the figure of Lieutenant Davidov, with his chest ripped open, and the moaning of Lieutenant Kostin, clutching the upper back of his right thigh, below his buttock, to stem the flow of blood. I sensed the stirring of other bodies back into consciousness. At once I was up in control of my own senses.

"We took a direct hit," I said. "We have to assess the situation and telephone the regiment's command bunker. Private Maciul, connect me with the regiment or brigade's bunker. Private Zielinski, tie a tourniquet above Lieutenant Kostin's wound and—" Maciul interrupted me, reporting our inability to get a connection. The phone was dead, our wires probably torn by exploding shells. I shouted, "Get them on the radio. Forget the radio silence order. Corporal Niedzielski, remove identification from the dead and cover the bodies." The radio came alive. I quickly reported the situation and received the orders: "We are regrouping. Abandon your position. Report to the Division Command bunker. Bring out the dead and injured. Follow and retrieve the telephone wires. Acknowledge!" I did.

I sent a detail with the bodies, accompanied by Kostin, who managed to walk with the support of a thick tree branch, and who assumed the command of the detail. The rest of the platoon followed shortly. We marched single-file through the thick forest, following and rolling up our telephone wires, when we unexpectedly heard the sound of the German language. We hugged the ground, our ears attuned to pinpoint the source. A German reconnaissance patrol was moving about a hundred feet to our left, heading in the same direction toward the positions of our batteries. We let it get ahead of us. Before it reached the edge of the woods, which would have given the German soldiers an unrestricted view and the chance to report the location of our heavy guns, I ordered an attack. Our guns blazing, for some of us for the first time, we surprised the enemy. With three of them dead, felled by our bullets, the remaining two Germans surrendered. One of them, a lieutenant, reached for his pistol, trying to avoid being taken prisoner alive, but a quick lunge by Niedzielski knocked it out of his hand. We scooped up their arms, tied their hands behind their backs, and triumphantly marched them to our regiment's command post. I reported our activity to Colonel Kosinski and handed over the pouch with maps, codes, and drawings I confiscated from the captured officer. He took note of my name and rank and praised our platoon's efforts. We parted to join the Division Command bunker, where we were apprised of our situation.

The artillery counterattack of the German forces reached its crescendo, mixing its salvos with our own continuous fire. Despite the urging of the members of his staff to take cover, General Nestorowicz stood at the edge of the tree line, refusing to go down to the safety of the specially reinforced command bunker, saying,

"At this moment the artillery is performing its most beautiful symphony, and a real artillery man has to be up here, on top, to be able to appreciate the sounds and detect any imperfect tunes." It was inspiring to be a part of this particular moment.

The attacks and the stubborn defense of the Germans slowed our forces in our attempt to capture the port of Szczecin in the battles to reach the Baltic Sea. My reconnaissance unit was involved in many of these activities, suffering further losses while being baptized under fire. By the time the orders came to transfer our division to the 1st Ukrainian Front under the command of Marshal Konev, twenty-five kilometers north of Wroclaw, which we reached in four days and nights, covering six hundred kilometers, we considered ourselves a hardened bunch of veterans. We were under the immediate command of the head of the 2nd Polish Army, General Karol Swierczewski. Our task was to cross the Nyssa River and proceed northwest. Our right wing was to take part in encircling and conquering Berlin, while the other part of our forces was to proceed west, in the direction of Wittenberg and Torgau, to join up with the American armies on the Elba River. An additional task was to secure the southern wing by capturing Dresden.

As we organized for our next offensive, our spirit was very upbeat. Our nourishment was quite rich, with plenty of meat and fats. We were low on tobacco, clean underwear, and mail, though some arrived. Unfortunately, I had no correspondents, and my platoon complained constantly. We found ourselves comfortably settled to celebrate the Easter holidays, yet somehow this early April was different from the past ones I remembered. It felt as if it didn't know whether its time had arrived. The forces of nature were pushing the grass to look up from the unfrozen ground, the trees to flex their branches and start their budding process, and the bushes to change their colors. There was something strange and different in the air, on the ground, and in the skies. Human fighting forces threatened the beauty and welcome of spring. Ugly and destructive, these forces clashed with the very essence of life and nature in its progress.

April 17 proved it.

2
The Southern Front

The first, faint light of the new day of April 17 found me at the forward observation point, directing fire of the mighty 122mm howitzers, pounding and decimating the ranks of the enemy soldiers. Over our heads, the noise of the German artillery shells, exploding into the treetops, breaking their crowns and limbs, blended into a symphony of sounds so familiar—as described by General Nestorowicz, exhilarating to the ear and soul of artillery men.

After a 155-minute barrage, our infantry units rose to push forward across the river Nyssa, the last natural obstacle on the final march on the German capital, under the slogan, "Next stop—Berlin!"

My reconnaissance platoon moved with the infantry to establish new observation points, radio-signaling the location of our advancing infantry units and direct artillery support. The rising sun on that April 17 cast a silver and gold reflection on the mirror of the flowing waters, soon mixed with the red of human blood, as the remaining German defenders shot at point-blank range at the rafts carrying us to their side of the riverbank. I landed, jumping on the ground and firing my automatic, which I stopped to suddenly confront a forest of upraised arms in the final act of surrender.

From many briefings, we perceived that the Germans relied substantially on the mobility and superior power of their armored, motorized, and airborne forces, but were no match in face-to-face combat. Their quick surrender seemed to give credence to this theory.

For two days, we marched unopposed. Our infantry advanced swiftly, leaving us with the heavy guns of our artillery units behind, a slow-moving mass of steel exposed as an easy target. We were soon tested by counterattacks of the enemy forces.

Field Marshal Schoerner, on Hitler's personal order, assembled the army group "Center." This consisted of two motorized divisions, the Hermann Goering armored-tank division and two infantry divisions, a force totaling 900,000 men, for a counterattack to disrupt our two objectives: a drive on Berlin and a march toward the Elba River to join up with the Americans. Units of this huge force engaged us in the region of the city of Bautzen.

Two days later, my unit, the 44th regiment of the 7th Howitzer Brigade of the 2nd Artillery Division, soon found itself under the bombing and machine-gun attack of twelve Junkers-87 planes. Powerless without antiaircraft weapons, we became sitting ducks. Their repeated raids and effective strafing fire inflicted heavy losses on our manpower, equipment, and supplies of ammunition. During one of their low-flying forays, two bullets hit my left shoulder. I felt the sting but didn't realize I was wounded until one of my men told me I was bleeding.

The next several days kept us engaged in heavy fighting, later referred to as the Battle for Bautzen. The village of Drei Kretschen, where our regiment was located, was attacked by motorized infantry units on the ground and by low-flying, unchallenged Messerschmitt planes from the air. Our division headquarters, aware of our plight, sent two hundred infantry troops as reinforcement. They were better outfitted, having machine guns, light mortars, and grenades to complement our light automatic weapons and side arms, which we used to repel the enemy in hand-to-hand combat. We suffered several casualties, lost three howitzers, and were separated from our food supplies. Withdrawing to the village of Neudorf, we found ourselves surrounded on three sides. We regrouped, setting up defenses, while the sun settled behind the horizon, ending a day of heavy fighting. My wounds bled intermittently without being properly treated. My men and I were hungry, weary to the bone, as we welcomed the darkness of the night.

Alas, the night did not give us the respite we had hoped for. A special courier from our division headquarters brought the news that we were to expect a morning attack by the Hermann Goering tank force. The orders we received were brief and emphatic: "Stop the bastards." We took turns napping, awaiting the light of an action-promising day. The thought that it might be our last day was not lost on some of us, but it did not enter my mind.

The sense of invincibility, the certainty of life's continuity, overwhelmed my entire being. Whether it was immaturity in assessing the dangers ahead, or the faith and enthusiasm of youth defying reality, still remains unsolved to this very day. I remembered reading that war was an exciting, dangerous, and challenging game that men love to play. I saw the picture of myself playing war games with my old friend Heinrich, and the memory of his violation of our friendship made me angry.

I led my platoon to the edge of an elevated wooded area most suitable as an observation point. We promptly installed the telephone connections to the batteries and the regiment's command post.

The sound of the roaring engines greeted us at daybreak. The first Tiger tank appeared, entering the open meadow spread in front of our freshly dug trenches, well-camouflaged by brush despite the black-on-white cross painted on its body. It was soon joined by ten others, moving lazily forward, assured of their power and safety in their armor of steel. The telephone message to my commanding officer, Captain Nikolai Vybornov, was short: "They are here, eleven of them. Let's give them hell!" The coordinates that followed the message sent the first salvo of the day, landing in the path of the steadily moving monsters. The Germans did not see us. They fired at random at no visible targets, overshooting our positions.

Our batteries were located at the bottom of a slope protected by the woods, from where my platoon operated. A direct hit immobilized the first German tank, then another. The infantry, which moved into the tanks' wake hesitantly, continued, only to be wiped out by the next cannon shell. Yet, stubbornly, the tanks kept moving under the rain of our shells, getting closer and closer to us. The situation was serious, calling for a desperate decision. My next coordinates shortened the distance to the lowest trajectory the howitzers were capable of delivering, which sent Captain Vybornov into a rage.

"You stupid son of a bitch, you are asking for fire on your own position. Forget it! If they get that close, we must save our ammunition for direct confrontation."

As calmly as I could, I repeated my coordinates, adding, "Captain, there will be no confrontation. If they pass us, we are all dead. And should we survive, I'll have you court-marshaled for your refusal. Give me the fucking fire from all batteries *now*!" And then, shouting at the top of my lungs, I repeated, "Fire now and don't stop!"

The barrage, which shook the earth, enveloping the meadow in a cloud of fire and smoke, was awesome. A couple of shells exploded over our heads, having made contact with the top of some taller trees, showering us with a rain of steel fragments and wounding two of my telephone men. Through the eyes of my youthful innocence, I looked at the scene in front of me with fascination, trying to savor every detail of the unfolding carnage and devastation. The classic duel between the two most powerful and destructive weapons of ground-war combat, tanks and howitzers, was frightening and fascinating, something I wanted engraved in my memory forever.

Soon more tanks stood still, with their gun turrets blown askew and their disabled guns grotesque in their limpness. The tank column stopped and turned south in the direction of the Czechoslovak border, away from their original northern course toward Berlin.

Our order to "stop the bastards" was carried out!

The platoon was jubilant. Smiles covered the signs of fatigue, weariness, and hunger.

"Lieutenant, we beat the Tigers. Can we call ourselves the Lions?"

"You certainly can," I said. "You are the greatest bunch of heroes. Thank you for all you have done and endured. I'll report it and recommend you for commendation. Don't ever forget this day."

I tried to reach our command post, but the telephone was dead, the wires cut by fragments of our own shells. I sent a courier with the battle report. He came back saying the regiment was folding up to join our main forces. We were to hurry back to board the trucks of our convoy. Quickly, we assembled our equipment and assisted the wounded.

As we emerged from the woods, we caught sight of the last of our trucks crossing the main road of the village. We yelled and gestured to catch their attention. In the chaos of retreat, they failed to see us. We ran, trying to catch up to them, when a sudden burst of machine-gun fire stopped us dead in our tracks. It came from a badly damaged church tower overlooking the only passage we had to rejoin our forces. We found ourselves pinned down on the wrong side of the road. Several attempts, exercised in intervals, failed to get us across. Without long-range weapons, we could not reach the tower to silence the machine gun. Without the risk of sacrificing human lives, there seemed no way to solve the impasse. Our situation made me wonder about the irony and whims of war. Here we were, a group of warriors coming off a victorious battle with a superior enemy force, which only a short while ago threatened us with total annihilation, only to be rendered helpless by one man with a gun. I wondered who he was. What motivated his lonely action? I had this strange desire to talk to him, as one would to a child, to explain the futility of his behavior in the face of a war that he had already lost and to persuade him to go home.

I split my platoon into three small parties, deploying them fifty feet apart. On command, the farthest one dashed across. As the gunman halted fire to adjust his aim, the group closest to him made the dash, and again, using the pause of his fire, the third one reached safety. We lost precious time and energy. Totally exhausted, we caught up with our column when it stopped for a rest to take stock of the losses.

It took me quite a while to find Capt. Vybornov to give him my report. I expected a reprimand and disciplinary action for my insolent behavior during our recent fighting. He looked at me sternly, and then he put his arms on my shoulders and gave me a friendly squeeze.

"I just heard about your encounter with the gunman," he said. "You did well."

I winced under the pressure of the squeeze over my wounds. He noticed it and shook his head, motioning me toward the ambulance truck. "Go, take care of yourself. We will talk later."

With my wounds freshly tended to, I joined my platoon stretched out on a slope by the main highway. Someone handed me a rolled-up cigarette. I inhaled deeply. The acrid taste in my mouth made me actually enjoy it. The sky was moonless, and the blanket of darkness enveloped us as we fell into a deep sleep. I dreamt about my childhood and family, whom I never was to see again. The face of my mother dominated my dream. She looked at me with a sad, loving expression. Somehow, I knew that she would always watch over me and protect me with her never-ending love.

I woke up sensing someone standing over me. It was Vybornov. He sat down next to me. Before I could chase the rest of my sleep and my dream away, he spoke.

"Lieutenant, I just communicated with the chief of staff of our division. I recommended you for the Cross Virtuti Militari for your calmness, command ability, and courage displayed facing a superior enemy force and for your bravery in willing to sacrifice your own life to save your unit. They already had the record of your action at the Northern front. My recommendation was accepted. Thank you and congratulations."

I was totally dumbfounded. Expecting a rebuke, I was quite unprepared for this unexpected turn of events.

In a flash, I remembered a discussion I had once had with my instructor Major Seredov, highly respected by all of the cadets at the officer's school. He had sustained severe wounds in the early stages of the war and was highly decorated for bravery in action.

"Bravery," he said, "is a youthful infatuation with danger, a powerful drive for adventure, and a challenge to one's ego combined with total ignorance of the consequence of one's actions. Some may call it stupidity." I did not share these recollections with Vybornov, as I was not really sure of the validity of Seredov's statement. I still had not solved the real and underlying cause of bravery.

A proud Major Seredov in August 1945 visiting his former cadets in Ostow Wielkopolski, including me, newly decorated with the Cross Virtuti Militari, the highest Polish military decoration.

I mumbled a thank-you. When I regained full clarity of mind, I said, "You are a good leader, Captain. I am proud to serve under your command." I extended my hand to shake his. "To our next stop—Berlin."

"There won't be 'next stop Berlin' for us. Our division is assigned to engage and destroy the army group of Field Marshall Schoerner. We will be heading south come morning." He got up and slowly walked away. I detected a feeling of disappointment in his voice and was surprised to find myself sharing it.

Our pursuit was uneventful, toward the Czechoslovakian border, along the banks of the Elbe River, through the neat and sleepy villages and small towns, with the Harz Mountains in the background. We encountered little resistance and no major confrontations. Most of the population had crossed the Elbe to be with their families and friends, in order not to fall under the Russian rule. The Americans were perceived as a safety blanket.

It surprised me when an order came for me to report to the division headquarters. I reached our battery position, where Lieutenant Szymanski intercepted me. "Get yourself cleaned up and shaved. A driver will pick you up in ten minutes." He turned away before I could ask him for the reason of my summons. My orderly, who became a dear friend, shaved me with his fine-honed pocketknife. It was sharp enough to make me bleed from a couple of cuts inflicted on my face, which was covered with five-day-old stubble. On the way to the headquarters, we encountered a burst of enemy artillery fire.

We veered off the road until the firing stopped. We lost almost a full hour. We reached the headquarters to find out that I had missed the purpose of my summons by ten minutes. General Swierczewski had just left after a field ceremony personally thanking, honoring, and decorating officers and soldiers for their deeds during the recent battles. Frustrated, I realized I would have to wait before the Cross Virtuti Militari would be pinned to my chest.

*　　*　　*

The month of May must be everyone's favorite month of the year. It symbolizes the promise of life and happiness. For me, this particular May had special importance and meaning. It was during the night between May 8 and 9 that the last shots in the European theatre of war were fired, granting a lease on life for its survivors and giving new hope to mankind.

Spring had finally broken out in full glory, covering the scarred earth of the battlegrounds with a carpet of vivid green grass, forcing bushes to flower in an explosion of colors enriched by the blood that had soaked into the soil.

When the order from the Division crackled over the radio—"Hold your fire, the war is over, victory is ours!"—we were stunned and overjoyed. We knew the war's end was near, but the meaning of the order was almost too powerful to perceive. Our caps flew into the air, hugs and shoulder-slapping ignored rank and position, and we became one family drunk with the happiness of survival and the sweet taste of victory.

Jan Mazenda, who one week earlier found out he had become the father of a little girl, jumped out of the bunker yelling, "I'm alive, I'll see my baby, I'll see my wife! Bless You, God, thank You, thank You, thank You!" He ran in circles, his arms waving, when a mine exploded, lifting Jan into the air before he hit the ground as a lifeless body.

I've witnessed death in many shapes and forms. I'd seen grotesque corpses in their charred, swollen shapes, burnt by the missiles of death-spreading, rocket-shooting "Katyushas," and I'd seen soldiers' bodies riddled with bullets or torn by explosives. I'd seen the looks of surprise, horror, and sadness in the eyes of the faces wearing the mask of death. Of all these gruesome images, Jan Mazenda's senseless end stands out as a symbol of cruelty, injustice, and tragedy that a war inflicts on humanity. It inspired me to deeply appreciate the value of peace and to devote my life to promoting it and fighting the causes of war.

We reached Bad Schandau on the Elbe River west of Dresden and southwest of Torgau, where American and Russian troops met to celebrate the end and the victory in the War of All Wars.

The elation of the troops eluded me. They were returning home. I was returning to what used to be my home, which no longer existed. I was returning to look, to probe, to search with a faint hope to find someone, anyone, to connect me with my previous life.

CHAPTER 15

THE POLISH INTERLUDE

Defying the unconditional capitulation of Germany, Field Marshal Schoerner refused to lay down arms. In his order to the troops, he stated that Germany had surrendered to the Western Allied Powers but that the fight against the Soviet Union must continue. His strategy was to break through our lines and surrender to the Americans across the Elba River. Our division was part of the forces assigned to stop and destroy his army. On May 12, the order to cease this operation reached us after we had chased the enemy into Czechoslovakia, where other units took over the pursuit. We regrouped in Decin on the Czechoslovak-German border, where, after a few days of rest, we moved north through German towns and villages on our victorious return to Poland.

Some of the places we passed through showed every sign of destruction, while others remained quite intact, although deserted. We spent nights in some of these deserted homes, choosing those that offered maximum comfort. Many were abandoned with all household items left behind. My new orderly, Bronek Mazur, kept busy loading my truck with abandoned bed linens, cutlery, some crystal glassware, and items of civilian clothing. In one place, he found a roll of the finest processed black leather. A Polish shoemaker later converted it for me into a pair of smart handmade officer boots.

We also enjoyed female company on our journey. We would give lifts to Polish women, who had been forcibly transported to Germany to be exploited as laborers in German factories or as maids in rich households. Now they would cook our meals and, on some occasions, gratefully accommodate us, their liberators, in the luxurious beds of their former oppressors. Strangely enough, we encountered German women of all ages, some of whom were most willing to share their bodies with our forces. I tried to analyze their motivation. Was it the homage of the vanquished paid to the conqueror? Was it an attraction to the victor? Was it a pure need for sex, of which they had been similarly deprived, as had Polish and Russian women, whose husbands went to fight the war? Or was it the fear that they might be raped and preferred to submit voluntarily to a chosen partner?

I was puzzled but not surprised by the eagerness with which some of our officers and troops took advantage of the situation. I wouldn't tolerate such behavior and was openly critical of it. In my mind, they were wives and daughters of the enemies I had been fighting against. My attitude won the appreciation of a Polish woman who, with her daughter Maryla, attached themselves to my unit. They had been deported from Poland to work in a German chemical plant. Maryla was very beautiful, with the looks of a young Susan Hayward, one of my favorite female Hollywood stars. We soon became intimate with the tacit approval of her mother. Our intense lovemaking took place in those luxurious bedrooms and in any other place where we would find privacy.

As we moved eastward, we encountered German men who were making their way to the west. They hardly deceived us in their ill-fitting civilian clothes; most were former soldiers.

Many Russian officers were merciless. They would force the German men to strip naked to check for their SS tattoos. Once found, they would escort the men to the divisional headquarters. Some officers were tempted to shoot them on the spot, hurling curses and obscenities at them. Captain Bondarenko was especially violent. He would pistol-whip them and show pictures of his family members, screaming, "You filthy fascist dung, do you recognize these faces? Pray you don't, or I will skin you alive. How many innocent children have you murdered? How many Russian women have you raped? How many Russian men have you killed?" There was no way to stop him when he would take his prisoner behind a building. The sounds of shots that echoed across the air were reminiscent of the Nazi's cruelties, executing innocent victims. I considered his action a bad example for our troops. Supported by fellow officers, I managed to have Bondarenko transferred out of our unit.

He left me to ponder revenge as a valid response to the enemy's unforgivable acts of brutality and injustice. I found it extremely difficult to maintain the promise I gave my grandfather to "never let hatred into my heart." But I remained true to my promise.

On May 25, 1945, we reached our new home. Ostrow Wielkopolski was a town about 230 kilometers southwest of Warsaw and about half this distance from my hometown Lodz.

The entire population of the town lined the streets in a heartfelt welcome to the returning victorious frontline troops. The white and red flags of Poland hoisted over all building entrances gave the town a festive look. A history-making moment was taking place, and all participants responded to its significance with shouts, bouquets of flowers sailing through the air to be caught by the marching troops, hand-thrown kisses, and the "V" for victory signs made famous by Britain's Winston Churchill.

Three weeks later, on June 15, the Second Artillery Division of Luzyce, as we were officially named, had an awards ceremony to decorate its officers and men. The Silver Cross Virtuti Militari was pinned over my heart. This order, the equivalent to the American Congressional Medal of Honor, is awarded for a deed of outstanding courage on the battlefield at the risk of one's own life. The award was created by the Polish King Stanislaw August in 1792. The official holiday of the order is May 3, Constitution Day.

Me as second lieutenant decorated with the Silver Cross Virtuti Militari in 1945.

Promoted to the position of our unit's deputy chief of staff, I took advantage of the privilege to live outside our military compound. I found a pleasantly located two-story house with a flowering garden and tall bushes in front shielding it from the quiet street. A wire fence surrounded the property. A bench was romantically placed on the edge of the narrow walkway between the house and the gate. The house belonged to two spinster sisters in their late thirties. I rented a large room on the ground floor arranged as a bedroom and dining room. A full bathroom was located across the hall. It was this privacy that allowed me many advantages I would have missed living in the compound. It also, as I found out later, provided an element of danger.

My relationship with Maryla had ended when her mother started planning our wedding. Before she contacted her priest at the local Catholic Church, I disclosed my Jewish origin. Maryla's mother, a devout Catholic, was both surprised and disappointed. She asked me to end my relationship with her daughter. While Maryla's feelings for me were not affected by my revelation, there was no question of her defying her mother. After what they had been through together during the war, they were very interdependent. We became resigned to the situation and parted as friends.

Soon after our unit had settled, I was asked to travel to Lodz to represent our regiment at an administrative meeting. My mission completed, I paid a visit to the city's Jewish Committee. Such volunteer committees were created in population centers where Jews had lived previously to help them connect with surviving relatives and friends. One could register as a survivor and be contacted by surviving kin. When I stated my name, a young typist asked me, "Did you have a sister by the name of Berta?"

"No, but I had a cousin and an aunt by that name. Do you have any information about them?"

"Follow me," she replied, leading me up a staircase to the third floor of the building. I was excited about the possibility of finding my favorite aunt, the sister of Roman, alive. I entered a spacious room occupied by several women bent at desks and tables, shuffling through various lists, and I immediately spotted Berta. She looked at me for a moment before she flung herself into my arms, sobbing uncontrollably.

"I gather she recognized you," said my escort with a broad smile.

"Thank you, may God bless you," was all I could manage to say, my vocal cords tight and my eyes watery.

"I wish I could do it more often," she said. With a friendly wave she disappeared.

Berta was deliriously happy with the news about the survival and new life of her brother Roman in Russia. But the next three hours were among the saddest of my life. One by one, she told me, with varying degrees of detail, about the demise of the majority of our family members. They were murdered in the Nazis' death camps of Auschwitz and Buchenwald. Berta had spent a short time in the ghetto of Czestochowa in Poland. She was then deported to Germany, where she was subjected to slave labor in a munitions factory. Freed by Russian troops, she had returned to Lodz in pursuit of any survivors. She volunteered to work for the Jewish Committee, and that was how she found Nadzia and her younger daughter Ada. She lived with them now, and she invited me for dinner that evening. I accepted the invitation but asked her not to disclose my identity to Nadzia except to say that she had known me before the war.

When I handed a bouquet of red roses to Nadzia, I was surprised to notice how kind the passage of six years had been to her. I could hardly detect any changes. Her slim figure maintained the delicate upper and lower swells of a woman's body, and her face showed no traces of the wear and tear of the suffering I would learn about later. The only change I noticed was that the spark from her beautiful blue eyes was gone, the spark that made them so alive. She invited me in with a smile and a friendly gesture. I complimented her on her appearance. I saw little Ada in the background, greeted her, and remarked how grown-up she had become. When she asked me my name, I said, "We have met in the past. I know it isn't polite to do so, but wouldn't you like to guess who I am?"

She looked at me with curiosity. I knew that I had gone through a physical transformation from my school days. I'd shed my glasses and lost the roundness of my face, which now assumed a manly look. It had become the face of a soldier, a determined face, yet void of masculine roughness, retaining its wistful quality. My body had slimmed down to fit the officer's uniform handsomely, the shiny silver cross of my medal adorning my chest.

"I'm sure I know you, but I wouldn't be able to recognize you." At this point I told her who I was. It opened a dam, memories flowing incessantly for hours, late into the night. I spent the night stretched out on a couch in the dining/living room and resumed our reminiscences at breakfast and lunch. Nadzia's husband Herman had perished in the death camp Treblinka. Her older daughter, the beautiful Tola, was taken away from their apartment in Warsaw. The thought that she might have been assigned to entertain the German officer corps drove Nadzia close to insanity throughout her entire life.

Taking advantage of her gentile looks, living as an Aryan woman, Nadzia managed to survive, despite being suspected of harboring a Jewish child. Ada bore no resemblance to her mother, having inherited her father's darker completion, brown eyes, and black hair. Neither of them was too forthcoming in sharing their experiences in the Warsaw ghetto and their flight from it to live as gentiles among the Poles. It was too fresh and painful. They did mention righteous Polish Christians who had helped them during the difficult period of their fight for survival. There was Ada's governess Telka, who took Ada in until her mother found a place to live. The judge Jaworski, their family friend, accepted Nadzia's jewelry, gold coins, and other precious items for safekeeping, always ready to supply them whenever she needed them to get along.

Many years later, in 1995, I was able to induce Ada to share a memory of one of her traumatic experiences. After she succumbed to cancer in New York, I managed to have her story published. I feel it is appropriate to insert it here.

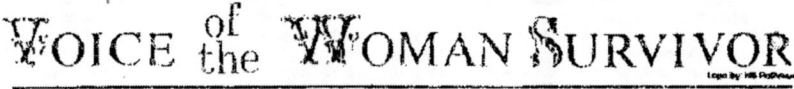

Voice of the Woman Survivor

Volume 12, Issue 1 — 122 West 30th St. — New York, N.Y. 10001 — Winter 1995

Published and presented by WAGRO's Women Auxiliary to the Community of Survivors, Holocaust Resource Centers and Libraries on a subscription and contribution basis.

TIME WAS AN ENEMY
by Ada Skowron*
(October 1932–May 1994)

It was a day like any other, although for me and many other Jewish people living in Poland during the year 1943, there were no days, just nightmares filled with struggle for survival. I was then eleven years old, living with my Mother in a one room summer cottage, in a small village an hour's journey away from Warsaw. The village was a place where the free Christian families came for summer months to get away from the heat of the city.

My Mother and I were hiding from the Nazis under an assumed name, after having miraculously escaped

*Ada was the daughter of Nadzia Harris deceased member of WAGRO.

from the Warsaw Ghetto, where the rest of our family was killed. The days or "nightmares" as I prefer to think of them, were filled with fear of the next minute which might bring death, should anybody discover our deception. We were Jewish, and it was then the only necessary fact for conviction and a death sentence. We spent our time in the one room cottage, which boasted neither plumbing nor electricity, trying always to be together and not wander among the people unnecessarily. There was little to do but sit on the porch in front and wait for the hours to pass, wait for that day which was long coming, to bring the end of the war. Hope was a scarce commodity in those days, with little or no good news to keep it alive.

From time to time my Mother would get up early, get ready and head for the commuter's train to Warsaw, which left the village at short intervals. It was a necessary trip, since our few valuable belongings were in safe keeping with Christian friends who lived in the city. This was one of those dreaded mornings, when it was necessary for my Mother to make the journey in order to sell something, which would make it possible for us to exist for another few weeks. Every trip meant endangering her life with each step of the way.

As I sat at the table joining my Mother in our very modest breakfast the prospect of the lonely, frightening day loomed in my mind. I wanted to beg her to take me along, but I sat silent knowing that she hated to leave me behind, yet could not risk the danger of attracting attention in any way. An adult person alone could get around more quickly and inconspicuously.

The waiting began as I watched my Mother walk away in the direction of the station with uneasiness and anxiety for her safe return. We were the hunted, we were not free, not free to walk down the street, not free to live. Any minute someone may step from around the corner and say: "come with me, you are Jewish"... This fear for my Mother who was always so full of courage, was my constant companion. As she went to face the danger of the Warsaw streets, my heart went with her. It was not easy to get around the city, which had become a jungle crawling with German soldiers of every branch and variety. There would be countless dangers to be faced; any minute an entire block might be cut off from all sides, each person's identification papers would be examined and one wrong word or gesture would mean a one way ticket to a Concentration Camp. The trucks would stand ready with their gaping mouths preparing to swallow anyone. There were those of the civilian population who made a business out of other people's misery. They knew just what to look for as they watched the passersby. Is somebody going down the street too fast? Do they look scared? Have they something to hide? The right answer would mean blackmail, money and maybe life.

Now she would be walking by the Ghetto walls, as the shots ring in the air and the red glow of fires is visible in the sky, she would fix her expression and with an extreme effort pretend indifference, so the lurking hoodlums can't read the truth. Mother would approach the friend's house slowly for fear she might be followed and so endanger her friends by leading the blackmailers right to their door. As she lingers on the street someone may pass who knew her before the war, who might recognize her. Danger took many shapes and forms as it sat ready to pounce, in every corner, every doorway.

I sat on the porch and the world around me was beautiful, summer in its glory with the sun shining on the newly blooming trees, the misery of my life as almost inconceivable in the face of such beauty. I went inside and reached for my faithful friend, my book. I owned one book which I had read countless times, but it was my most cherished possession, it could still keep the minutes moving as I lived with the gay and carefree characters.

I sat on and time somehow managed to pass. It was noon and I could hear the pleasant sound of my friend "Blackie", a watchdog kept by the people next door, who were permanent residents of the village. I thought of the times "Blackie" came to visit me, he would sit on the porch, wag his tail and lick my hand and I would love him with all my heart for being my friend; for not caring who I was. I had a piece of bread for my lunch and feeling a little better decided to walk among the trees surrounding our house. As I walked I imagined my Mother returning down the street, by the low fence and through the gate. Suddenly I froze, I could feel someone's presence. A man was standing by the gate with briefcase under his arm, looking at the house. My legs refused to move, I was terrified, all I could do was to remain rooted to the spot praying that my Mother was all right and this had nothing to do with her, they would just take me. The man hesitated and moved on. I shook all over as I made my way back toward the porch. I began to worry about my Mother, what was she doing? was she being careful as she promised me? I tried to clear my mind and tell myself that in a few hours she would be back, she always came back between five and six p.m. so that I would not worry when I saw the commuters returning from work. Very soon I could start watching for her among the people coming down the street from the station. Since I knew the train schedule by heart, I had a little game, I would try to guess which train she would be on and then pass the time by watching the groups of people, who came like clockwork at the appointed intervals.

As 4.30 came around my little game began, she would be on the 5.10, no, today it will be the 5.25, that way if she came early I would be thrilled and if later the disappointments not too many. The people came slowly at first, returning early and leisurely strolling toward their homes. At five o'clock the groups moved just a little faster, "time for dinner" you could almost hear them thinking, "have to hurry a bit". My anticipation grew steadily, may be the next train, she might surprise me today. By now people rushed down the street, faster with each coming train. My guess was wrong, 5.30. In between trains I counted seconds over and over until the next one. Here they come again, a big group, then a smaller and then just a few stragglers. Mother had many things to take care of, next train for sure.

Time was now becoming my outright enemy, it was growing horribly close to the curfew hour, which would kill all hopes. In Warsaw and all over Poland nine o' clock was synonymous with empty streets, deserted trolleys and busses. "Any civilian found on the street after 9 p.m. will be shot on sight", declared the German proclamation. Often on a late evening shots would pierce the silence and people would shudder in their homes and look around their family for a quick check.

Mother's eyes fell on the proclamation announcing the police hour as she was being dragged down the street by three young hoodlums full of alcohol. They wanted money, they wanted the very thing she was planning to sell that day. They had gathered good and thorough information, now they wanted to be paid for their trouble. They had been waiting as my Mother came down the street, just a block away from her destination.

Mother knew an old judge from her native city now living in Warsaw. From time to time she would talk to him and seek advice and he would try to help all he could. Unfortunately the judge had a stepson who managed to overhear the last conversation and decided to cash in with the help of his friends.

"One wrong step, they warned "and the information of your origin will be passed to the nearest Gestapo officer". As they pulled and pushed her down the streets she racked her brain for a way to obtain the valuables in question, without giving away her friends' address, which would lead to certain trouble for them. Three youths pushing a woman around was a sure thing to attract attention. After long hours of struggle she managed to induce them to allow her a phone call, dialing the number without revealing it to those watching was a difficult problem. Finally the reassuring click of someone answering on the other side. "No, they are not home" says the maid, "didn't say when they would be back". One look at her tormentors, who finally abandoned the phone in favor of the bar, convinced Mother to call back. They were drinking and keeping a close watch on her, time was moving fast, too fast if she were to get back before the curfew. After much pleading and long explanations the maid agreed to bring the requested articles and meet Mother on the staircase of a house a block away from their residence.

It was nine o'clock and this train was my last hope. Already I worried how Mother would make it from the station going through the wooded areas. Suppose somebody shoots? I was glued to the porch railing now, my hands were numb as I held on peering into the darkness of the street. Almost nobody came new from the train, I had nobody in the whole world and nowhere to turn, and no reason to go on living. The intense desire to live another day and another, till the end of the war, was gone. There was no more hope for Mother's return, if she was not with me at this time she was not alive. Nothing could keep her from coming back, because she knew the agony I would go through waiting for her.

The hours wore on as I stared into the night, time mattered no longer, tears came and then dried and came again. There was no reason to move, nowhere to go, I felt no necessity for thought, I felt nothing but the complete numbness of despair.

The shrill voice of the air raid siren cut the silence, people stirred in the next house, I felt a familiar stab of fear someplace deep inside but almost instantly it subsided. Nothing mattered, I have lost what was dearest to me, there was no more to lose.

I moved and was surprised that I could still walk, inside our room I sat in the dark and shivered uncontrollably. There was silence again all around, the moon was very bright looking in, I shut the door and lit a candle while a dog howled outside. As I laid on the bed I think I prayed and the tears came down completely unchecked now. Suddenly there was a slight noise on the porch, I could swear somebody was outside my door, I didn't dare to hope and yet I had to see, I was compelled to look out. As I opened the door in front of me stood Blackie in a pool of moonlight, around us everything was still, the trees bloomed in silver, it was the most beautiful night I had ever seen. Blackie looked up at me and his eyes were sad, he seemed to be crying with me as we stood together. I could feel a cry escaping my throat as I quickly shut the door and faced the little stub of candle feebly burning inside. It was as if the candle represented all the courage I had left, as long as it flickered I would keep existing.

1.30 a.m., minutes passed as I stared at the flame, there were no more tears left, no more feelings. The candle began to die down and a voice outside called softly, I sat on. It could have been hours before I became aware that the voice was calling my name. I stumbled to the door and tore it open, on the doorstep stood my Mother.

Ada's story "Time is my Enemy," published in "Voice of the Woman Survivor" in 1995

There is a touch of irony attached to this episode. Radosc, the name of the village Ada described, translates into English as joy, gladness, pleasure, and exultation.

Having used up all her material resources, Nadzia was supporting herself and Ada by selling women's cosmetics and underwear on consignment. She traveled by train to various cities where she established connections with local distributors. She carried heavy suitcases filled with merchandise. As a woman traveling alone, she was easy prey for the thieves and robbers Poland was full of in the immediate postwar period. Taking advantage of my position in the regiment, I made arrangements for Bronek to accompany her on these trips to help her with the heavy luggage and to protect her. At first, she would not hear of it. When I pointed out that this was the time for survivors to help one another, her opposition softened. It was not until Ada remarked, "Mother, you should be thankful to the lieutenant and accept his offer," that she gratefully did so. It took some time to have Ada call me by my first name. When it happened, it initiated a lifelong friendship.

I had learned from the Jewish Committee of some of my old friends who had returned to the city, and the next day Nadzia accompanied me on a visit to look them up. Unfortunately, I was able to locate only one family, the Szladkowski brothers, in addition to Benek Markowicz, whom I had encountered earlier in my old apartment building that late night as my unit and I were on the way to the front. Ben, who was leaving Poland for Palestine, urged me to do the same. "You will find out that this is not our country anymore. We are not wanted here, and your uniform will not protect you."

I heard the same message after a long session with the three Szladkowski brothers, who had lost their parents but managed to survive and reunite in Lodz. They intended to immigrate to Australia. They found nothing to make them want to stay in a country where they felt unwelcome. The youngest, Abek, supplied me with the most crushing news. He had been interned together with my brother Ignac in the death camp Majdanek, the very one I had visited on my way from Russia to the battlefront. Abek related to me that he was in the last transport of Majdanek inmates sent to Germany. After that, all those left in the camp presumably perished. Maybe it was naïve of me to ask, "The two of you were the closest friends. How come you could not manage to have him join you?" The minute I asked the question, I knew by his facial expression that I had touched a raw nerve. I knew from stories told by others that there was no rhyme or reason in the Nazis' capricious selections of those who were to die and those who would get another day of false hope. I also learned from Benek that Ignac was in deplorable physical condition when he was deported from Warsaw, which surely did not improve in the camp. I also knew that physical condition was often a decisive factor in the Nazis' selection process. Yet the question I asked, the absence of an answer, and the lack of an eyewitness account of Ignac's fate, never stopped bothering my conscience. Somehow, I still wait for a miracle of finding him alive, fully realizing it may never occur.

After the visit, Nadzia and I walked down Piotrkowska Street. I was lost in deep thoughts and did not notice the figure of a colonel walking toward me. I was jolted out of my lethargy when, with a smile on his face, he saluted me. Stunned, I responded in kind, feeling guilty about having failed to salute a higher-ranking officer first. The realization and pride that he was saluting the Cross Virtuti Militari borne by an officer junior in rank conflicted with my dark mood. I was troubled by the feelings of disappointment with Poland, expressed by Benek as well as Heniek and Abek. I soon found out how accurate their pronouncements would be.

In 1945, for the first time in its long history, a communist government would rule Poland, while the London based anti-communist government in exile would refuse to recognize it and would continue its own existence. This situation gave rise and support to Poland's various underground forces opposing the ruling communist government. These forces were composed of some former military underground units, who fought the Nazis during their occupation of Poland. Their resentment toward the Soviet Union spilled over to include the Polish Army, which they now saw as the military arm of the Soviet Union embraced by the Polish communist government. This resentment turned to hatred and was intensified by the memory of the heroic Warsaw uprising in August 1944, when Stalin's orders prevented the Polish Division, fighting alongside the Red Army, from crossing the Vistula River to help their brave compatriots. The Germans' cruel suppression of the Warsaw uprising and their destruction of Warsaw became an unforgotten—and never forgiven—Russian sin. Unjustly, the Polish Army units were blamed as well, even though they could not act independently of the Soviet Command. The attitude of the underground forces did not take into consideration the fact that the Polish units were composed of Poles freed from the same Soviet gulags. They were the same element as the Poles of General Anders' units based in England. The various underground groups disregarded these facts and labeled the Polish Army an enemy. Although there were no open confrontations, sporadic raids and assassinations of some targets took place. Targeted were mostly the army's *politruks* (Politichesky Rukovoditel, translated as Political Leader-Commissar), as well as some Jewish officers.

Conversely, the Polish communist government conducted reprisals through its army by sending commandos into forests and villages serving as hideouts for the underground military groups. These actions exacerbated further the tensions existing between the Russian and Polish officers, transmitting serious antagonism to the ranks. The Russian officers who had been fighting alongside Poles in the same units of the Polish Army had no interest in continuing as a part of that army, now that the fighting was over and the war had been won. Most of the Poles, who had never liked Soviet dominance, especially the indoctrination conducted by the *politruks*, were hostile and critical of having Russians in their army, even out of necessity. We respected our fellow Russian officers who had fought bravely against our mutual enemy, but we recognized the gap separating the two cultures. Polish national pride and the aspiration for a truly independent Poland could not be reached with the Russians around; we had lost the commonality of purpose in our relationship. This tension led to a number of incidents, and I became deeply involved in one.

September 15 marked our division's anniversary. The day started with a Holy Mass at the town's largest church, followed by speeches in the large city square by the mayor and members of the country's government delegation from Warsaw. The division was honored, and decorations were presented to the division's commander. It ended with a parade. Warsaw officials and a delegation representing the chief and the general staff of the Polish Army joined General Nestorowicz on the reviewing stand.

That evening, many parties were held at different bars and restaurants and some private homes. I attended one at my favorite hangout, the restaurant Europa. I knew the owners and the staff well from drinking sessions in which I frequently participated. As I entered the place, it was jammed. One could hardly hear the renditions of the piano player. A haze of alcohol enveloped the room and everyone in it. The proprietor, who handed me a glass of ice-cold vodka, greeted me warmly. We chatted for a moment before a handsome Polish major from the Warsaw delegation approached me. He looked at the decoration on my chest, shaking his head in a disbelieving manner. His voice, slightly slurred, penetrated the din of the drinking crowd. "So you are saying you are a Pole?" In his ironic smile and in the expression in his watery, opaque, gray eyes, I unmistakably perceived him silently asking yet another question, "*So you are a Jew?*" I was dumbfounded by this bold approach and tried to recall if our paths had crossed in the past. My memory drew a complete blank. Facing him, meeting his gaze, half-smiling and half-mocking him, I replied, "Major, I didn't hear myself *saying* anything, but to answer your implied question, of course *I'm a Pole, as I presume are you?*"

Without waiting for his reaction, I turned my back to him and joined a group of my fellow officers' table at the wall. My festive mood was gone, giving in to a feeling of tension. As soon as I sat down, my attention was drawn to the table next to ours, where Lieutenant Sergey Mironov held court. He was known for his hot temper, heavy drinking, and womanizing. The commander of our regiment had once publicly reprimanded him for this. I didn't particularly like him, but we never had any problems with each other. Seeing me, he snapped his finger against his throat in the familiar Russian gesture of invitation for a drink. The bottle of vodka that was making the rounds found its way to me. As custom dictated, I took a slug from it and raised it in a thank-you salute to Sergey. My attention was drawn to his table a few minutes later, when I heard our waitress Danuta scream loud enough to be heard over the ever-increasing noise level in the room. Danuta was a pretty, solidly built young woman with a supple upper body and a bottom that caused men to give her that second look. Sergey Mironov had his hand under her skirt, with the other holding her close to prevent her escape. While his companions laughed, enjoying the scene, I stood up and turned to him and said, "Sergey, let go of her." Taken by surprise, he eased his hold on Danuta, who freed herself from his grasp and darted for the kitchen, sobbing. I could see the anger rising in Sergey's face. He looked at me with hatred, lifted his body from the chair, and reached for his gun, spitting, "You Polish swine, who do you think you are! You will pay for it!"

While he fumbled for his weapon, I drew my pistol and pointed it at him. I had hoped that someone would intervene, but his buddies sat transfixed as if paralyzed by the scene developing before their eyes. "Don't do it, Sergey," I said. "Put your gun down. Remember we are friends." I tried to keep calm and calm him down.

"I'm no friend of Polish swine!" he sputtered, his face contorted and his eyes full of contempt. In that one moment, the antagonism between the Russians and the Poles surfaced in full force.

My shot rang out before he pulled his trigger, the bullet grazing his cheek. I was aiming for his upper arm, but he had moved too quickly for me to adjust my aim. It was only then that his companions and fellow officers from the adjacent table sprang into action, overpowering Sergey.

I holstered my gun and left the restaurant, filled with confusing emotions. I felt surprised and relieved that no one followed me as I walked slowly away, trying to sort things out in my mind. I sensed someone behind me, and cautiously I turned around to face Danuta. Silently she placed a kiss on my cheek, slipped her arm under mine, and started to walk. "Where are you going, Danuta?" I asked.

"To be with you," she replied, snuggling up to me. I stopped, took her hands, and said, "Danuta, what had happened in there puts you under no obligation to spend the night with me. I appreciate your gesture of gratitude. I like you a lot, but I would find it improper to take advantage of you. Besides, I'm in a foul mood and need to be alone. Please forgive me."

She looked at me promisingly, kissed me on the mouth, and whispered, "Thank you and good night." I embraced her and gave her a friendly pat on the bottom. It felt good and surprisingly gave me an instant erection. I didn't yield to the sudden temptation, even though I realized that I might not get another chance.

I could hardly fall asleep that night. The events of the day and the evening were whirling in my mind. The pride and elation at the division celebration, the gentile Polish major, Mironov, Danuta's bottom and my reaction to touching her, were dancing in my head.

It seemed incredible that in a time span of one hour, I was made unwelcome as a Jew, challenged as a fellow officer, and insulted as a Pole. This combination of insult and assault on my identity created a myriad of questions.

Who am I? Which insult hurt more? Why do I deserve this? Do I belong any more in this environment? Where would I go? Where could I go?

I got up to get a drink only to find out I was out of vodka. I made a mental note to tell Bronek in the morning to barter another item of my front-line loot for some more of the lethal brew the local peasants provided from their primitive moonshine stills, called *bimber*. He had been bartering regularly to keep me supplied. I found a bottle of Armenian cognac and downed half a glass of it, the Russian way, bottoms up. The cognac felt raw and scratchy as it hit the back of my throat. I was too lazy to get some water to chase it and instead poured another shot and sent it down to join the first one. My mouth felt hot, and soon the heat of the cognac spread over my insides, then traveled up, reaching the perimeters of my consciousness. I fell asleep visualizing myself holding onto Danuta's bottom, the last and only pleasant feeling I could remember of that emotion-laden day.

*   *   *

Our division counted three hundred and sixty three officers: two hundred Russians, 129 Poles, fourteen Belorussians, ten Ukrainians, and ten Jews. By my count, there were at least twenty-one Jews. The news about the shooting spread like wildfire over the entire division.

The next day I was greeted at the regiment with cold, hostile stares from my Russian fellow officers and congratulatory handshakes by the Polish contingent. To the soldiers I became an instant hero.

I prepared a written report of the incident at the restaurant and delivered it to the regiment commander's aide. As expected, I was summoned to him that afternoon. He was firm in his condemnation of my action and dismissed me with an order to report to the division prosecutor's office at nine o'clock the next morning.

I was met by second lieutenant Stefan Tarnowski, assistant to the prosecutor, who escorted me to the office of his boss, Captain Boleslaw Glowacki. I did not expect to face two Polish officers of relatively low rank, expecting a rather higher-ranking Russian in this position. I was not sure which would have been more favorable to my case. As it happened, I needn't have worried. After the initial formalities were over, I was asked to give my account of the incident. I pointed out my report, which rested on the prosecutor's desk, saying, "To add to my report, I wish I could express my apologies and regrets for my action, but I really cannot do it with a clear conscience. I would probably act the same way again in similar circumstances, if the dignity of my uniform and my Polish nationality were intentionally maligned. Besides, I was acting in self-defense, which can be corroborated by witnesses. I'm sorry that the incident took place, but I will not accept the responsibility for its outcome."

"There is no need for you, Lieutenant, to be so dramatic. We are fully aware of the circumstances from reports of witnesses. We also have a written apology from Lieutenant Mironov. He is well and wishes to apologize personally. We shall close the file on this case as soon as you reciprocate by offering your apology. Both of you have a distinguished battlefront record. Your Order Virtuti Militari grants you a favorable treatment. You can't be penalized without being stripped of your order by the army's high command. However, in lieu of a reprimand, your superior's pending recommendation for your promotion to the rank of captain is hereby denied."

With these words, Tarnowski opened the door to let Sergey Mironov into the room. A thickly padded bandage covered his left cheek. He was the first to extend his hand in a greeting and an apology. I shook it and said, "Lieutenant, please accept my apologies for losing control and causing you pain. I hope your recovery will be quick and complete."

"*Nitshevo*, Aleksandr, let's forget it and have a drink tonight to our friendship."

We parted and went our separate ways. I had no intention of having a friendship drink with Mironov.

The entire encounter left a bitter taste in my mouth. My promotion denied, I felt I no longer belonged in the army, even though it provided me with temporary sanctuary. More and more, I felt my life must move on along a new track I had to find or create. The events that followed transformed this feeling into a course of action.

The activities of the underground groups and the responses of the Polish secret security and military troops intensified over the next few weeks. There was evidence of infiltration on both sides. One couldn't trust one's own comrades in arms anymore. Sitting in my second-floor staff office in the three-story building where my units were lodged, I was writing my daily report and studying the orders from the chief of staff of the division. As lunch hour approached, I started my descent to the ground floor officer's mess hall. Halfway down, I noticed Sergeant Niedzielski, whom I had promoted from the rank of corporal after our northern front battles.

He was my favorite non-commissioned officer, and I relied on him a lot. My rapport with my enlisted men was excellent. They treated me with respect, and I enjoyed training them, displaying patience with those who were slow in learning how to use the intricate equipment for reconnaissance observation and communication. At the same time, I was strict, demanding discipline and respect for each other and their superiors. I emphasized in particular tolerance for the different backgrounds of the members of our troops. I would not allow ethnic jokes or derogatory ethnic remarks. Sergeant Niedzielski supported me in this effort. At one time during our platoon's free discussion session, which I conducted once a week, one of the privates, in a display of anger, called the politruks a "communist band of fucking Russians and scabby Jews." It was Niedzielski who immediately slapped the offender across the face, asking for an immediate retraction and an apology. It was no secret that these communist indoctrinators were intensely disliked by everyone, including even their Russian fellow officers. My method was to undermine their influence by using humor rather than inflammatory rhetoric. Niedzielski understood my approach, and in his own way he transmitted it to the enlisted men.

It struck me as unusual to see him at this hour in the compound away from his platoon.

He was standing at the staircase, resting against a window ledge, with his head down on his chest as if dozing. I addressed him. "Sergeant, are you well? Are you waiting for someone?" He lifted his head. I immediately noticed his tear-filled eyes. They conveyed suffering and compassion.

"Lieutenant, you will be perishing," he told me. "I couldn't do it, but someone will." Before I could react, he descended the staircase, skipping two steps at a time. It was my turn to lean against the window ledge to steady myself and absorb the full meaning of what had transpired. When I reached the mess hall, I related the incident to my second in command, First Lieutenant Marek Kaczur, who said,

"You must report it immediately. We must weed out the underground infiltrators from our midst before you, me, and others will indeed perish."

I followed his advice. Within an hour, Sergeant Niedzielski was taken away for interrogations. He never rejoined our unit. My efforts to find out his whereabouts hit a dead end. I regretted losing a good non-commissioned officer and an obviously loyal comrade in arms, however misled he might have become.

The commander of our brigade assured me that he had spoken to the commander of our regiment, urging him to secure my safety. I soon found out that this message was in turn transmitted to my immediate superior and friend, Captain Vybornov. I realized that I was witnessing the classic pass-the-buck routine. I knew I was on my own, with my safety depending on nothing other than my own ability to protect myself. Being on some sort of death list made me nervous and jumpy.

In all my encounters since I had left home, I had never submitted to the power of fear. I stood up against my persecutors, took all kinds of risks, defied the rules imposed by an autocratic regime, and fought against odds at the war's battlefronts. Now, for the first time, an enemy I could not meet face to face, an enemy I never opposed or harmed, threatened me. I had to learn to respect the power of fear and learn how to live with it.

Nadzia, who visited me a couple of times, became adamant in urging me to leave the army and the country. She had a brother in Birmingham, England, and a brother and sister in Brussels, Belgium. We decided that she would explore the possibilities of emigrating to either of the two countries. I promised to keep an open mind and discuss the subject with her during our next visit.

On one of my visits to Lodz, I presented her with a gift for thirteen year old Ada, a powerful large Telefunken radio equipped with a pair of earphones, to cheer her up during the long days and evenings of her solitude. Ada refused to attend school after a bitter disappointment she experienced shortly after the liberation of Warsaw. Her mother had enrolled her as a Christian child in the local school in the city of Lublin, their temporary residence. Having lived as a Christian in Radosc, where she attended church services and learned the prayers and rituals of the Catholic Church, the pretense became a habit, and the habit turned into reality. Ada became overwhelmed by the ornate richness of the church and the powerful doctrine of Catholicism. Feeling rejected and having been subjected to suffering, she identified with Christ's rejection and suffering. She found solace and comfort in the prayers and was awed by the ceremonial nature of the faith. Readying for a communion, she went to the confessional. In her innocence and sense of honesty, confident in the secrecy of the confession that she had been taught to believe, she confessed to the Polish priest of being born a Jewess.

"To save my life, I lied about my identity, but I don't believe I would be a good Catholic if I wouldn't tell you the truth," she whispered to her confessor.

She was shocked, humiliated, and shamed the following day in school at the Morning Prayer when the teacher asked her to be excluded as a Jew. The priest had broken the sanctimony of the confessional by sharing Ada's secret with the teacher, and with it he had destroyed Ada's trust in her newfound faith. She never went back to her class and vowed to eliminate any religion from her life. She avoided people and wouldn't go to school after her mother resettled in Lodz in their spacious prewar apartment, which she succeeded in reclaiming. A lady teacher who rented a small room from Nadzia became Ada's tutor. My gift of the radio restored the feeling that someone cared about her. Without knowing it then, I was accepted in the new world Ada would be building for herself.

In my present situation, I decided to limit my exposure as a target by no longer living outside our regimental quarters. I started to carry a hidden second gun, confiscated from a German officer near Bautzen, and eliminated my visits to the public drinking places I used to patronize. I became a solitary drinker. I befriended another Jewish lieutenant from the 50th regiment, Henryk Sobel, who confided in me about his plans to leave the country. In turn, I told him about the recent incidents I went through and my confusion about the future. One day he approached me, saying, "You have access to your regimental seal and blank traveling order forms. Would you fill one out for me, granting me a two-week traveling absence on the ground, and say that I would be studying athletic facilities to introduce them to our brigade? We must help each other any way we can." I hesitated for some time, but in the end I obliged him. My decision proved to be, to my regret, most unfortunate. It started a flow of similar requests from a number of officers, who through gossip found out about my assistance to Henryk. I was mad as hell at him for disclosing the fact that I had helped him. My anger reached a peak when I began to be offered money for privileged documents. I turned off the spigot and refused to be the nice guy.

I transferred my modest possessions to my new quarters in the compound. Within two days, I would be leaving my little nest and my two friendly spinsters. I was thinking about the new change on my way home. I usually was on alert studying the street ahead, approaching corners with caution. This particular evening, I enjoyed the full moon's pale light spread over the low houses along my way. I approached my house, and as I opened the gate, I froze in place. I noticed a figure of a man sitting on the bench in front of the rhododendron bushes with a rifle resting between his legs. Cautiously, with my gun drawn, I slowly crossed the gate and took small steps to cut the distance between the potential assassin and myself to ten feet. With my cocked gun pointed at the sitting figure, I yelled out, "Drop your rifle and get up slowly with your hands raised above your head. I will shoot at any sudden motion!" The man raised his head and laid a crutch down on the walkway. I had mistaken it for a rifle. His head turned to face me, and a soft voice called out my name. "Olek, I'm your friend, Julek Bader."

I stood transfixed, my adrenalin level dropping to zero, my limbs almost paralyzed. I lowered my arm; the gun hit the grass as my hand relaxed its grip. I felt momentarily disconnected from reality. I stared at the person before me as if I had seen a ghost. It seemed to be an eternity before I regained my voice and heard myself saying, "You stupid son of a bitch. I could have killed you. How did you find me? What has happened to you?"

Without waiting for an answer, I threw my arms around Julek and pressed my cheek against his unshaven face. We were locked in this embrace for a long moment, before we found ourselves facing each other at the dining room table with glasses of vodka clutched in our hands, stories and accounts drowning us in a flow of bittersweet memories. Julek, an infantryman, had lost his leg on the Northern Front. While in the hospital, he had met Lieutenant Kostin of my platoon, who told him about me and identified my unit.

After his release from the hospital, Julek located my unit and decided to visit me before moving east to stay with his sister. She had survived the Holocaust hidden by a Pole, a righteous gentile, whom she had married after liberation. The Pole had invited Julek to live with them on their farm in eastern Poland. We parted after a two-day visit, wishing each other peace and tranquility.

Tranquility was furthest removed from my present state of mind. The last incident with Julek left my nerves shattered. I now knew that leaving the army and the country was only a matter of time and opportunity. Lady Luck smiled at me with the arrival of orders to demobilize our division. I requested and received the approval for a one-week leave and left for Lodz.

Nadzia, pleased with the turn of events, arranged for a festive dinner. The guests were my cousin Berta; Ada's tutor and her brother; the brother's friend, Captain Artur Alter, who was currently courting Nadzia; and a couple of her business suppliers.

The evening before the dinner, I had asked Nadzia to marry me. She was taken aback with my proposal, and, resting her hand on mine, said,

"Olek, you are twenty years my junior. Ada is only eleven years younger than you. I'm very fond of you; I know you are a good person. But marriage is too serious to be a spontaneous decision. I know I'm a link to your past, but you cannot marry your past. We can be friends, we can plan on leaving Poland and staying together, but I wouldn't want to burden you for life. I will age a great deal sooner than you and Ada would become your responsibility."

"I have already thought about this," I said. "My feelings for you are based on honest love and admiration. I feel that if you asked Ada, she would approve of our marriage. She is at a very impressionable age. Having gone through so much already, she needs the protection and the feeling that she is a part of a legal loving family. I need a family to care for. I would like you to reconsider your reservations."

She gave me a warm embrace, and with a deep sigh, she said, "You are a good man indeed, and a persuasive person to top it. We shall talk again soon. I do love you."

At the evening of the dinner party, to my delight, two more people appeared unannounced. They were Nadzia's brother-in-law Marek and his wife Stella, who had let me stay at their home in Warsaw after I'd left my family and home in 1939. It created a problem at the table, with no room for Ada to sit. Her uncle Marek and Captain Alter each invited her to sit on their laps. With her face turning red, she approached the table, and with a bashful smile she settled in my lap. I caught Nadzia's eyes, which all of a sudden became moist. It was a telling moment.

The next day, to Ada's delight, Nadzia accepted my marriage proposal. We got married a month later, in September 1945 in Kalisz, her hometown, and returned to Lodz. That night our bodies joined in a bond that would last for twenty years.

While Nadzia busied herself with liquidation of her business matters, the disposal of the apartment, and purchases of various items we thought would be necessary for our planned departure, I decided to wander one last time through my city.

I was thrown five years back and became transformed into the youth I had been then, turning the past into the present. My city stretched before me in its somber melancholy, faded like an old photograph in a family album. I recognized the familiar surroundings. My excitement mounted, my pulse increased, and I felt the throbbing of my heart. In my mind's eye I saw them all. My father, as he paced the floor of his factory, intermingling with his workers, with a smile and a good word for everyone. And then the forlorn look on his face and the trembling of his lips as he kissed me at the bus terminal at Ogrodowa Street.

My mother's voice saying "I'll miss you and I'll watch over you always" still lingered on and echoed in the air. My grandfather's grip on my hand and his words, "Promise me, you will never let hatred into your heart," resounded in the quietness of the street where we walked together.

Heinrich's arrogant and cruel face and his words to the Gestapo officer as he pointed to me and said "That's him," followed my grandfather's image. My brother Ignac's face pulsating with vitality and happiness, looking up to me for recognition and praise, after scoring a goal in a soccer game.

The magic moment was gone. No one was there. My heart cried for all those who did not come to greet me, and once again my hopes were shattered forever.

My home, the old building in need of new face, exuded sadness. Not even the magnitude of colorful flowers hanging from every windowsill could take away the ever-present gloom. Stillness filled the air in the dismal yard, and the wind gently whispered ballads of the traders that came every morning, the performers, the magicians, and fire-eaters, the children whose voices were silenced forever.

My friends. How young they were before they ceased to exist, scattered in unknown pits of the earth, swallowed by unmarked graves into eternal darkness, leaving behind a trail of unspoken accusations.

The city awakened to a new day. Crowds of strangers passed me on the streets, and in vain I searched for one familiar face. I met with indifferent, at times curious stares. Grey clouds and smoke from the freshly ignited factories hovered over the city. The buildings aged, looking shabbier, and the trees grew taller. They bore witness to the tragedy that befell my people, and they bowed in silence. I saw ghosts peering out of every doorway, and in the omnipresent spirit of mystery, each house told me incredible tales. The sole survivor of a lost world, I wandered through the streets invaded by death, unrecognized and nameless. I followed the familiar path to my school. In front of the old building that was once the pride of every student, I looked in awe at the only peaceful oasis in the doomed city. Untouched by the turbulent years, it retained its gracefulness.

My steps led me back to my house. Tender memories crowded my mind in front of the closed doors that led into the intricate alleys of my past. Only the walls, standing proud and erect, greeted me silently. They still remembered. I stopped across the street, my house in full view. Inside those walls, behind the neatly curtained windows, my life was formed, and I knew that I could never discard my past. For it was here that the treasures of my youth were hidden; it was here that I first learned how to think, how to feel, and how to love.

I shook my head to break the mood and returned to reality, zeroing in on the present.

The time had come for me to leave this city now fading in the dusk, and this country rich with memories, bitter and sweet. My pride in my wartime accomplishments and my courage to deal with life-threatening difficulties disappeared, leaving the realization that my life had turned from that of a victor to that of a victim.

CHAPTER 16

DISPLACED PERSONS

It was an army truck that carried my new family and me on our journey across the recently conquered German territory, leaving Poland as a distant memory. After weeks of discussions, we agreed that there was no future for us as individuals or as a family to stay in a country that had become one vast graveyard for all who were dear to us and for our hopes to rebuild our shattered lives. As uncertain as we were of the future, we were willing to build it together and start afresh with whatever opportunity fate would provide us. We would join the multitudes that had been physically uprooted from their homelands. Many of these "displaced persons," DPs as they were called, were forced laborers from occupied Poland, the Soviet Union, and other conquered nations. Several hundred thousand DPs had survived the Nazi concentration camps, including as many as 100,000 Jews. Special camps were established under the auspices of UNRRA, the United Nations Relief and Rehabilitation Administration. Our goal was to reach one of these camps in the American sector in a Germany divided administratively between the four powers—American, British, French, and Russian. We had hoped to establish contact with Nadzia's and my family members residing in Belgium, England, France, Palestine, Canada, Australia, and the United States in order to emigrate. The overwhelming irony was that it would be on German soil that the efforts, visions, and hopes for a better life and future were to become a reality for the victims of Nazi aggression.

I selected the same route I had traveled once before as a participant in the bloody fighting for Szczecin on the Northern Front. Although demobilized, I retained my army uniform and equipped myself with blank forms carrying my old regimental seal. They were to serve me should I need them to facilitate my travel. We reached the Russian sector of divided Berlin late in the evening. With no place to stay overnight, I decided to brave it out by approaching the Russian command headquarters and filled out one of my forms with the appropriate travel orders. The captain in charge who received us couldn't have been nicer.

"I see you have been decorated with the Order Virtuti Militari. May I ask under whose command were you fighting?" he asked with a friendly smile.

"I had the privilege to fight under Marshal Zhukov and Marshal Konev, Captain. It is kind of you to ask."

"I salute you. How can I be of help?"

"I would need for us to overnight here and get a pass to cross into the French sector tomorrow. Mrs. Skowron found out that her husband is there after having been freed from a Nazi concentration camp. She and her daughter would like to help him get home to Poland. They are relatives of Colonel Zaborski, who delegated me to assist them. Here are the orders," I lied, reaching for the previously prepared papers. It was a lie even my father would approve.

"No need to bother. I'll arrange for sleeping quarters for the ladies and hope you are not too tired to have a drink with me. Would you, please?"

I made sure the ladies were comfortably settled before I rejoined the Captain in a storytelling session about our war exploits, interrupted by frequent vodka toasts. It was toward the morning that I would have the opportunity to get some sleep. Later that morning, using the zone-crossing permit into the French zone, we headed for the Jewish Committee at the address I had obtained before leaving Poland. There were few undamaged buildings in Berlin. The results of bombing and heavy fighting were evident everywhere. The committee was lodged in one of those less-damaged buildings.

The room we entered was filled with people milling around a single desk. My uniform got the attention of the man behind the desk. Briefly I explained our situation, asking to be accommodated by the committee until we established contacts abroad. He smiled suspiciously, looking at Nadzia, and asked, "Is this lady your Christian friend?" Flabbergasted, I returned his look and said angrily, "No, she is my wife and this is her daughter," pointing to Ada.

"Yes, yes, yes, they all say that." He addressed Nadzia in Yiddish. When she answered in the same language fluently, it was his turn to become flabbergasted. By now my patience was running out, and I turned to our interviewer and said, "I thought that we are past the time when identities have to be proven by men having to lower their pants or women reciting Catholic prayers. It seems bad habits are contagious."

A man approached us and addressed Nadzia. "Aren't you Herman Skowron's wife? I used to deal with him before the war. My name is Aron Segal." A conversation ensued about Nadzia's recent past and of Herman's death. I was introduced and joined in expressions of wishes for a brighter future.

"I can vouch for this woman's Jewish identity. Please treat them with courtesy," said Mr. Segal, addressing the man behind the desk. We found out that Segal was an executive of the committee.

We were given an assignment to a house at Iranische Strasse Number Three, maintained by the committee. I was asked to donate my uniform, which would be used as a disguise for some of the field workers involved in guiding Jewish refugees across borders. I changed into a civilian suit, which I carried in my duffel, but retained my gun, decorations, and fancy officer's boots. When I reappeared from the adjacent room, where this transformation took place, I had shed my past, assumed a new name, received new identity papers, and entered a no-man's-land of my life, retaining only the bittersweet memories of my childhood and adolescence.

Over the next several days, any thoughts of the future were drowned by the minute, uneventful, yet necessary details of our new daily existence. We couldn't get used to the routine of eating together with a group of strangers from different walks of life. Arguments, complaints, taunts, and hostilities ruling the mealtime made us tense and depressed. Arranging our living quarters in the tiny room, with one bed and a cot for Ada, taking care of our hygienic needs in the limited common facilities, made me question the wisdom of our decision to abandon Poland.

"Poland was no home to us anymore," Nadzia kept saying, trying to nip in the bud my oncoming nostalgia. "Our home is where we are as a family. We will settle permanently sooner or later. Have patience and hope. I know it is hard on you. You fought for Poland under its flag; you speak, think, dream, and feel Polish. Believe me, it will pass." I was grateful for her words of wisdom and encouragement. I shook off my mood and realized I was now the head of a family that depended on me. I pushed aside the little problems that annoyed me and took charge of our planning.

The next day, I took a commuter train ride to Schlachtensee, a large DP camp on the outskirts of Berlin, located in the American-occupied zone. En route, the train stopped briefly at Wannsee. Here, on January 20, 1942, Reinhardt Heydrich, Himmler's second in command of the SS, convened the Wannsee Conference with fifteen top Nazi bureaucrats. They coordinated the Final Solution, in which the Nazis would attempt to exterminate the entire Jewish population of Europe, an estimated 11 million human beings. I shuddered seeing the Wannsee station sign. It brought instant thoughts of all my family members who perished in the concentration camps. At the same time,

I heard an inner voice saying, "You Nazi bastards did not succeed. You did not get all of us. You bestowed on future innocent German generations a bloody heritage of shame, with a heavy burden to atone for. And we shall bear witness to your crimes."

I scouted the D.P. camp and went to the management building to find out how to register our family. To my surprise, I spotted Henryk (Henry or Heinie) Sobel jauntily emerging from the gym next door. I had last seen him when I supplied him with a travel permit allowing him to leave our army unit in Poland. We greeted each other warmly. He was the physical culture trainer and a boxing coach of the camp and expected to depart soon to the United States to join his sister, who had sponsored his immigration. Running into him gave me hope that I might experience such an unexpected encounter with some members of my family or my old schoolmates or army buddies.

The following day, we moved into our new transitory home. Ada, whom I had made the custodian of my gun, meekly confessed that she had buried it in my absence under a heap of rubble in Berlin. She had heard that there would be an inspection by the French authorities of the hospice on Iranishe Street where we had been. Thus, the last vestige of my military service joined my discarded uniform and my soldierly career. Losing my weapon depressed me.

The camp was composed of old military barracks and a main building housing the management, a gym, a medical facility, and a small area equipped for meetings of the various committees of the residents. I volunteered to serve on the judicial committee and was designated as the public prosecutor. It amazed me that in this rootless situation, people were able to return to a semblance of normalcy as a "society." The kitchen, a small dining area with food storage, occupied the other brick building. We usually ate in our room, which, in addition to the sleeping accommodations, contained a dining room table, a closet, and a sink with hot and cold running water. A bank of toilets and showers located on the floor took care of our hygienic needs.

1946—Displaced Persons Camp in Schlachtensee (Berlin).
I'm in the first row, sixth from left.

The camp was filling rapidly, and after a short time we were transferred out of Berlin to Eschwege, another DP camp in the American zone near the town of Kassel. Once proud and stately, Berlin was still in piles of rubble, and with my parting glances I was overcome with feelings of sympathy for its inhabitants. At the same time, conflicting thoughts surfaced as I remembered the destruction of Warsaw and countless other cities and villages in Eastern Europe. I didn't know if I would see Berlin again. I tried to push my conflicting thoughts away and discard symbols of a traumatic past.

Now, while in Eschwege, we knew that life in a DP camp was transitory. The vast majority of those who found themselves in these assembly centers hated being there. Unfortunately, they had no other place to go. Our immediate objective was to notify our relatives abroad about our existence and whereabouts and explore ways of joining them. We were very explicit that by joining them we did not intend to become their burden. We were simply looking for a sponsor so that we could establish a new home, with both of us being able and willing to work as hard as necessary toward this goal. We soon found out how difficult a task we were facing. The immigration restrictions governing entry to most European countries, Palestine, Canada, and the United States were insurmountable obstacles. The world had shut its borders on us. I remembered the question I had asked my father two decades earlier about the meaning of "borders of freedom and oppression." I was now experiencing firsthand the answer to my question. We were the victims of the world's indifference to human suffering and the tragedy of being persecuted and uprooted. We weren't wanted anywhere. Waiting for conditions to change over time became our ally if we were to find a welcome home, our enemy if nothing should turn up.

We plunged into the thriving culture that evolved in our DP camp. Ada joined a school formed by a group of experienced teachers and a dance and theatre ensemble, where she continued to pursue her first priority and love, dancing with aplomb on stage before a live audience. Nadzia became involved in community work with preschool children, and I joined the camp's Betar chapter, the organization I had belonged to during my years at school. I quickly advanced to become a member of the party's executive committee and an instructor in conducting military training of the young refugees, who had managed to leave Poland and other Eastern European countries. Most of them did not understand the commands in Hebrew, and some of them spoke very primitive Polish, hailing from ultra religious Orthodox homes where Yiddish was spoken exclusively. My Yiddish was very poor, but I could understand German after studying it in school and listening to it. The training was conducted in the open fields surrounding the camp and on the runways of what was once a Luftwaffe airbase. We were able to obtain light arms from the American units stationed in the region, who were most supportive and sympathetic to our cause and program. Another part of their training was to take classes in the mechanical school established by Paul Geyer, a top-notch mechanical engineer whose courses included dismantling and assembling of engines, basic physics, mathematics, and driving instruction. My trainees were smuggled to Palestine to join the Irgun, the underground fighting units under the command of Menachem Begin, the future prime minister of the State of Israel. Their goal was to force the British to end their mandate over Palestine and stop denying the Jews the Right of Return to their historical homeland. Israel would declare statehood in 1948, recognized by President Truman and other members of the United Nations. Some of the Irgun became heroes in the fight for Israel's survival when the infant State of Israel was attacked by six Arab states.

In the training of my young charges, I encountered a psychological problem. All of them were survivors of Soviet gulags or German concentration camps. They resented authority and orders, the two basic foundations of military education. They survived by their wits, cunning, perseverance, and courage. It was my job to channel these assets into an organized behavior with respect for discipline as well as recognition and acceptance of the chain of command. Major Seredov's lectures on tactics and strategy took on a new dimension as I applied them in my present task. It made me think of him with renewed fondness.

I was occupied with the training, but my predominant concern was to secure for Ada the right conditions for her development as a teenager. She was growing up in primitive surroundings and an abnormal environment. For most of our stay in the camp, we shared our room, which was common for most of the inhabitants. Our fellow occupants were a young couple whose loud, intense lovemaking was embarrassing and could not be ignored. It might seem odd after all we'd been through that a complete lack of privacy and other inconveniences would demoralize us, but they did, and we sought to get Ada out of these conditions. Using my connections, I was able to change our accommodations to a much smaller room that nevertheless offered us the privacy of living as a family. Then, surreptitiously, I worked on another solution to this problem. Using my contacts, I succeeded in obtaining a place for Ada on a planeload of children who would be admitted by the British as legal immigrants to Palestine. This planeload was one of the few exceptions granted by the British since they had banned legal Jewish immigration to Palestine. Knowing that Nadzia would never let Ada go alone, I secured a seat for her as one of the chaperones of the children. This was a great accomplishment, and I felt very good being able to arrange it. When I proudly presented the official documentation of my accomplishment, Nadzia's immediate reaction was, "How about you? Wouldn't you be going with us?"

"You know well that this is impossible. The British would never admit me as a legal immigrant. I would have to get there illegally, like other Jewish immigrants, and join you there. Your family would know where you are, and they would be my point of contact. Don't worry, I've thought it all through," I said reassuringly.

She looked at me with amazement and handed the documents to me, saying, "Don't deprive someone more deserving of this precious opportunity. I separated from one husband and never saw him again alive or dead. I wouldn't do the same ever again. Remember that we married to stay as a family together. Whatever the future has in store, it would have to be for all of us together. You are a caring person, and I'm so grateful to you." She embraced me warmly and shook her head, repeating, "We must stay together."

I looked at Ada, who listened quietly to our conversation. She nodded her head, and in a faint voice, almost a whisper, said, "Mother is right, we both love you."

I now realized I would have to find a route out for the three of us together and decided to register for immigration to the United States. The next morning, I returned Nadzia and Ada's papers to our Betar leader, telling him of my wife's reaction. I also offered to resign from the organization to avoid embarrassment to our chapter when it became known that I had abandoned my duty as a Betar leader to reach Palestine one way or another.

"Let's discuss it at our Board meeting," Liberman said. "You are doing a good job with the kids, and we would hate to lose you. I understand your situation, and I'm sure others will as well."

In a sense, our Board acted as an extended family. The members, Liberman, Palewski, Mejerson, Krajtman, Hecht, Stolowicki, Majerowicz, and the Pech brothers, hailed from various regions of Poland, with different intellectual and economic backgrounds and a variety of opinions that made our sessions lively and interesting. The theme and range of our discussions would naturally be tainted by the experiences gained during the war and the persecution we had suffered. The questions haunting us most were, "Why were we spared and not our parents and siblings? Why would God inflict this tragedy on *His chosen people?* What great sins had they committed to deserve such enormous punishment? What are we to learn from this tragedy if we don't know the answers to these questions?"

But we had no answers or solutions except to pour out our bitterness and take solace in the sharing of these moments among ourselves, knowing that we also shared compassion for each other.

The Board decided that I should continue as an instructor. At the time of my departure, the Board would find a way to handle the public relations aspect of my action.

I realized that I had sentenced us to a long wait for an opportunity to leave the camp, but the dice were rolled, and all we could do was to hope for the right number to come up.

That afternoon, I sat across the desk of our camp secretary, Ms. Block, intending to register. She instead pulled out a file and handed it to me. It was our registration to immigrate to the United States, which Nadzia filed the first week after our arrival in Eschwege. Ms. Block noticed my surprise and said, "I'm sure it must have slipped your mind that you have already registered. But it is always good to check on our office work." I absorbed her subtle rebuke and offered my apology. I decided not to make an issue of my encounter with Ms. Block when I faced Nadzia at the evening meal. In a way, I felt that she had been more pragmatic and decisive about our future than I was. I had gotten involved in an ideological cause rather than concentrate on personal priorities.

About a week later, Ms. Block asked to see us. She held a thick envelope that she handed to me, saying, "You are very fortunate. You just received an invitation to appear for a hearing at the American Consulate in Frankfurt. Fill out these forms, and I will take care of your arrangements to go to Frankfurt for an interview. Congratulations." She handed us a second envelope with a copy of our original registration containing all pertinent information about the three of us, which Nadzia had previously supplied her with. We thanked her and left her office overwhelmed by this unexpected turns of events.

It took three visits within the next two months before our priceless visas were issued to us at the American Consulate in Frankfurt. In our visits, we noticed that the city was greatly damaged by the bombing air raids of the Allied Air Forces, but not to the same extent as Berlin. The Consulate of Taunus Anlage was located in a solid impressive building in a prestigious part of the city. It became our fountain of hope and a fond memory for us. We transferred to another camp in Zeilsheim near Frankfurt to wait for our turn to depart for Bremenhaven, the seaport of the northern city of Bremen. From there, we would board an American navy vessel on our sea voyage to the New World.

It was a dreary, drizzly day in January 1947 when the call came for us to line up in alphabetical order with our meager belongings to be transported to yet another transitory camp in Bremen. We found ourselves next to Henry and Lola Helman, who would become our roommates in Bremenhaven. They hailed from Czestochowa, a city in Poland known for its Pauline Brothers Monastery, Jasna Gora, housing the world-famous picture of the Black Madonna and serving as a pilgrimage center for the predominately Roman Catholic Polish population. Our acquaintance turned into a lifelong friendship. One week after the Helmans' departure for New York, our turn came, and we boarded the former troopship *Ernie Pyle* for an eleven-day transatlantic crossing. We were separated by gender; women were accommodated in staterooms, twenty-four to a room, while men stayed in one enormous area of countless two-tiered bunks. The February weather was not conducive to smooth sailing.

Nadzia and Ada, suffering severe seasickness, wouldn't leave their bunks, taking water only as their nourishment. They rejected heavy food, so I tried to get some fruit for them. The cafeteria-style dining room was buried in the lower guts of the ship. To get there with the heaving and swaying motion of the ship was an ordeal. The smell of fried sausages, the mainstay of the menu, would make anybody sick. I braved these obstacles only to have to bribe the cooks for oranges and grapefruits. My entire fortune amounted to forty-five dollars. This included a pocket money allowance of fifteen dollars per person, kindly provided by our sponsors, the United Service for New Americans. My meager supply of precious fruit became a lifesaver for my family.

I also learned the essence of willpower. For a fellow who had been susceptible to motion sickness since childhood, I hadn't gotten seasick through the entire voyage. Every moment not spent with Nadzia and Ada, including the nights, I would spend on the upper deck of the ship sucking the cool, moist sea air deep into my lungs. It became a competition, mind over body, and the mind won.

By the sixth day, I succeeded in getting my two women out on the deck. Once they tasted the fresh ocean breeze, they never returned to their dormitory. We made our bedding on the deck, and for the remainder of the crossing we lived there. I was able to provide them with bread and cheese, and this sustained them.

On the eleventh day, the vastness of the ocean gave way to distant buildings, and the Statue of Liberty came into view. The *ooohs and aaahs* and the push toward the railings of the ship to view this incredible sight did not stop until the ship docked at New York's Pier 61. We were welcomed into freedom, and the gates were opened to a future filled with hope for a normal life, shedding the stigma of feeling inferior as "displaced persons."

Now, having crossed another border, the expansive Atlantic Ocean that separated the Old and New worlds, Europe seemed to fade into a distant memory. I wondered if I'd ever miss the Poland of my childhood and youth, and Russia, where I suffered pain and indignation as a human being, and Germany, where I shed my blood, gaining a new lease on life.

Having bid farewell to these countries, I felt as if the waves of the Atlantic washed away the ties to my past, cleansing and preparing me for crossing the threshold into a new future. And yet the idea that a thin thread would always keep alive a connection with my past and the old continent kept lurking in my mind.

I thought of all the places I'd journeyed through, all the good, compassionate people who had crossed my path, the ones I'd learned so much from, the ones I grew to cherish and respect, the good souls who shared with me shelter, warmth, good advice, and kindness.

This connecting thread was given substance by the nagging thought that somehow I needed to repay this debt.

CHAPTER 17

A NEW BEGINNING

As we descended the gangplank to set foot on American soil that memorable February 18, 1947, bidding our farewell to Europe and giving one last friendly wave to the hulk of the *Ernie Pyle*, I spotted the familiar figure of Henry Sobel, a big smile beaming from his face. I remembered giving him the address of my uncle and recognized the short man standing next to him as Uncle Maurice Harrison. The tall, strongly built young man next to them was my cousin Alan, older son of my deceased uncle Max. The evident family resemblance provided me with a warm feeling.

For a moment, I stopped in my tracks to absorb the scene unfolding before my eyes. Some of my shipmates knelt on the cement floor of the pier, kissing the ground. With tearful eyes, others recited prayers in various languages. Still others buried themselves in the embraces of those who came to welcome them. The scene even surpassed the emotional outpouring when we had first spotted the Statue of Liberty. As symbolic as she was, her sight could not override everyone's elation at physically setting foot on American soil. I felt it so strongly that my throat tightened, making it momentarily impossible for me to speak. When I regained my voice and composure, I introduced Nadzia and Ada to Alan. I immediately realized that language barrier with my relatives would be a tremendous hindrance. Alan spoke English only, and my uncle spoke Polish haltingly. But another barrier crept into my consciousness with the first words my uncle uttered after greeting me. "Oles, where is your hat?"

"I don't own one," I answered.

"Well, I'll buy you one for Passover," he said earnestly.

"Thank you for your concern, but I do not wear hats," I responded. He looked at me, puzzled. Perhaps he hadn't known what to say.

"But this is winter, it is February. One should wear a hat as a protection against the cold."

I was tempted to reply that if he really were concerned, why would he wait until Passover in April to buy me one? I thought better of it and said nothing. Instinctively I perceived that this good man, whom my mother felt so close to, and who had tried so hard to help me secure an American visa in 1940, lived in a world of his own, devoid of a sense of priorities and practicality. I recalled that he had always been considered a romantic and adventurer. I made a subconscious decision right then and there to cultivate a warm, family relationship with him, without expecting sound advice or material support to help us settle in this new environment.

The three of us were put on a bus, which turned up Broadway heading north to Hotel Marseilles at the corner of West 103rd Street, our temporary home provided by our sponsors. My relatives and Henry were to join us there. The streets of the city were covered with snow grown dirty and shoveled into piles at the edge of sidewalks, creating an uninviting, ugly wall. Cats were rummaging through trash cans not yet emptied by the sanitation department crews. Shabby-looking buildings and small stores completed this picture, transposed against the street sign "Broadway." It seemed so odd and unbelievable to me.

Is this the famous Broadway depicted in the glamorous movie scenes of the American films I had watched as a youth with passion and a child's overactive imagination? Would my concept and expectation of America be as disappointing as the failed glamour of Broadway? Would I be able to adjust to my cultural past being pitted against the culture of a new society?

The visit in our hotel room was brief for lack of a common language. We parted with promises to keep in touch. Our accommodation was modest but not uncomfortable. One double bed and a sofa bed in an alcove, a small table, three chairs, a night table, and a closet seemed luxurious compared to what we had in the recent past. The fact that we would enjoy our own bathroom and bathing facilities seemed like a gift from heaven.

The lobby of the hotel was teeming with people. The newly arrived refugees, or greenhorns as we were called, met their families with tears intermingled with smiles. The sounds of various languages and accents turned the place into a modern-day Tower of Babel. I listened for a while to the conversations, amazed by the range of subjects they covered.

"So you are the son of Aunt Hannah. That makes you my first cousin. *So how do you like America?*"

"This is my wife, Frieda. She is a wonderful cook. You will come on Saturday to taste her apple cake. I will pick you up in my new Buick. It is a beautiful car," bubbled a man to his newly discovered nephew.

"President Roosevelt should have bombed Auschwitz and destroyed this death factory. Those Jews who would have perished in the bombing died anyway, but think how many future deaths would have been prevented," philosophized an elderly scholarly looking gentleman, talking to his brother, a well-dressed man of about the same age.

"It is easy to criticize the actions of leaders not knowing the circumstances under which they were forced to make their decisions. Americans were helpful in winning the war and saving countless potential victims. They deserve gratitude, not criticism, so let's not talk about it." A shrug of shoulders would put an end to this discussion.

"Oh, sure, I remember Poland. Did you still have to haul water in buckets from the well?"

rambled on another relative.

"No, uncle," was the reply. "You left your village fifty years ago, a village with a population of a few hundred people with no electricity and no sewage system. I lived in a city of three quarters of a million inhabitants, with all modern facilities, educational institutions, and recreational establishments. Did you have in America all these facilities fifty years ago that you enjoy today?"

"Of course not, but this is America, the land of progress. *So how do you like America?*" The scornful look on the face of the young man was a telling answer to his inquiring uncle. I couldn't help suppressing a chuckle taking in these first encounters of the two culturally divided groups. The breath and depth of the conversations sprinkled with ignorance and naiveté amazed and amused me. The provincialism of the earlier immigrants made them think that time stood still in their old countries, while time in America leapt forward, propelling them into a life of opulence and progress. And those older immigrants, who had never shed the philosophy and way of life of the villages, *shtetls,* or the poor slums of the big cities, welcomed the new arrivals as if they had fled from the same conditions of persecution and religious intolerance that they themselves had been exposed to and had run away from. The real, enormous extent of the tragedy of the Holocaust had not penetrated our psyches until later, when it became universally publicized, known, and acknowledged.

I approached the middle-aged woman sitting behind a desk with a sign displaying the name of our sponsoring agency to find out the procedures we were to follow.

She introduced herself as Miss Greta, a German-speaking social worker we would keep in touch with for any questions and needs. She handed me an envelope with vouchers to Rosenbloom's delicatessen restaurant, located diagonally across Broadway. In exchange for the coupons, we would be fed lunches and dinners. Another set of coupons would provide us with breakfasts in a place located on the west side of Broadway half a block away. The envelope also contained thirty dollars in cash for our pocket money. Considering that we had seven dollars and fifty cents between the three of us that we had saved from our Bremen pre-departure subsidy, we felt rich and lucky. That was the feeling that lulled us to sleep that first night in America.

After the luxury of a shower *and* bath the next morning, we headed to our designated breakfast spot. We found a drugstore at the address indicated on our voucher. We continued walking another block, convinced we had the wrong street number. We still could not find a restaurant and returned to the hotel for verification. Greta burst out laughing when we confronted her with our problem. "The address is correct. Go back there and have a pleasant breakfast. The food counter is in the back of the drugstore." *What a strange country,* we thought. The idea of eating in a pharmacy seemed very odd to us. As it happened, the eggs, the crisp bacon, and the steaming hot coffee more than made up for our apprehension and became our first discovery of the unconventional way of life in New York. This experience was matched by our first meal at Rosenbloom's Delicatessen. The sandwiches we ordered were so huge, with layers upon layers of delicious meat between slices of rye bread that we could hardly bite into them. We managed by splitting and separating the layers. Of course, there was no way for us to consume the full sandwich. When we shyly confided our dilemma to the waiter, he laughed and suggested that we order less of the prepared food and take the balance of our voucher value in dry food. We welcomed the idea and stocked up on canned fruits, spreads, and jars of pickles, whole dry salamis, and other tasty items. Later on, when the time came for us to leave the hotel, we were well equipped with food that lasted us a long time.

We kept stumbling along every day, subjected to more laughter on many other occasions, facing unfamiliar customs to which we reacted with innocent surprise and disbelief. We were not the only ones who struggled to learn the culture; one of the new arrivals, passing a bakery, noticed a sign "sugar free" in the window. Attracted to the offer, he asked for five pounds of sugar and was dismayed at the laughter in response.

Although Nadzia and Ada took these incidents seriously, my sense of humor prevailed, and I absorbed these situations as part of my new education. But one incident caused me to become quickly disillusioned about the compassion of some of the locals and the attitude of some of the refugees.

I was not prepared for the experience I encountered the following day. I left the hotel to deliver messages for my DP friends who were left behind in Eschwege. I considered it my duty and an important priority. The first visit paid that dreary day was to the Colomby Watch Company on Fifth Avenue and 47th Street. And what a dreary day it was. Wet snow was falling that early morning, lasting throughout the day. I walked all the way from 103rd Street and Broadway, as I was unfamiliar with the subways and surface transportation system of the city. After a while, the soles of my shoes would soak in the moisture from the snow-covered sidewalks, making my feet wet and cold. I smiled recalling Uncle Harrison's warning about the need for a hat in February. It would surely be wise to be wearing one. I was grateful to have retained my army rain-parka with a hood, which turned out to be a real savior in this weather. I had my route outlined on a piece of paper, which I followed, walking down Broadway to Columbus Circle, east to Fifth Avenue, and down to 47th Street. My original poor impression of New York gave way to admiration of the city's splendor. The mighty buildings challenging the sky, the shop-windows with their opulence of wares decorated with taste and imagination, the special sight of Atlas supporting the earth's globe resting on his shoulders in front of the Rockefeller Center complex facing the impressive St. Patrick's Cathedral, and the multitudes of humans, oblivious of the weather, scurrying hastily around, made my head spin in wonder. *This was the New York I imagined!*

Mr. Colomby's secretary understood my request, delivered in German, to see her boss. I preempted her questions by stating that I had no appointment and had come to deliver a message from his nephews in Germany. After a short wait, I was admitted to the lavishly furnished office, where Mr. Colomby lounged in a high-back black leather chair behind a huge mahogany desk. Dressed in a charcoal dark three-piece suit with gold-rimmed glasses dominating his ascetic-looking face and receding blond hairline, he looked at me with curiosity, taking in my vintage DP clothing. He finally stood up, pointed to a chair across his desk, and invited me to sit down.

"You *claim* you know my nephews. Where are they?"

"I don't *claim* to know your nephews. I *do* know them. We were in the same DP camp, where they still are. According to them, they have written you several times receiving no answer. They asked me to deliver this message to you," I said, handing him an envelope containing a letter and their photographs.

"How can I be sure they are my nephews?" he asked, his head cocked to one side in a challenging position.

"I'm sorry, but this is something you have to figure out yourself, Mr. Golombek." I called him by his old name before he had changed it in America.

"How do you know this name?" he asked, by now quite piqued.

"From those who *claim* to be your nephews, Sir," I replied, standing up ready to leave.

"What do I owe you for your trouble?" he asked, reaching for his pocket.

"You owe me just a simple thank-you for bringing you the good news about the survival of your close blood relatives. It is they who need your moral and financial support. Good day, Sir."

"I do thank you for coming. Let me know if I can be of help to you," he said softly.

The answer "not in a million years" was on my tongue, but I managed to check my impulse and left the office with a bitter taste in my mouth. I almost wished I could erase this visit from my mind. This suspicion, callousness, and indifference of many American relatives to the plight of their survived European kin bothered me for the longest time.

When I reached my hotel room, I was bone-tired and mentally exhausted. I didn't realize that I had walked almost seven miles on this snowy, gloomy day. I was greeted with the news that my Uncle Emile and his wife Lucy would be paying us a visit that evening. Exhausted and disappointed as I was with my day's activity, I had to prepare myself for yet another experience.

The idea that I would be facing the relatives who were indirectly responsible for the tragic fate of my family filled me with anxiety and apprehension. This clashed with the anticipation of meeting my uncle, this legendary midget-sized giant of our family.

Our eyes locked on each other's faces as we stood across the threshold of our hotel room. I saw in his face the likeness of my mother emerging from the darkness of eight years that could as easily have been ages. The softness of his face, with a trace of strength, matched a low voice of quiet dignity as he uttered his first words that sounded like a question as well as an affirmation. "You are Mala's son. You are my nephew."

It immediately became clear to me that I would never hate this man. I felt no sense of forgiveness, either. It was an odd moment, bringing past memories and the reality of our meeting into a closed circle without an escape.

We had no language problem, as they both spoke fluent Polish. Within a short time, without elaborating on details, we caught up on events from the past to the present. Uncle Emile offered to contact our sponsors to take over financial responsibility for us. I emphatically argued against such a move. I explained that we met the requirements of the agency's charitable program, and that we, as a family, would be able to repay them as we become financially capable of doing so. We would not accept charity from the family under any circumstances. Persuaded and impressed, but showing disappointment, Uncle Emile offered Ada thirty dollars so she could buy some winter accessories. The very sight of her wearing knee socks in the blustery February weather made him shiver. Ada refused his offer, looking shyly to me for support. Nadzia (or Natty, as Aunt Lucy renamed her), not wanting to be ungracious, accepted their gift to buy Ada some clothing.

The next several weeks bristled with activity. Looking for a place to live, finding a job, and starting to learn English filled our days. I quickly concluded that I should not rely on the bureaucracy of the United Service for New Americans, having been sent several times on a wild goose chase for jobs that didn't exist or were already filled. In the evenings, groups of refugees would gather in the lobby of our hotel to relate and discuss their experiences. There was a common bond that united us, a group of strangers sharing the same problems and frustrations. Yet I discovered among us different attitudes about establishing a new existence. Some believed that they had suffered enough in a world that had turned a cold shoulder on them and that the world owed them a comfortable existence. Others, possessing an extraordinary sense for evaluating and seizing opportunities, spent time beating the pavements of the city, listening, observing, and talking to strangers in order to find business ventures to invest in. I was curious about how they would finance such investments. Some had money saved, while others simply expected the agency to lend them the money. Quite a number of them became early millionaires by buying the decaying buildings in the Bronx, on the Bowery and uptown Third Avenue, anticipating the elimination of the "El," the aboveground metro line running the length of the avenue. Their instincts proved right when they sold these rat-infested buildings to developers, making their fortunes. Their contempt for work, which most of us pursued, made me feel uncomfortable. I stayed away from them. But later on I learned to respect their determination and the application of their business acumen in carving out their successful futures in a new environment. Some of these tycoons wouldn't even bother to learn English once they acquired their wealth. They would say with a chuckle, "Money speaks louder than words, and everybody understands and respects it."

While we wouldn't subscribe to this theory, we realized that we had arrived in a country that placed no restrictions on individual initiative and offered all people an opportunity to set their own goals and pursue their own ways of achieving them.

We made learning the language of our new country our utmost priority. However, the language course for refugees, which we attended one evening, left us confused and disappointed. The variety of accents the students used to pronounce English became so overwhelming that they drowned out the teacher's correct pronunciation. We knew that we would never learn how to speak properly in this environment. Ada was adamant about not attending another class, arguing that once we settled she would enter a neighborhood school to start her regular education. Natty argued that once we assimilated life in normal circumstances, it would be more natural and easier for us to learn. I was the impatient one. The following day I purchased a Polish/English dictionary. I cut out a front-page article from the *New York Times* containing eight hundred words and started a self-taught course of the English language. My next problem was to learn not only the meaning of the words but the proper sounds, the essential melody of the language. This I solved by purchasing a small Philco radio and focusing on listening intently to any spoken program. My two ladies complained about feeling deprived of any entertainment, shut off from the musical programs they loved. They longed for some diversion, and the pleasure they would derive from listening to opera performances, concerts, and other forms of American music that the little radio could offer. I was relentless in my insistence on listening to lectures, monologues, dialogues, soap operas, and sports broadcasting. They started calling me a tyrant, a dictator, and many other uncomplimentary names. As a compromise, I offered them my absence for a few hours every day when I would walk the streets listening, absorbing, and learning the habits and the sounds of the city while they listened to the radio.

In the course of these forays, after two months, I found an apartment on the city's Lower East Side between Delancey and Rivington streets, one block from the East River, adjacent to the Williamsburg Bridge connecting Manhattan and Brooklyn. Number 61 Mangin Street became our first home in America.

For years, the five-floor walkup building had been abandoned, serving as a shelter for families of rats, mice, and cockroaches. The waves of postwar immigrants provided the ideal element for the building owners to revive its human occupancy. This apartment building offered its new residents nothing but a roof over their heads with a minimum of comfort and service. The flip sign of the coin was that for a monthly rent of sixteen dollars, one could not expect more. Yet when we climbed the five sets of stairs to the top floor and entered the apartment, Natty broke out in sobs she could not control. The front door opened into the kitchen, which happened to be the largest room. Immediately to the left of the door, recessed into a niche, was a sink and bathtub resting on cast-iron legs and covered with a flat metal cover so it could also serve as a working table. Across the room, in the corner next to a gas range, stood an icebox. A metal cabinet with shelves on top bordered a narrow window that overlooked an empty lot littered with garbage. Rust was evident on all of these furnishings, suggesting their age and lack of use. To the left of the kitchen, an open doorway led to a room with two windows facing Brooklyn across the East River, with the Williamsburg Bridge to the right. A rusty fire escape outside the windows led all the way down to the street level. A narrow, shallow built-in closet completed the room. Across the kitchen, to the right of the entrance, a door led to a tiny narrow room, probably meant to be a closet or a bathroom, with an oblong narrow window giving an illusion of light. Ada's eyes lit up when she spotted it. "Could I have this room for myself?" she asked pleadingly.

"But of course you can have it. It was meant for you when I first found this place," I replied. Her arms embraced me, and kisses mixed with tears landed on my face. I thought at that moment of the irony of the two reactions: Natty's despair and humiliation for a life stripped of dignity versus Ada's outburst of happiness at the prospect of privacy. I understood both of them, and I made a silent promise to do everything possible to improve our living conditions. When I explained to them that the toilet was located outside the apartment on the landing of the staircase, and that it was to be shared with the occupants of the other apartment across the hall, their reaction of horror was visible. I strengthened my resolve to do all possible to improve our living conditions.

Our sponsors supplied us with an approved list of used furniture dealers, where we purchased the necessary items on long-term repayment plans guaranteed by the agency. Since we were limited by the size of the apartment, our task was relatively easy. For our combined living room/bedroom area, we picked a pull-out sofa bed, a chest of drawers, and a small stand for my Philco radio. For the kitchen, we picked a table and six folding chairs, and for Ada, an armchair that converted into a pull-out bed. We were able to find a narrow desktop, which we installed for her. Since there was no room for a chair, she used the arm of the armchair to sit on when doing her homework. A hanging rack fastened to the door and a chest of drawers in our bedroom accommodated her limited clothing.

I had once more declined the offer of Uncle Emile to help me out financially. Asked to visit him and Aunt Lucy by myself in their Manhattan apartment at East 81st Street, they drew me into a discussion of my future in America. Lucy proposed that I divorce Natty, freeing myself from the burden of supporting her and Ada, a burden the Paulins would assume until Natty would become self-sufficient. I would be free to enroll in a college to continue my education. With their connections, they would be able to arrange for admission based on my educational records from my school in Poland. I was shocked by their ideas of reshaping our lives and unequivocally stated that my marriage and my family's love and support supplied me with all the strength, respect, and values that I needed. I did not miss mentioning that it was Natty who was reluctant to marry me, and that she relented only upon my insistence. Uncle Emile then offered a ten-thousand-dollar loan with no immediate repayment schedule in order to set up a newsstand and candy store, which Natty would manage while I studied a profession of my choice. Touched by their offer, realizing that it was partly driven by a guilt feeling, or to test my integrity, I again declined. My refusal didn't anger my relatives. On the contrary, I detected a sign of approval mixed with pride at my determination to be the master of my own future. This produced the next offer for a partnership in my Uncle Maurice's small knitting plant located on lower Broadway, where he and my cousin Alan were eking out a modest living.

"Your father was a successful textile manufacturer, so you would uphold the family tradition and possibly contribute to the development of the business. I would help financially," Uncle Emile suggested.

"I'm sorry, but I was too young to be involved in my father's business," I replied. "I could not contribute any professional expertise to people who have been doing it for a long time, know the market, and possess the required skills."

"What a pity," said Uncle Emile. "They certainly could use some help and a stabilizing element in their relationship and their working attitude."

I did not want to probe the meaning of his comments, which I later discovered for myself. Indeed, there was constant bickering and disagreements between my uncle and my cousin. I was lucky and grateful that I followed my instincts and principles in staying away from this project.

In the meantime, Uncle Maurice, unaware of his brother Emile's ideas, secured a job for me at a clothing factory owned by a distant relative named Ben Gans. My job would be to press the edges of jackets on a steam press, after which the coats would be processed on chest, shoulder, and collar presses.

Thus, two months after my arrival in America, I had a job, an income, and a place to live. These conditions set the stage for a new beginning in my so-far turbulent life, opening a new chapter filled with the hope for stability in a normal environment in a society that valued freedom and an individual's human rights.

I could now affirmatively answer the well-meant but naïvely timed question asked of the newly arrived newcomers to the American shores: *"So how do you like America?"*

CHAPTER 18

EAST BOUND–WEST BOUND

My job at Ben Gans' factory was short-lived. His foreman hated me from the first moment we met. He perceived me as a threat, since I was introduced as a distant relative of the boss. Of Hungarian origin, he had no particular love for Poles, which further intensified his resentment of me. He concocted a series of lies about my being critical of the owners and implied that my work lacked the quality required. To avoid creating complications for my benefactor, I decided to quit my job and look for another employer. I looked up the address of the local office of the Amalgamated Clothing and Textile Workers Union on 14th Street and paid it a visit. Mr. Weiss, who received me, understood my Polish, while I understood his Yiddish. He said, "I would like to help you, but cannot since my primary duty is to find jobs for unemployed union members."

"I propose that you enroll me as a member," I said.

"I can't do that, because the rules specify that you can join the union only while working in a unionized shop or one which is about to be unionized."

"Why not recommend me to a non-unionized shop?" I asked.

He shrugged. "That would be against Union's rules!"

At this point, I became extremely frustrated and angry. "Where were you during the war, Mr. Weiss?" I asked.

"Here doing the job I'm doing now. Why do you need to know?"

"Because alongside your bravest countrymen I fought on the battlefields of Europe to make sure that you enjoy your job and safety. Is it too much for you to assist me in my predicament?"

I knew that my argument was obviously self-serving. To my surprise, it proved effective. I walked out with an address of a large clothing factory on Livingston Street in Brooklyn producing suits for the men's retail clothing chain Robert Hall. I got the job and was able to secure one for Natty as a seamstress.

The factory was a full-fledged, all-encompassing enterprise employing a cross section of New York's ethnic population, recent immigrants, and native born. Every phase of the production was performed on the premises. None was sent to outside sources known as "jobbers." The cutters were the elite, considering themselves artists of the trade. They converted the bales of fabric by cutting them into shaped parts that would make up the suit. The sewing section performed the second phase. Rows upon rows of sewing machines ticked and hummed, stitching and sewing the loose pieces of cloth. The collar-stitching section was next. Natty worked here, while I started as a presser. Both of us were paid in accordance with our output rather than a fixed salary. We were qualified as "piece workers." This created an unexpected problem. Natty was faster than the other women in her section. They threatened her with physical harm unless she adjusted to their pace. To protect her, I accompanied her to and from the subway, carrying in my breast pocket large scissors as a weapon. Fortunately, I was spared the occasion to use them.

As a presser, I progressed to operating three Hoffman presses, and within a short time Natty and I started accumulating an impressive savings in our bank account. Ada started her studies at the Seward Park High School on Essex Street, where she progressed rapidly. One of her teachers discovered that she was a dancer. He recommended her to Mrs. Dvora Lapson, a dance teacher and choreographer, who took Ada under her wings. This initiated her dancing career with Martha Graham, the famous doyenne of modern dance.

I stuck to my program of self-education. The constant chatter of my co-workers in the factory augmented it, and before I could blink an eye, I knew how to swear and curse using the juiciest English-language expressions. I also became familiar with the American national pastime, baseball, winding up as a devoted fan of the Brooklyn Dodgers. The names Duke Snider, Carl Furillo, Sandy Amoros, Gil Hodges, Jackie Robinson, Peewee Reese, Billy Cox, Roy Campanella, Preacher Roe, Don Newcombe, Carl Erskine, Joe Black, Ralph Branca, and Johnny Padres remain imbedded in my memory.

After several months, I had less fear and doubt about being able to cope with the new environment, language, habits, and behavior. I began to develop confidence and a sense of belonging, although some memories and sentiments for Poland still remained strong. I found myself rooting for Polish soccer, basketball, and hockey teams, except when they played the Americans. I took pleasure in the accomplishments of Poland in the different fields of science, literature, and fine arts whenever they became known and recognized. At the same time, my pride as a Pole suffered, especially when reports of Polish anti-Semitism would keep appearing in the news media. My sentiments for Poland were not exactly shared by Natty and Ada, who, unlike me, had lived in Poland through the entire war and were exposed to the worst behavior of their Polish countrymen, with the exceptions of a few righteous Poles who harbored and protected them.

The many members of our new social circle, whom we met through Henry and Lola Helman—the couple we were next to in the Bremenhaffen camp prior to sailing to America—shared Natty's feelings. We spent our free time with the Birmans, Zelkowiczs, Tenenbaums, Haydens, Zlotowskis, Golds, Bruns, and Jasons. This group expanded to include the three Uffner families, the Cadmons, Zandels, Joan Wren, and my old army friend Julian Feingold, who had selected me for the officer's school during the war, and his buxom wife Ada. Stanley and Zosia Stebel and their two sons Henry and Michael became my closest friends and my adopted family. In our frequent gatherings, which took place in our modest apartments, we were insatiable in our need for sharing the joy of living. Animated discussions of our tragic pasts intermingled with singing, dancing, drinking and feasting, playing poker, and flirting. These activities became essential for breaking out of our shell as victims, humiliated and persecuted by the terror and brutality of war. We were overwhelmed by the miracle of survival, by being free to do, to think, and to behave as we pleased without restrictions and penalties.

We were human again!

We often reminisced about the early days when we newly arrived refugees were met by our American relatives and friends with that first question popping out of their mouths, *"So how do you like America?"* The lack of sensitivity and timing of the question bothered us at first. As time passed, we put it in the column of humorous naiveté as well as an expression of their own pride as Americans.

We had lived through evil times of degradation and denial of fundamental rights and benefits of human beings. The Nazis tried to reduce and eliminate us as an inferior people. Those of us under the Marxist Soviets were reduced to being slaves of the State or rotted in prisons and camps accused as enemies of the State.

Yes, we were humans again! Yes, we did like America! We were grateful to the country that gathered us to its warm heart, returning our human dignity and offering us the opportunity as individuals to use our skills and abilities to realize our potential to achieve prosperity and become loyal members of a great democratic society.

I was especially fond of the children in our circle. They were the foundation of our perpetuity and a testament to the eternal hope and faith in the future we were all eager to share. For the survivors of the Holocaust, creating new families symbolized this continuity of life, denying Hitler his plan to exterminate all Jews. I loved to communicate and play with the kids; they filled the gap that life had created for me. In turn, I was rewarded by their love and acceptance as a mentor, as their buddy, and as a favorite Uncle Alex.

I marveled at the capacity and ability of human beings to reconcile the extremes of existence we were exposed to. Moments playing with the children and social activities contrasted to our return home to face the army of cockroaches; the basin under the icebox overflowing from leaks of melting ice; the mice that roamed undisturbed, even in the bright light; and the screams of "Murder!"—which sounded like "moyda"—from our next-door neighbor's wife being abused by her husband. I learned to handle these crises. I became adept with a swatter. I developed a sense of timing to empty the basin in accordance with the prevailing temperature. I hauled the chunks of ice five floors up myself, not relying on the tramps, who would stop at the local bar to get drunk during their ice deliveries and cause it to partially melt on the way. At night, I hunted the mice by throwing my heavy workman shoes, reinforced with metal tips, in the direction of peeping sounds they would make. My ratio of kills became quite impressive.

I used to clean up the "battlefield" before Natty would wake up to avoid her hysterical reaction. I took long walks while my girls were using the bathtub in the kitchen and took my baths later that evening while they were asleep. Bathing involved lifting the heavy metal top and thorough scrubbing of the bathtub, a chore I assumed voluntarily. New York's summer heat and oppressive humidity made it unbearable in our apartment; we adjusted by occasionally sleeping on the park benches along the East River. This would not be possible later on when the crime rate in the city rose out of control.

There was only one remaining problem: we were helpless to control our neighbors' fights and screams. When we notified our police precinct to intervene, our request was met with laughter. "The Grichkos have been killing each other for as long as they've lived there. Relax and pay no attention to them," was their advice. We started paying less attention, but we found it hard to relax.

This was especially true when Uncle Emile and Aunt Lucy planned to visit. I anticipated they would be breathless after climbing to the fifth floor, only to be greeted by blood-curdling screams of "moyda." I feared this would be too much of an experience for both of them.

They walked the several blocks to reach Rivington Street from the subway station on the corner of Essex and Delancey streets. The streets were teaming with pushcart vendors selling a variety of household items, articles of clothing, fresh produce, and samplings of foods and delicacies from the old countries. The fragrances, the sounds of many languages, the clothing, and the faces bearing unmistakable signs of their origins made up an ethnic mosaic alien to them. The chants of the afternoon prayers from the tiny synagogues Uncle Emile and Lucy passed may have triggered some old memories from their childhood years in Poland, which I'm sure they now also considered alien.

"When are you going to move from this God-forsaken place?" they exclaimed, out of breath after climbing five flights.

"As soon as we can afford it, after we find steady and secure employment."

"This may take a long time. How can you live here?" asked Lucy.

"We lived through worse conditions and survived," Natty said. "We shall survive this one as well. And when we do find a suitable place to live, we will appreciate it that much more having lived here. We have learned the virtue of patience and the rewards it can bring." I was surprised to hear it from her, knowing how much she resented our present living conditions. Our eyes met, and I'm sure she could read in mine my gratitude and approval.

The meal that Natty prepared surpassed everyone's expectations. Our modest kitchen was transformed into a top-class dining room. The burning candles gave it a sense of intimacy and dignity. For a change I tuned our Philco radio to WQXR, the *New York Times* station, which was broadcasting a concert from Carnegie Hall. Even our crawling creatures took a leave of absence, and our neighbors ceased screaming as if sensing the importance and the spirit of the moment. The compliments my aunt and uncle gave Natty were genuine, and a new, warm feeling of acceptance replaced our guests' initial concept of breaking up our small family unit. By the time I accompanied them downstairs and hailed a taxi, Aunt Lucy said, "You married a fine woman. In the face of poverty, she maintains her dignity. Poverty is a passing economic stage; dignity is part of a person's character. Stick to her."

"I intend to. Thanks for your visit and your advice."

As we parted, I had the premonition that the recognition and respect expressed would produce a bond that would enhance our so-far distant relationship. In the meantime, our lives turned into a routine, and time seemed to stand still for a while. We were both working hard, earning enough money to see our savings account grow appreciably. We paid back our sponsors and were told we were an exception, since the majority of the new immigrants considered the agency's contribution as charity they were entitled to. We had no obligations to anyone and were proud to live our modest lives unencumbered by debts. At the same time, I realized that being a jacket presser wasn't a high point in the career I was looking forward to. I needed a change. Fortunately, new developments enabled me to resolve this situation.

The factory kept expanding by installing several new presses. Victor Silvano, a young Italian from Brooklyn, was hired to work alongside me on the added equipment. We quickly became good friends. He was the one to take me out to my first baseball game at Ebbets Field to see my favorite Brooklyn Dodgers defeat the New York Giants, their perennial foes. He asked me how much I was paid per coat and was genuinely shocked by my answer. As a union member, he was paid more than double my remuneration. On his advice, I confronted our foreman, protesting this inequity. The next day, I was called in to the plant manager's office to meet with the union delegate. To my surprise, I found myself facing none other than Mr. Weiss. He greeted me effusively, a big smile on his face, which disappeared the moment I stated my demand for a raise to equal Victor's wages. After a half-hour argument, he made a vague promise to admit me to the union "sometime soon" and to have my pay adjusted. I came to the conclusion that an unholy alliance existed between the union and the factory management. I was being exploited, and they shared the benefits of my being underpaid.

It was the first of several experiences that challenged my idealistic image of purity and fair play in the conduct of business in America. Angrily, I devised my own plan to get even, to outwit this corrupt alliance. In my weekly summaries, I started submitting advanced numbers for loads of coats or "lots," as they were called, getting paid for work I had not yet performed.

Natty supplied me with these numbers as each of these lots, consisting of several hundred coats, was being processed in her section before being passed on to me for pressing. When I felt that I had reached the limit of my deception before I might be caught, I quit my job with a feeling of justifiable revenge and a bundle of unearned money, though not nearly enough to cover the months of work as an underpaid employee.

The experience of Natty being threatened for being too diligent and ambitious in her work, and my case of being exploited by the labor union in tandem with my bosses, left me confused and disappointed. It affected my evaluation of labor and corporate interests and the choice between the Democratic and Republican parties.

As if arranged by providence, in the mysterious way in which it operates, it was at this precise moment that my uncle Emile approached me offering me a job in the newly incorporated branch of his travel agency Generaltour-Agence Generale de Tourisme. The offer carried several conditions:

First: I must never disclose that I was related to him.

Second: I must learn English within one year to his satisfaction and approval.

Third: My salary would be forty dollars per week with no demands for increase unless offered by him.

Fourth: He would reserve the right of dismissal for any cause without compensation.

The job would start immediately, since he was to leave soon for his permanent home in France, where he and Aunt Lucy spent the better part of the year. They split between their residence at the fashionable Neuilly sur Seine in Paris, overlooking the famous Bois du Buologne, and their villa at Chantilly. I was to work with Mlle Boucher, the secretary and the only employee of the company.

At the time, my income was in excess of one hundred twenty dollars per week. Reduction by two-thirds was hardly tempting. In addition, the harsh conditions, and especially the way in which they were presented, struck me as heartless, bordering on cruel. I tried to ignore the lingering memory of the way Uncle Emile had treated my father in our moment of need several years ago, but it stayed vivid in my mind. I shared my feelings with Natty. Her reaction was instantaneous:

"Forget your pride and the past, bury your pain, and consider only what it would mean to your future. He is challenging you, because you have proven that you are honest, proud, and independent. You have turned down his offer of help, his money, and his ideas of how to live your life. You made it clear that you are not made to run a candy store or rot in an insignificant knitting shop with your relatives. He is testing you and your character now. I know you can rise to his challenge. Accept it. You will succeed."

I had not seen Natty as firm and determined before. When I brought up the subject of financial inequity, she replied without hesitation. "Don't forget that you quit your job. We managed to accumulate a decent savings, and I'm earning enough to keep us going. Once you learn your new profession, you will do well. Don't be discouraged. Treat him the way he treats you, as a stranger with no family connection. In the long run, it will work out to your advantage."

It was the middle of April 1948 when I paid full price for a suit and tie from Robert Hall Clothing, and this would become my new uniform for the rest of my working days. I reported to the one-room office at 55 West 42nd Street ready and eager to start my new job. After introducing me to Miss Boucher, my new boss, Mr. Paulin, led me to the office's only filing cabinet. "The top drawer contains files of clients traveling by steamships, the lower one is for train and airplane clients, and the third is for accounting and correspondence. The bottom one contains brochures, schedules, and printed matter. Take your time to acquaint yourself with their contents. Ask if you have any questions." This was Paulin's brief introduction.

As I browsed through the files, I found a common denominator in them. The symbols EB and WB appeared in every file. I considered them to be the key to my understanding of the new business. Discretely, I asked Paulin their meaning.

"Eastbound, Westbound," he replied dryly.

The East and West portion I understood, but "bound" was the part that gave me trouble. I connected it with being tied by ropes or some kind of a restraint. I wouldn't dare to bring my English-Polish dictionary to the office and innocently confessed to Paulin that this key descriptive term perplexed me.

He raised his brows and said loud enough for Mlle Boucher to hear, "You really don't understand? Well, then you are an idiot." He turned his back to me and resumed reading. I felt as if I'd been hit by lightning. I counted off sixty seconds, reached for the key to the men's room, and left the office. It took me a while to regain my composure and return to my small desk to resume my "education." At the end of the working day, I managed to act natural, bidding both a pleasant evening. I felt that it would be a permanent good-bye.

The subway ride gave me a chance to evaluate my situation. By the time I reached home, I was relatively calm. My Polish-English dictionary helped me to relieve my frustration. At dinner, I shared my experience with Natty. She listened attentively before asking what I had decided to do. In turn, I asked for her opinion. "My dear," she said, "this must be your decision. All I can say is to repeat what I said before about your pride, your pain, and your future. I will respect your decision."

That night, when I threw my boot at the noisy mouse, it was Paulin's face that I saw. In a nightmare, I screamed curses at Captain Vybornov: "Give me the fucking fire from all batteries now. Fire now and don't stop." This yielded to another image of my defiance in the face of my Russian tormentors when I said, *I will not sign!*

The next morning, I dropped the anchor of my future in the shallow waters of Generaltour with the determination never to ask Mr. Paulin another question. His challenge became a foundation for me, directing me in the way I built the company's and my personal future, earning honors, respect, prestige, and financial independence.

CHAPTER 19

THE MARSHALL PLAN IN ACTION COURSE

I returned to work with a new attitude, hell-bent on learning and absorbing the intricacies of the business. Without expressing it, Mr. Paulin was proud of my quick progress in acquiring a command of the English language and learning the tricks of the trade from him. I was learning not only how to conduct business but also how not to. When I tried to please a demanding or difficult client, he would scold me by saying, "Don't waste your time and energy on this one. There are 165 million people in America. You will always find enough of them to sell to." When I replied that a satisfied client was the best source of repeat and potential new business, he would call me naïve.

One morning, as he was preparing to leave for France, he came to the office all flushed with excitement. He explained that he was taking the noon train to Burlington, Vermont, to get a contract for a large group movement to Europe, which was being organized by the University of Vermont. He handed me the front page of the New York Times, pointing to an eight-line announcement of an educational credit-earning trip to Europe for teachers and students to study the effects of the Marshall Plan.

"How do you expect to get a contract for this group?" I asked. "They must have completed all arrangements for this trip, since it is so close to the end of the school year."

He again called me naïve and said, "If they had any detailed facts and a date for this trip, they would have included it in the announcement. I'm sure they have the idea, but it will be I who will supply the know-how to turn it into reality."

His reasoning based on instinct and sharp business sense proved correct. He returned with a contract. We quickly chartered a troopship from Holland America Line, the M/V Tapinta, for the round-trip crossings of the Atlantic. I was assigned the responsibility for the Vermont University project.

Ralph Darnell of Holland America Line spent countless hours with me poring over the name lists of my large group. He would teach me to properly pronounce the English names. I was humbled and grateful to him for his patience and forbearance. Occasionally I would have my moments of fun when we would come upon a Polish or Slavic name, which I in turn would help him to pronounce correctly.

Mr. Paulin left for our Paris headquarters to organize the group's land arrangements. Just before his departure, he hired an office manager to conduct the day-to-day business.

Frank "Nicki" Adelberg was the first and only manager of our firm before I assumed full control of the company. An Austrian-born American, a most disorderly person, he did not acknowledge the existence and usefulness of filing cabinets. He hoarded all files, papers, and tickets in layers upon layers on top of his desk. Yet he would find the appropriate document in seconds, when needed.

His mind was similarly crammed with travel information, facts, and photographic ability to describe places he has been to, as well as the ability to invent description of places he had never visited.

"When asked, don't hesitate," he coached me. "Any answer or description given promptly with conviction and authority carries more weight than delayed answers based on research and accuracy. Once they travel, people make up their own minds and form their own impressions anyway. They would hardly remember your comments," he used to say half-apologetically with an impish smirk on his face.

I used his technique up to a point, avoiding gross misrepresentations, and found it very effective. He taught me more about retail travel than anyone else. With the daily business under his control, I concentrated on the University of Vermont project under the name "Marshall Plan in Action Course."

* * *

With the English-Polish dictionary by my side, I read and reread the excerpt of Secretary Marshall's address until I understood every word of it. However, it wouldn't be the words that spoke to me from the inside cover page of the University of Vermont brochure, but the thoughts they expressed.

THE MARSHALL PLAN

☆   ☆   ☆   "I THINK ONE DIFFICULTY is that the problem [of world economic and political recovery] is one of such enormous complexity that the very mass of facts presented to the public by press and radio make it exceedingly difficult for the man in the street to reach a clear appraisement of the situation. Furthermore, the people of this country are distant from the troubled areas of the earth and it is hard for them to comprehend the plight and consequent reactions of the long-suffering peoples, and the effect of those reactions on their governments in connection with our efforts to promote peace in the world."

"An essential part of any successful action on the part of the United States is an understanding on the part of the people of America of the character of the problem and the remedies to be applied. Political passion and prejudice should have no part. With foresight, and a willingness on the part of our people to face up to the vast responsibilities which history has clearly placed upon our country, the difficulties I have outlined can and will be overcome."

From the Address of Secretary Marshall at Harvard University, June 6, 1947, as reported in the "New York Times."

---☆---

General Marshall's speech

☆ ☆ ☆ ☆ ☆ ☆ ☆

THE
MARSHALL PLAN IN ACTION
COURSE

A unique opportunity for study and travel
during the summer of 1948 sponsored by the

UNIVERSITY OF VERMONT
and State Agricultural College

In cooperation with the United States Department of State; the New York City Board of Education; and the governments of Belgium, France, Great Britain, and the Netherlands.

The University of Vermont and State Agricultural College believes that the problems of economic, political, and cultural recovery of Europe can be fully understood only by study at first hand. Therefore, the University, in cooperation with the several agencies listed above, has created an integrated course of study known as the MARSHALL PLAN IN ACTION. Advanced students and teachers of social science will travel through Europe, where they will observe directly the problems of recovery under actual local conditions. Instruction will be given on board ship by a carefully selected faculty of American scholars. The courses will be continued and supplemented through lectures in the several European universities by professors, government officials, trade union officers, and business men. In addition, five field trips to critical areas will be the basis for on-the-spot seminars and group reports. By these means each student will gain an appreciation of the importance to peace of the European Recovery Program and an understanding of the role which the several countries must play.

John S. Millis
President

☆ ☆ ☆ ☆ ☆ ☆ ☆

University of Vermont President Millis' message

In a world still obsessed with suspicion and fear based on mistrust and ignorance, travel and tourism seemed a natural catalyst to overcome these negative forces. It might provide the opportunity for Americans to see others not as a faceless mass of victims or enemies, but as human beings longing for the same peaceful existence that Americans enjoyed and cherished. It also would offer the people of other countries and cultures a chance to see Americans not as victors or the proverbial "rich uncle," or, for some, "capitalist imperialists," eager to impose their system on others. Instead they would see people interested in progress and development in many fields of endeavor under a democratic system of laws and curious about other countries and peoples, their cultures, habits, and ways of life.

In short, it provided an educational experience with the overwhelming message that we all are part and parcel of the human race, with the same needs, the same longings and hopes, the same feelings, ambitions, and desires.

Given the enormous task, I became engrossed in the project. It was my first experience in tour planning and operation, and by preparing and attending to every need and operational detail, I cut my teeth on it.

What I also later learned was the tremendous value and power of on-site education in forming and reforming various perceptions, convictions, and prejudices.

The participants, 180 women and 120 men, were divided into five field groups that participated in seminars and lectures for the full summer study program traveling through Europe. The courses included "Germany and Europe," "Education for the World Community," "Social and Political Implications of the Atomic Age," "The Church in World Affairs," "Democracy vs. Communism," and others. Respected members of academia delivered the lectures, as well as did cultural attaches of the American Embassies and Foreign Office representatives of Great Britain, France, Belgium, and the Netherlands. Additional lecturers were recruited among industrialists, labor leaders, and political parties from the ultra-conservative to the communist.

When the inclusion of the communist was announced, a female tour member from Texas asked to be shipped home with a full refund of the cost of the trip. "My father fought communism, and I will not attend a lecture by a communist enemy of our democracy," she stated with conviction.

"How would you fight enemies not knowing them, their arguments, and methods?" Dr. Grosscup, the project organizer, replied. "You owe it to your father to educate yourself so you can intelligently oppose your enemies. Otherwise he would have fought in vain."

She stayed for the rest of the tour and filed one of the best papers, earning maximum credit toward her degree. I drew a lesson from this story, which I used later during one of my own seminars. What especially appealed to me was the wide range of the program, in which every segment of political thought and ideology was represented and exposed, challenging one's own thinking. In addition, language studies, art, and cultural programs were offered, and participants' experiences were enriched and livened by personal meetings with artists and prominent figures from the world of music. The diversity and experience made possible by travel, the escape from the familiar surroundings of home, getting to know how our allies and enemies lived and thought, sealed my future in tourism.

The words of Mark Twain from his book *Innocents Abroad* guided and inspired me: *"Travel is fatal to prejudice, bigotry, and narrow-mindedness, and many of our people need it sorely on these accounts. Broad, wholesome, charitable views of men and things cannot be acquired by vegetating in one little corner of the earth all one's lifetime."* He also pointed out, *"The best way to learn about one's country is to visit another."*

The tour of Europe was an outstanding success performed to the total satisfaction of the leaders, Dr. George C. Grosscup Jr. and Dr. Fritz Kaufmann. These two couldn't have been more different from each other. George, of medium height, built like a sailor, with his light-blond hair and Nordic look, represented the typical American Anglo-Saxon Protestant. He spoke slowly, always to the point, and was inquisitive and detailed in his requests for clarity and perfection. He earned my respect, which he reciprocated, and in the years to come he became my close friend. Conversely, Dr. Kaufmann, with his Jewish countenance, spoke quickly and with a heavy Austrian accent. He had an erratically creative mind and was hard to please, often confusing matters. Connected with the New School for Social Research in New York, he later founded Academic Travel Abroad in Washington DC, a well-known tour operator specializing in educational travel. It would become prestigious under David T. Parry. David became my friend and an active associate in founding the American Tourism Society. He has contributed significantly to this organization, especially with his unique ability to create visual presentations of statistical data that is unsurpassed in its usefulness to the travel industry.

Dr. Grosscup accepted a position with Miami University in Oxford, Ohio, and continued the study tour program for almost two decades under the name Miami University Abroad, with our company providing all travel services.

One of the participants in the original tour, Lynne R. Smith, became the dean of Howard University in Washington DC, and for years organized educational trips for African Americans to Europe, West Africa, and the Holy Land. She also became a close and cherished friend who liked me to address her as Lynnie.

In 1951, while promoting a tour to Europe for teachers, she invited me to come to Newport News, Virginia, to describe and answer questions relating to the forthcoming tour she was promoting. To my surprise, I found myself the lone white person facing a black audience of several hundred in the university auditorium. I felt challenged and uncomfortable until Lynnie introduced me, put her arms around my shoulders, and said, "Mr. Harris, you are among friends." The applause, the smiles, and the friendly questions and comments made me relax. I would soon repeat this seminar many times before religious Baptist audiences, promoting pilgrimages to the Holy Land. Thanks to Lynne R. Smith, I gained an understanding of and developed respect for African American culture. I started reading up on African American history in the United States, cultivating friendships with members of the community.

When Mr. Paulin returned from Europe in the early fall, he acknowledged my part in the successful management of the Marshall Plan in Action Course project.

During his absence, I connected with Steve Lohr, a partner of Nicky Adelberg from their old days in Vienna. I introduced him to Mr. Paulin, who agreed to employ him to boost our retail business in Europe. Steve was well-known among the members of Austrian, Swiss, and German communities, and was able to recruit many of them as clients. He was an avid skier, which prompted us to create a branch of the company called "Europe on Skis," specializing in ski tour packages to the Alps; later we added ski tours to South America. The branch became extremely successful as the leader in the ski tour market, attractive enough for the airline Swissair to acquire it in the late '70s. Although we considered ourselves friends, there was a certain aloofness in our relationship. Steve was very much focused on maintaining his image as a sportsman, party hopper, and a ladies' man. Tall and lean, always properly dressed with his inseparable pilot-type sunglasses casually resting high on his forehead, he achieved a debonair look. Even though he would get involved in the firm's activities only when it affected his department, I appreciated his indirect contribution to the firm. His immense self-assurance rubbed off on me, and I became worldlier in my manner of dress and demeanor. He worked until the last moment of his vivid life and died at the ripe age of ninety.

Lucille Murko was our secretary. She had been brought up in a French Canadian Catholic convent, so she had a prim demeanor. She took command of the office, introducing a strict working regime. Lucille and I became great friends. She was the one most responsible for the elevation of my understanding and command of the English language. She had reached the ripe age of ninety-five when she passed away.

Shortly after Lucille joined the company, Nikki decided to start an airline ticketing business on his own and departed on good terms. In his absence, I assumed management of the day-to-day operations. It puzzled Paulin that I was able to get the most difficult steamship accommodations at the height of the season, May through September, using friendly relations instead of the commonly used tactic of bribery. Most steamship lines were located next to the U.S. Custom House on the southern tip of Manhattan at Battery Park. Every Friday, I would travel by subway downtown to position myself at noon sharp at the bar of the restaurant Pier #1 at One Broadway. There, the steamship companies' managers and reservation clerks of tourist and cabin classes, as well as some less pretentious first-class managers, would congregate to end the week's work. Anchored at the bar, I established the tradition of treating each of them to a couple of drinks.

They all appreciated my generosity and would never take advantage by expecting me to pay for any additional drinks. We would chitchat and share details of their private lives, their problems, dreams, and desires as well as disappointments. My English became peppered with new expressions. I made it my business to remember the birthdays of their wives and children with token gifts. It was a wonderful period of my life that drew me deeper into travel and tourism, with its easy access to people and the joy of intimacy and sharing. When Paulin found out about my popularity, he proudly confessed to the general manager of Holland America Line, Mr. Elliot Lyman, his friend and bridge partner, that I was his nephew. I was caught totally unaware when, one day during my negotiations for steamship space allotment for the peak season, Mr. Lyman addressed me as Paulin's nephew. That afternoon, I dared to ask Mr. Paulin for a substantial increase in my salary, which he brushed aside. I handed him my resignation. Taking it as a joke, he asked, "Where do you think you would find a job?"

"I'm sure Mr. Lyman would recommend me to some of his agents." I rattled off several names of travel agents who had offered me positions. He smiled, asking how much of a raise I expected. I gave him the figure, and, seizing the opportunity, asked for 25 percent of the firm's annual profits. His quick consent proved to me how satisfied he was with my development. I knew then that my career in travel had been cemented. His recognition of my progress paved the way to a contract granting me 49 percent of the firm's stock in 1951. Aunt Lucy was to hold the other 49 percent, and 2 percent was deposited in escrow with the company's attorney. I was granted the buyout right of the 51 percent in the case of Uncle's death.

The time had arrived for us to move out of Mangin Street. When I announced to the Paulins that we would be moving and disclosed the rent we would be paying, ten times higher than the Mangin Street dump, my uncle's comment was, "Don't count on other adjustments in your salary. If you won't be able to manage, you may have to sleep under the bridge." I had gotten used to his constant challenges and cutting remarks, taking them in stride. "Well, if that happens, you won't have to climb stairs when you come to visit," was my tongue-in-cheek reply.

We rented an upper floor of a two-family house in the then-fancy neighborhood of Richmond Hill, Queens. We didn't mind the slow pace of furnishing it piece by piece for over two years. We played soccer and catch, and partied and danced in the empty, unfurnished living room. Most of the time we spent in the spacious kitchen and the adjacent huge open-air terrace. In the kitchen, we would sit glued to the little radio, listening to our favorite programs. On the terrace, we entertained our friends, and their kids loved to hang out. The men played poker, and the ladies canasta.

My uncle and I became closer. He treated me to lunch at the Horn & Hardart Automat on 57th Street, where we could purchase ready-made sandwiches by depositing nickels and dimes into the food dispenser. Later he would invite me twice a week for lunch at his favorite French restaurant on 56th Street off Fifth Avenue. One day, in a tearful confession, he admitted that he was henpecked by Aunt Lucy and was unhappy in his marriage. It broke my heart to see this intellectual giant reduced to tears. His pride and joy were Lucy's two nieces, Lucette and Colette, with whom we socialized occasionally. I liked them very much.

In 1957, Dr. Emile Paulin passed away in Paris after a long battle with cancer, which had kept him bedridden. During his illness, I paid him several visits. His mind was as sharp and alert as ever, and I was able to discuss with him the company's business activities and future plans.

> Le Conseil d'Administration,
>
> Le Personnel de L'AGENCE GÉNÉRALE DE TOURISME
>
> ont le profond regret de vous faire part du décès de leur Président
>
> **Monsieur Emile PAULIN**
>
> survenu le 26 Mai 1957, en son domicile, 8 bis, Boulevard Maillot, à Neuilly-sur-Seine.
>
> 23, Rue de la Paix, PARIS-2ᵉ.   19, Avenue Kléber, PARIS-16ᵉ.

Uncle Emile Paulin's obituary, 1957

I was surprised at the amount of pain his departure inflicted on me. Despite his negative characteristics, he was my uncle, my mother's youngest brother, and a pillar of strength and wisdom, my mentor and benefactor. With much sadness and a great deal of gratitude for the opportunity he gave me and the knowledge he imparted to me, I assumed the presidency and exercised my option to buy the outstanding shares to become the owner of the company.

I immediately Americanized its corporate name to General Tours Inc., joined important trade associations, and became involved in the industry, intermingling with its leaders. I converted the company from a retail travel agency into a wholesale tour operation.

To my immigrant friends, I became a kind of role model. As the first to learn the new language, to have a white-collar job, to replace the subway commute with my first car (a new, flashy Oldsmobile 88), to own a business, and to travel the world over, rubbing shoulders with heads of states and royalty, I was seen as a "pacesetter." Yet I tried to remain humble and fond of my compatriots and their families and gratefully mindful of my good fortune.

* * *

The Oldsmobile 88 brings back a bittersweet memory of Ada. After completing her second year at Brooklyn College, she decided to concentrate on her dancing career by joining the school and dance company of Martha Graham.

Ada's life was filled with tragedy. She married her dancing partner John Stacey, reaching a decent level of success with him, only to lose him to cancer at the age of forty. I liked him a lot for his quick wit, good manners, and strength of character, After a long time of mourning and loneliness, Ada married one of her early suitors and admirers, Denard "Denny" Clark. She gave up dancing and became one of the most sought-after tour escorts for my company, capturing the respect and approval of her charges. She perceived her job as a continuation of her stage career, performing and interacting with different live audiences. She performed until cancer confined her to bed.

VARIETY
Wednesday, April 29, 1964

STACEY & SKOWRON
Dance
12 Mins.
Monticello, Framingham, Mass.

Bright, youthful, personable and enthusiastic dance team essay clean, sharp overhead lifts and spins in a torrid stint that runs gamut with jazz, musical comedy and adagio. The team has plenty going for it visually and artistically. Femme half, Ada, is a 5-1 brownette looker with a figger who studied her ballet terp in Poland, and then the dance with Jose Limon and Martha Graham in U.S., and has done her homework well. They open with "Merry Widow" in which comes the first of series of continuing one arm overhead lifts. Male half of act, though slight of build, is heavily arm-powered and his timing is expert.

Act's costuming is good showmanship. He wears tight fitting black leather trousers and jersey and she's in ice-blue breakaway gown. Their tricks have continuity and as they go into flare, femme is lifted by partner with rises carousel music, and goes into a one leg spin, an applausegetter. Pair go into a boy-girl "Honeysuckle Rose" bit; femme flips skirt and lad dons derby for musicomedy skit; then segue into their big offering, "Man With Golden Arm." It's a jazz number, in which femme demos snake-like movements, slithering up partner's back and around to a culmination of pantherlike movements to windup for heavy mitting.

Dance team shows lots of grace too, and should do well in nightclubs, hotels, and posh spots. Their act looks also very suitable for tv and musicomedy. *Guy.*

STACEY and SKOWRON

For Engagements: Write, Wire or Phone

STACEY and SKOWRON, 103 Moonachie Avenue
Moonachie, New Jersey - Code (201) 939-1450

Write-up of Ada and Johnny in a "Variety" column

Ada and Johnny Stacey's wedding in 1961 at the Waldorf Astoria Hotel in New York

Shortly before she died, she thanked me for being in her life. She told me that her most memorable happy moment was the surprise I prepared for her after her Broadway debut as a soloist in Nina Fonaroff's production of "Lazarus" at the Alvin Theatre, where she danced the part of Mary Magdalene. After the performance, Ada and Natty emerged from the dressing room, and I met them outside the theatre. Instead of hailing a taxi, I invited them into a brand-new shiny black Oldsmobile 88 bought the day before without Ada's knowledge. When we arrived home, our living room was filled with flowers and all her dancing companions and friends, whom I'd secretly invited, assembled to cheer her on.

The memory of her tears of happiness and the grateful hug she gave me, combined with that happy memory she shared as she was dying, left me shattered with pain and a feeling of helplessness and anger at the scourge of cancer. My confusion with the ways of God was deepened. Unlike Lazarus, she did not rise from the dead.

Ada and Denny Clark in New York in 1985

CHAPTER 20

REFLECTIONS ON AMERICA

Reaching back in my memory, June 24, 1952 was my most memorable and poignant day. At the Eastern District Court in Brooklyn, together with Natty, I took an oath as an American citizen. My two American close friends, Maxwell Davidson, my accountant, and Marty Lublin, our company's printer, were my witnesses and joined me at home to celebrate my new citizenship. I felt rewarded for the time I spent reading and rereading the Constitution and the Bill of Rights of my new country, a country with its arms and heart open to embrace and adopt the multitudes of the underprivileged and oppressed, offering them the ultimate of human values—*freedom*. To me, the most precious was the right and freedom to move across borders.

So I relished the moment when, as a new American citizen, I crossed into Canada to supervise our group's departure for Europe aboard a Dutch boat leaving from Montreal. Not even the beastly heat that day in late June could dampen my enthusiasm. That evening, in my hotel room, clad only in bathing trunks, with the ceiling fan working limply to move the air around, I listened with excitement to the blow-by-blow reporting of the fight between Sugar Ray Robinson and Joey Maxim for the light-heavyweight boxing championship of the world. Sugar Ray, whom I considered the best "pound-for-pound" boxer, lost the fight due to the oppressive heat, failing to capture the championship of the third weight division. He already ruled the light and middleweight classes.

Relishing my new freedom to travel, I took a trip to Israel in 1955. I had the address of my old schoolmate Benek Markowicz and corresponded with him in Haifa. With his and Moniek Szapowal's help, I managed to assemble the other surviving classmates, accompanied by their wives, at the Dan Hotel in Tel Aviv for an emotion-filled reunion. There we were, smiling, hugging, shoulder-slapping, caught in a happy moment, sharing memories of the good old times at school and filling in the gap of time since our parting in 1939.

I looked at the red-haired, freckled face of Ben Rosen, who luckily left Lodz immediately after graduation to study in Dublin, Ireland. He succeeded in organizing an Irish commando of volunteers to fight the British in Palestine for the establishment of a Jewish State. There was the bulky, muscular figure of Witek Zylberbogen, the unruly son of our physics teacher, who with a small group of underground fighters helped secure the northern border with Lebanon against the assault of overwhelming enemy force in the 1948 war of Israel's independence.

There was Rafal Borensztajn, his stooped, slow-moving, bear-like body just as I remembered it. He was now a professor of chemistry at the prestigious Hebrew University in Jerusalem. I accepted his invitation to ride in his two-seater motorcycle, and for the next two days we covered the breadth and length of Israel, absorbing its beauty and the images and spirit of the people we were meeting. I was amazed at their sense of reality matched against the history of this ancient land of the Bible, the cradle of civilization, which gave the world the three religions of Judaism, Christianity, and Islam. The experience and thrill of this trip was beyond description.

Olek Tabaksblat, known as Alexander Tarski, had made his claim to fame as a conductor with appearances at the Tel Aviv Philharmonic Hall. Jacek Orbach was chided by everyone for his job as a director of the Israeli equivalent of our Internal Revenue Service. He was apparently used to it and took it in stride. Salek Kleinman-Katoni chose his career as an expert in statistical science, which he later pursued in the United States when he immigrated. Adam Schweig-Shatkai couldn't join us for security reasons. He had become one of the leading scientists of the Israeli nuclear development program. Gideon Silberstrom-Shoshani also was absent, pursuing his diplomatic career in the Israeli consulates in Washington and other European capitals. Also absent was my buddy Haim Grynbaum-Gueron, renowned architect, who built the round Shalom Tower in the heart of Tel Aviv, and a number of other architectural gems in Africa and Central and South America. He later hosted a second reunion at his home. My old geography teacher, Lola Perelman, was one of the guests who couldn't hide her surprise that I had chosen a profession in which the knowledge of worldwide geography was essential. She had almost failed me in that subject.

My class reunion at the Dan Hotel, Tel Aviv, Israel, in 1955. Top row: Lolek Litwin, Witek Zylberbogen, Olek Tabaksblat, Salek Kleinman, Moniek Szapowal. Front row: Wislicki, Rafal Borensztajn, me, Benek Rosen, and Benek Markowicz.

I was proud of our small group of survivors of World War II, each of us grateful and conscious of being spared the fate of our less fortunate colleagues and families, all of us determined to make an impression and contribute to the building of a better future.

Yet that night, as elated as I was in having arranged for this meaningful reunion, I walked away with the feeling that despite the promises we all made to keep in touch with one another, the evening was more of a farewell to memories, comradeship, and friendship. With a great deal of sadness, I recognized that the damage that the war inflicted, the passage of time, the distance separating us, and the involvement in new realities that fate and everyday life heaped upon us would not let us reestablish the old close ties and spirit.

After my exposure to the various aspects and problems of life in Israel, I found the country and a good many of its people very much rooted in the horrors of the past and the feeling of being surrounded by enemies who were united against it. It made me sad and unwilling to live there, having to be constantly conscious of this history and threat.

Having tasted the American way of life and the principles on which it was founded and by which it existed, I considered it impossible to even entertain the idea of living anywhere outside the United States.

I returned to New York in a state of euphoria. My dream of being able to travel and cross borders as a free man had finally come true. My pride at being an American had penetrated my very being. A poem, "Reflection on America," which I wrote to commemorate the fiftieth anniversary of my arrival in the United States, sums up these feelings.

REFLECTION ON AMERICA

February eighteenth nineteen forty-seven,
A date I shall cherish the rest of my days
When you welcomed me, Lady Liberty, into your blessed heaven
Your crown shining with hope's promise in the wintry haze

I looked at you from troopship's deck named for Ernie Pyle,
As it was slowly plying into Hudson's final mile
To pier 61-Bremen-New York, our journey's end
"Welcome to America"—you were saying—freedom's torch in your hand

Fifty years have flown by from that day of days
I still feel breathless living out the dream, amazed
At the turn of fate and the invisible hand
That steered my way to settle in this chosen land

I remember well the days of early struggle
Sweatshop smells and noises will forever haunt me
The English class for newcomers made my mind boggle
With strange tongues, accents, a mixed cacophony

Instead, in my fifth floor walkup, on the Lower East Side,
A little Philco radio perched on a narrow shelf
Would become my teacher, my American guide
Into the new society and faith in myself

Eight hundred-word columns from the New York Times
Provided a vocabulary, which I learned by heart
With a roof over my head, work to save nickels and dimes
I blessed you, America, for my second chance and new start.

Brooklyn Dodgers became my very early symbol
Of American culture and competitive spirit
Jackie Robinson, his resolve, courage and gall
Laying ground and example for us all to live it

I hailed eight presidents and their leadership
Harry Truman, Warrior Ike and young JFK
LBJ, Nixon, Ford, Carter whose stewardship
Made room for Reagan, Bush and Bill Clinton today

There were strikes and wars, young people have died
There was King and Bobby Kennedy, who valiantly tried
For a bright future based on rights and equality
Giving their lives fighting ignorance and brutality

There were ups and downs in the life of our Nation
From the Man on the Moon to Oklahoma Damnation
Regimes had fallen, down came Berlin Wall
Changing the world while America stood tall

Witnessing it all enriched my very life
Never, not for a moment, did I stop to strive
To contribute in my own field of endeavor
To the USA's well being, which holds my loyalty forever.

February 18, 1997

While reflecting on my years in America and composing this poem, I was deeply conscious of key historical moments and how leaders rose courageously to the occasion, breaking conventional borders that were part of our national habits and rules of conduct. These reflections had a lasting influence on my own rules of conduct and inspired me in my professional goals, which became my life's mission.

I thought of President Truman's courage to defy Soviet political intimidation, challenging Stalin by launching the Berlin Airlift; his origination of the Marshall Plan, which helped break America free from its borders of isolation and indifference to Europe; the creation of the United Nations, where the

United States was the first world power to recognize the creation of the State of Israel; Truman's dismissal of General MacArthur, reinforcing civilian control of the U.S. military establishment; and his many other bold actions.

I was moved by President Eisenhower's record as commander of Allied forces in World War II-Europe and his compassion for the survivors of Hitler's death camps, breaking the borders of America's indifference to human suffering and sacrifice; and his disgust with the abominable behavior of Senator Joseph McCarthy in his witch hunt for so-called communists.

The Cold War years of the 1950s certainly were not conducive for me to advocate and start tourism to countries under communist rule. Without President Eisenhower's desire to build bridges of understanding between countries and peoples of the politically divided world, it would have been unthinkable. But he made it possible.

I was bothered by the concept of a divided Europe. I remembered Sir Winston Churchill's famous 1946 speech at Westminster College in Fulton, Missouri, in which he coined the term "Iron Curtain" to describe the separation of West Germany from the East and the isolation of Poland, Hungary, Czechoslovakia, Romania, and Bulgaria as well as the Baltic states of Latvia, Lithuania, and Estonia. These were Stalin's spoils of war, and they became hostages to his absolute rule.

Much later, I admired President Kennedy's defiance of Khrushchev in 1961 in the Cuban missile crisis, President Johnson's breaking the borders of racial prejudice, President Reagan's challenge to Mikhail Gorbachev, *Tear down this wall*, referring to the Berlin Wall and Gorbachev's courage to implement that challenge—all of these events and the political and personal courage these leaders exemplified gave me the satisfaction that I chose the right way to direct my life's efforts.

CHAPTER 21

THE POLISH CONNECTION

During the years I spent in Russia as a prisoner and a laborer, I observed the level of misinformation and misperception that the Soviet government spread about the United States. Later on, I was surprised to discover the same characteristics in reverse among Americans.

Consequently, I saw tourism as the most effective way to break down the political and ideological barriers separating the two societies. I looked for a way, an opportunity, and some connection that would help me start the penetration of Eastern Europe.

The Polish connection walked into my office in 1955 in the person of Leopold Dende, a journalist, editor, and publisher of a monthly magazine, the *Polonia Reporter*, who was active in Polish circles in the United States. KLM Royal Dutch Airlines, the air carrier my company favored, recommended my company to him.

He informed me that Rome's Polish Archbishop Gawlina had decided to visit the Polish communities in the United States, commonly referred to as the "American Polonia." Leopold was entrusted with the choice of a travel agency, which would arrange the Archbishop's trip in the States. I accepted the assignment and was in turn introduced to Monsignor Wojciech Arthur Rojek, the U.S. coordinator for the Archbishop's trip.

Tall and handsome, with an air of authority and a booming baritone voice to reinforce it, Monsignor proved difficult to work with, demanding total submission to his requirements and commands. A military chaplain of the Polish Army, one of the defenders of Warsaw until it fell to the Germans in 1939, he had lost two fingers of his left hand as an inmate in Buchenwald, one of the infamous Nazi concentration camps.

He was decorated with Poland's Order of Virtuti Militari, an honor I shared with him. Working together, we gained respect for each other and initiated a long-lasting friendship. It was at his parish in Staten Island where I had the privilege and honor to meet with the then-archbishop Karol Wojtyla, who later became Pope John Paul II. The Archbishop's charm, sense of humor, modesty, and brilliance of mind made the afternoon at Monsignor's parish an inspiring and unforgettable experience.

Monsignor's younger brother Jozek and I developed a close friendship. He lived in Warsaw. During my visits with him, we would frequent nightclubs and restaurants, browse through Warsaw's Old City's antique shops, and flirt with pretty women in the crowded smoke-filled cafés. I bonded with his wife Celina, their daughter Krystyna, and especially with their son Wojtek. When Jozek died unexpectedly after a massive heart attack, the family chose me, as Monsignor's closest friend, to break the sad news to him. To this day, I consider the Rojeks my adopted Polish family.

Following the success of Archbishop Gawlina's tour in America, I revealed to Leopold my desire to develop travel to countries behind the Iron Curtain and decided on Poland for the first phase of my plan.

We carefully evaluated the Polish market in the United States. Most Americans of Polish descent used Polish agencies, which acted mostly as outlets for sending food and clothing packages and money transfers to their families in Poland.

Polish Americans resented traveling to Poland under the communist regime. The highly nationalistic and anticommunist Polish Catholic churches, civic organizations, fraternities, and veteran associations discouraged such travel as unpatriotic, some equating it with treason. Unfortunately, this attitude made it impossible for American Poles to grasp the greater good in face-to-face contacts—and the penetration of these artificially erected political and mental barriers—by visiting Poland and promoting the superiority of our democratic system. I warned Leopold that these barriers would likely be compounded because the Poles would be reluctant to deal with a Jewish-owned travel agency. He did not share my concern and asked for some evidence of my theory.

I soon encountered one. Ruth Thompson, my reservation agent who successfully managed the trip of Archbishop Gawlina and Monsignor Rojek, was assigned to handle our Polish clients. She possessed excellent manners and patience. Tall and blond with a short, shapely coiffure and the trim figure of a skier, she projected her WASP personality with ease and grace.

One day, she was working with a Polish couple that spoke English haltingly. It took all of her charm and patience to guide them through the bureaucratic process of requesting a Polish visa in order to book their trip to Poland. The man had never learned to read or write. His wife did all the talking. Ruth extracted the necessary information from them and completed all the paperwork, which the man signed by placing three crosses next to his typed name with the co-signature of his wife. He reached for his wallet, asking what he owed for these services. Ruth answered that since they were buying the air tickets and the required per-day hard currency coupons, both commissionable to us, there would be no charge for our services. He looked quizzically at his wife and said in Polish, "The Polish agency in New Jersey charges fifty dollars to fill out the application, twenty-five dollars for authorizing the signature, and a twenty-five dollar booking fee. How come this agency is doing it for free?"

"Don't be silly," the wife answered. "It is not free. These Jews must have an angle. They have a way to make money from us and then some. You should have never listened to the Monsignor and come here."

Having overheard this exchange, I was amazed at the depth of ignorance and prejudice of the segment of population this couple represented. This incident made me decide to change the nature of our agency from dealing directly with an ethnic market to packaging and operating tours as a wholesale tour operator, dealing with retail travel agents as our distributors and sales outlets.

I was able to convince Leopold of the wisdom of my decision. He in turn introduced me to his friend Jan Pargiello, who under the name Polonia International serviced the Polish community as a distributor of food parcels and money transfers to Poland. We explored the possibility of joining forces under his firm's name, acceptable to the discriminating Polish Americans. We paid Jan a visit, and in turn I invited both to join me for dinner at home. Natty served us a gourmet five-course dinner, which we enriched with frequent toasts of vodka. Jan boasted of his capacity for alcohol tolerance, which, interpreting this as a challenge, made me state that I could match him drink for drink. We started a drinking duel, with each of us alternating in calling the next round. Leopold bid us good-bye, leaving us to our foolishness. After untold shots of vodka, Jan called for Grand Marnier. He remembered from previous conversations that I didn't like liquor as a chaser after vodka. In turn, I called for a Remy Martin, remembering his dislike for brandy. We were becoming seriously inebriated when Natty scooped up all bottles and said, "I'm sorry, but this bar closes at midnight. Besides, we don't serve children, and you surely behave like them. I suggest that you sleep it off." She turned to Jan. "I'll prepare your bed in the study."

Jan wouldn't hear about staying overnight, insisting on driving home. I accompanied him to his car, down in the garage of my building. Very drunk, he was unable to insert the key to unlock the car door. I led him to my car and drove him to his home about twenty minutes away. I handed Jan's keys to his nephew, asking him to pick up Jan's car at his convenience. When I returned home, Natty was on the phone with our daughter Ada. She was frantic at my long absence, visualizing Jan and me in the city morgue. It took a whole week before she would speak to me again.

It was late in the afternoon when Jan called me at my office.

"Olek, I called you at home. I can't believe you are at work today. I slept through most of the day, and I'm ready to crash into bed again. You were crazy to risk driving me home, being dead drunk yourself. But I was even more stupid to let you do it. I never met a Jew who could outdrink a Polish peasant. I think we can work well together. Let's conclude our deal." I didn't take offense at his ethnic remark, nor did I take pride in his accolade to my drinking powers.

Polonia International started promoting tour packages to Poland with General Tours, operating the travel and touring arrangements of Polonia's clients.

We initiated an advertising campaign in the *Polonia Reporter* and American travel trade publications and printed attractive tour brochures, which were distributed to the retail agents in areas of the country heavily populated by Polish Americans. These activities drew the attention of government security agencies as well as the political leadership of American-based Polish organizations. In the process of convincing the authorities of the positive intent and beneficial aspects of our work and ideas, I met Walter Zachariasiewicz, a prominent, influential leader in the Polish American community. A broadminded man of high intellect, he understood my concept. We met frequently and developed a relationship based on mutual respect. While ideologically opposed to contacts with countries dominated by communist rule, he intellectually perceived the potential political benefits of penetrating the Iron Curtain. His association with the Voice of America broadcasting service, which disseminated an American point of view in countries behind the Iron Curtain, was compatible with my efforts.

His tacit approval provided me with the moral support I needed in my mission of breaking barriers and borders of ignorance and prejudice. I was delighted when Walter's qualities and efforts were recognized by his appointment as deputy postmaster general of the United States in March 1965. I maintain the highest respect for Walter.

The year 1954 produced the opportunity I was hoping for, the July peace conference in Geneva, Switzerland. President Eisenhower and Secretary of State

John Foster Dulles, British Prime Minister Harold McMillan, Soviet Foreign Minister Vyacheslav M. Molotov, and French Foreign Minister Antoine Pinay represented the Four Powers.

After the conference, I drafted a letter to the White House on Polonia International's letterhead, outlining the goals and strategy for developing tourism to Poland.

The letter we received in reply from the president's press secretary, James C. Hagerty—which was later endorsed and blessed by the primate of Poland, Stefan Cardinal Wyszynski—became my seal of approval. It was the guiding beacon for what was to become my life's mission, as well as obsession.

THE WHITE HOUSE
WASHINGTON

October 13, 1956

Dear Mr. Pargiello:

On behalf of the President, I would like to acknowledge the letter you wrote to him.

The President wanted me to tell you that he was delighted to receive a report of the activities of your associates and hopes that you will continue your work of good will.

With best regards,

Sincerely,

James C. Hagerty
Press Secretary
to the President

Mr. Jan S. Pargiello
President
Polonia International, Inc.
335 East 14th Street
New York, New York

White House letter from James Hagerty endorsed by Stefan Cardinal Wyszynski

Against the prevailing cold-war mentality and the atmosphere of hostility toward the communist-ruled countries of Eastern Europe, I created tour programs to Poland and later to Czechoslovakia, Hungary, Bulgaria, and Romania, designed for their respective ethnic groups in America, as well as for the general public.

By establishing and developing a healthy flow of American tourists to those countries, as human messengers of goodwill and friendship, we were breaking barrier after barrier of indifference, suspicion, and hostility of the communist bureaucracies.

Religious pilgrimages broke barriers and created bonds between the Poles in America with their brethren in Poland. Monsignor Rojek and Father Michael Zembrzuski, the head of the Catholic Order of Pauline Fathers in Doylestown, Pennsylvania, led such pilgrimage tours. Father Zembrzuski was responsible for the creation of Doylestown's modern replica of Poland's Jasna Gora Monastery in Czestochowa, where the image of the Black Madonna is housed. These pilgrimages were joined by the Order of the Felician Sisters from Lodi, New Jersey, followed by lay institutions.

Some Polish American travel agents became jealous; they resented the fact that Monsignor and Father Michael would choose a Jewish-owned agency to operate Catholic pilgrimages to the Vatican, Lourdes, and Fatima, as well as the Shrine at Jasna Gora, rather than use their services.

Monsignor Rojek lived in Manhattan's Leo House, a Catholic hospice opened in 1889 under the care of the Sisters of Saint Agnes, a religious community headquartered in Wisconsin. His critics, acting anonymously, harassed him by mailing soft- and hard-core pornographic magazines showing his name as the subscriber. It caused Monsignor a great deal of anguish and frustration at the inability of the post office to prevent this. Embarrassed, he appealed to the nuns to destroy the magazines as they were delivered. The vicious campaign reached its peak when Archbishop Gawlina at the Vatican received a letter from a group of Polish American travel agents protesting Monsignor's choice.

Monsignor responded that he was ashamed of the actions of his fellow countrymen. He pointed out that he had chosen to work with me as a Pole who happens to be of Jewish faith but whom he respects as a true patriot, and as a skilled, devoted, and trustworthy professional. He expressed his regrets at the lack of these attributes by the protesters. He showed me his copy of the letter to the Archbishop but wouldn't let me have a copy, embarrassed by the behavior of his countrymen.

Monsignor's honorability was further exemplified by his open letter addressed to President Reagan in 1985.

Open letter to president on the SS

The following is an open letter to President Reagan in response to his observation that "there is nothing wrong with visiting that cemetery where those young men are victims of Nazism also, even though they were fighting in the German uniform, drafted into service to carry out the hateful wishes of the Nazis. They were victims, just as surely as the victims in the concentration camps."

The author, Msgr. Arthur Rojek, pastor of St. Stanislaus Kostka R.C. Church in New Brighton, was chief chaplain of Warsaw during World War II and was taken captive when the Nazis overran Poland. He and 57 fellow chaplains spent the duration of World War II in Nazi-run concentration camps and he was at Dachau the day Allied forces liberated the surviving prisoners.

Dear Mr. President:

I have the greatest admiration for you as a president who is trying to do everything possible to make our United States of America the greatest country in the world.

May I ask you to consider the voices of others, apart from your advisers, especially those who during the Holocaust experienced atrocities at the hands of the Nazis.

You stated in your speech on April 18, 1985 that the German soldiers fighting in the German uniform "were victims as surely as the victims in the concentration camps."

Monsignor Arthur Rojek

Mr. President, do you know that all chaplains of the Polish forces were taken from detention camps by the Wehrmacht (the regular army of the Third Reich) and given into the hands of the SS?

This, after a promise that we would be set free because we did not resist the Nazi invasion with guns; we spent most of our time praying over the bodies of those killed in the invasion.

All 57 of us were captured and eventually taken to Buchenwald.

"Jedem das seine," or "everyone will get what he deserves" was the slogan of the camp There were two ways out of the camp, we were told: Through the grace of the great Fuhrer or through the chimneys.

Monsignor Rojek's open letter to President Reagan, 1985

On our arrival, the SS men pretended they were going to kill us right away and lined us up against the wall and pointed machine guns at us. They played with us for an hour like this. These were the German youth in SS uniform you stated were as much victims as those in the camps.

Here is only one example of how your advisers misinformed you:

One afternoon on a Sunday, the 57 Polish chaplains were resting after the long hours of work that began every day at 3 a.m. One young SS man around 18 or 19 years old was coming toward our group. The young soldier called to someone. The young Polish prisoner went.

Then the "victim of Nazism" took his gun and killed the prisoner without any reason.

The very next day, this SS man got a higher rank and some gifts because, of his own free will, he killed the "enemy" of the Reich. This was the way of educating young SS men in the concentration camps.

Then on July 7, 1942 they took us again by trucks to Dachau, where they were doing all these horrible experiments on human bodies. Over half the chaplains died in the camp.

On the day we were liberated by the 7th American Army on April 29, 1945, I weighed 80 pounds. That's why when I read what you said, I could not have peace.

I am absolutely for reconciliation, but I am not for changing history. The so-called Fourth Reich should know the truth.

We shouldn't hate them. We should cooperate and take them into the family of nations.

But that is no reason for the president of the United States to put on the same level those who were killed with those who were killing us.

As a nation we should forgive but we cannot forget what has happened.

In my humble opinion, it was not only the people in uniform but the whole nation that was absolutely responsible for the crime. Teachers and school children threw stones at the trucks that carried us across Germany on our way to the camps. The nation went after what Hitler called them to: *"Deutschland, Deutschland, uber alles."*

There is almost no Polish family that did not suffer at the hands of the Nazis. But after the Second Vatican Council in 1965, the Polish bishops went to Germany and forgave the nation as such. I am absolutely for forgiving. But the truth should be known, so that this will never happen again.

That's why, in admiration for you, Mr. President, I am asking you to listen to the voices of those who know, a voice in addition to the Jews and the veterans, to one who was there and is so happy to be a citizen of this great country.

— MSGR. ARTHUR ROJEK

Monsignor Rojek's open letter to President Reagan, 1985

More than thirty years after we had met, Monsignor passed away. His Eminence John Cardinal O'Connor, head of the New York Archdiocese, in the presence of fifty-white clad priests and a Polish Honor Guard, delivered the eulogy. While it failed to lessen my feeling of personal loss, I felt elated by the recognition given my mentor, compatriot, fellow soldier, and dear friend.

The success of the first stage of my obsession-driven initiative to penetrate the Iron Curtain gave me the incentive to continue working on my adopted cause. Determined, I was on my way to expand tourism, especially to the Soviet Union but also to all of Central and Eastern Europe.

We needed a reliable Eastern European motor coach company to take me to Berlin again to sign a contract with a company called BBS. I was hosted by the operations manager Werner Homelius, who took me on a comprehensive tour of West Berlin, followed the next morning by a full-day tour of East Berlin, still separated by the infamous Wall. We crossed through Checkpoint Charlie, immortalized in John le Carre's book *The Spy Who Came In from the Cold*, later made into a movie with Richard Burton playing the role of the spy. I hungrily took in all the sights on my two-day tour: the bomb-damaged Capital Memorial Church, left as a symbol of the war; the Rathaus Schoeneberg, where President Kennedy delivered his famous "Ich bin ein Berliner" speech from the balcony; the Reichstag, on top of which a lone Russian soldier hoisted the Soviet flag on that memorable day in May 1945; the Schloss Charlottenburg, an ornate Prussian palace begun in 1695, taking over a hundred years to complete; the glittering shopping street called the Kurfuerstendamm, Germany's Broadway, Piccadilly, and Champs Elysees all rolled into one; Unter der Linden Boulevard and the Brandenburg Gate, a symbol of Berlin, crowned with the Quadriga and Goddess of Victory in 1794; the Soviet War Memorial, commemorating the five thousand Soviet soldiers who fell in the battle for Berlin in 1945; the Pergamon Museum, home to one of the best examples of ancient Grecian altars; and the Olympiastadion, where, during the 1936 Olympics, the black American runner Jesse Owens defied Hitler's racial superiority theory by winning the hundred-meter dash and several other events.

I was struck by the difference between the two Berlins: one full of vitality, people moving with a sense of purpose in a place pulsating with life; and the other sunk in gray drabness that even the bright sunshine didn't bring to life. It was like watching a color TV show's sudden change to black and white.

Werner was a knowledgeable guide and a good companion. After our stimulating sightseeing tour, he asked if I'd like to dine in his favorite neighborhood restaurant frequented by locals rather than tourists. I loved the idea and soon enough was enjoying the ambiance of the small, warm, and cozy bistro. We had herring swimming in cream sauce, genuine Caspian Sea caviar served with thick, dark bread accompanied by cold glasses of schnapps, chased by the rich local brew. We relaxed and dropped the last vestiges of officialdom, our conversation turning more personal.

"Werner, your accent is not that of a Berliner. Where are you from?" I asked.

"Oh, I am from the eastern part of Germany. And where are you from?"

"From Poland. I arrived in the United States after the war."

"Hmm. You were in Poland during the war?"

"Not quite. I was in Russia and then in the Polish Army until the end of the war."

"Ja, the war was terrible. Let's have another drink for peace. *Prosit!*"

Our dinner arrived. We dove into bratwurst with sauerkraut and veal in thick gravy in which we soaked chunks of hearty peasant bread, cleaning our plates. We topped the meal with heavy chocolate cake buried under a cloud of whipped cream. A number of Werner's friends stopped by our table, and Werner kept introducing me as his American friend who had fought in the war. We shook hands and exchanged friendly greetings. Werner's choice of introduction made me feel a bit awkward, but the cordiality that flowed dispelled my discomfort. Yet somewhere in the deepest recesses of my mind, I doubted his friends' cordiality. Our conversation resumed when Werner asked me what military rank I carried.

"I was a lieutenant. How about you?" I asked.

"I was too young to be in the army. Toward the very end of the war, as a teenager, I was drafted into a local civilian unit to defend our town after the regular army withdrew."

"And what town did you live in?" I asked.

"Oh, you wouldn't know it. It wasn't big, but there was a lot of fighting there."

"What was the name of the town?" I persisted. A strange feeling came over me as if I sensed the answer, and I wasn't a bit surprised when he replied, "Bautzen."

"I was there," I said. It was his turn to feel a foreboding of what was to come. "Our units were engaged there for several days toward the end of the war. Has the church with the badly damaged tower been repaired?" I asked.

"Yes, but why do you ask?"

I related the incident of the machine gunner in the tower, adding, "That son of a bitch caused me a lot of grief and could have cost me my life and those of my men."

The silence that followed couldn't have been more telling. Werner looked at me and almost inaudibly said, "I was that son of a bitch."

We looked at each other for a long moment. Werner broke the silence. "Alex, I'm glad I missed you there, and I'm glad to have met you here." His hand stretched across the table and found mine in a spontaneous clasp and a squeeze.

"So am I," I heard myself saying before we both burst into uncontrollable laughter. The incredibility of our meeting made us reflect on the inexplicable ways and twists of destiny that brought two former enemies together as partners in business and companions across a dinner table. The proverbial soldier's camaraderie that had developed between fate, supported by additional doses of cognac and coffee, and us during the evening's discussion about duty, courage, lasted until the bistros closed at about three o'clock in the morning.

At the lobby of the Steigenberger Hotel, we bid each other good-bye, expressing the hope to meet again. That night, and later as I continued on my journey to Warsaw and Moscow, I kept thinking about the forces and causes of conflicts that turn nations and peoples into enemies and killers, and conversely reflected on the capacity of individual human beings to communicate, to understand one another, and to forgive. I keep wishing for a way to exploit these qualities to make them the standard code of mankind's behavior.

I never saw Werner again, but our incredible meeting etched itself in the history of my war experience as my one-in-a-million memory.

CHAPTER 22

GLIMPSES OF YUGOSLAVIA

1
Mirko

The tall, handsome figure of an American Serb, Trajan Voynovich, emanated energy and a sense of excitement as he entered my office in 1962. My KLM friend Gus Mize had given him my name over drinks while they watched a soccer game on television in his neighborhood bar in Queens. He told him about my pioneering of tourism to Poland and other countries in Eastern Europe.

This piqued Trajan's interest in doing this for Yugoslavia. He had little regard for the few Serbian and Croatian neighborhood travel agents who handled the ethnic airline ticket business and forwarded food packages and money transfers. He wanted to connect with an American firm that would take charge of what he envisioned as a flowing river of people and dollars to his mother country.

"Where would you find the source of water for your river?" I asked, picking up on his metaphor.

"My friends and patrons," he replied with self-assurance.

I took a liking to this handsome Serb and accepted his idea as a challenge. It suited my concept of building bridges between the two prevailing opposite ideologies. Even though Yugoslavian leader Marshall Tito defied Stalin in charting an independent course for the six federal republics and two autonomous regions comprising Yugoslavia, he was nonetheless a part of the communist camp.

I prepared an itinerary for a fact-finding study of the country to set up and market an attractive tour program. I invited Natty to come along to alleviate her growing discomfort of my frequent business-generated absences from home, which had started to seriously strain our marriage.

Due to the many inviting spots in Yugoslavia, I worked hard to limit our itinerary to places having an adequate hotel capacity and an availability of efficient ground services.

Unlike Russia and other Eastern European countries, which operated through one mega travel agency such as Intourist, Orbis, Ibusz, or Cedok, Yugoslavia had a variety of separate government-controlled entities in each of the regions that could carry out my programs throughout the country. I postponed my choice of a local ground tour operator until I had tested their services and their ability to satisfy the requirements of American clients, whose habits and demands varied greatly from European tourists.

As we approached the registration counter, a young, handsome man came forward and greeted us by name, introducing himself as Mirko Ilich. Although he was a reception clerk, he projected an air of both authority and hospitality. His appearance, manners, and the way he carried himself projected charm, efficiency, and pride in his job. He sparkled against the drabness of the environment and the system in which he functioned.

He collected our passports and invited us to follow him to our suite. He graciously indicated that we could take time to prepare our registration forms, and he would collect our signatures whenever we were ready after we unpacked and took a rest. We appreciated this departure from the expected lifeless routine check-in procedure at the reception counter.

His robust greeting, "Good morning, Mr. and Mrs. Harris," and his smiling eyes welcomed us the next morning as we descended to the hotel lobby on our way to the restaurant for breakfast. I again noticed how far apart he stood from the glumness and indifferent service generally prevailing in the communist countries. Against my sense of propriety, I could not restrain myself from asking him, "What are you doing here? You don't belong here. Your place is in America." He looked at me intently as if to test the seriousness of my remark and said with a smile, "Thank you, Mr. Harris."

Three days later, before we left, I handed Mirko my business card and wrote, "I hope you will come to see me," and bid him good-bye. I was struck by the firmness of his handshake, the fiery look in his eyes, and the strong voice wishing us a safe journey.

Several years later, I picked up the phone and heard Mirko's resounding voice. "You probably don't remember me, but being in New York I thought of calling you," he said.

"Mirko Ilich," was my instantaneous response, "Of course I remember you. Why don't you come over to my office? My address is still the same." I was thoroughly delighted, and I quickly decided on the position in my company I would offer Mirko.

"Of course I have your address, but to my regrets, I can't visit you on this trip. I'll do so on my next visit in New York. I'm catching a plane to Los Angeles to return to my office at American Express, where I'm working as vice president for the West Coast."

Speechless for a moment, I congratulated him on his success. It took several weeks until we finally met in New York to fill the gap of the years that had passed.

I asked why he hadn't contacted me for assistance or advice when he first arrived in the United States. He answered in an emotion-filled voice. "Alex, you have done more than enough for me. You recognized my potential, and you gave me pride in my self-worth and confidence. You gave me encouragement and a direction to follow. Why would I expect more from anyone?"

This combination of a strong self-image, matched with humility, became his life's trademark. His vision, intelligence, ability to face challenges, and a drive to succeed led him to set up his own business. He became a prominent and wealthy entrepreneur as president and publisher of *Traveling Times*, a publication that provides private labels and promotional materials for subscribing travel agencies. He loves to refer to himself as an American capitalist.

Our personal ties progressed to a family-like relationship that included his wife Karen and his daughters Tara and Angela. Our friendship became my invaluable reward for our inspired and memorable meeting in Belgrade and my first glimpse of Yugoslavia.

2
The Maiden Voyage

In the spring of 1965, Captain Boris Markoc of the Jadrolinja, a Yugoslav cruise company, invited me to sail on the maiden voyage of the newest addition to its fleet, the MV *Dalmatjia*. The timing was ideal considering the current circumstances of my life.

My total immersion into the business world had placed a heavy burden on my marriage. Natty felt left out, even though I had her accompany me on many of my foreign trips. My frequent travels, long hours at work, and easy interaction with men as well as women in the industry made her feel uneasy. The twenty-year age difference drove her insecurity and suspicions beyond a tolerable level for both of us. Her constant jealous outbursts and unfounded accusations drove me to heavy drinking. I lost my drive and enthusiasm for work and soon realized that my business would be lost if I didn't quickly resolve this unhealthy situation.

I reached out to a business friend, Haskel Tydor, who managed the New York branch of a travel agency, Patra. I kept supplying Haskel with steamship tickets since Patra had no license from the Transatlantic Steamship Conference as a ticketing agent. We worked well together. I respected him as an elder, a learned and wise individual, while he respected me for my honesty and genuine effort to be of help to him. Much older than I, born in the part of Poland under the Austrian occupation, he immigrated to Germany, where he established a metal smelting business in Frankfurt. During the war he was interned in Auschwitz and then in Buchenwald, where American forces freed him. I invited Haskel to my office, offered him 30 percent of my company, and asked him to manage it in order to give me time to regain control of myself. He looked at me benignly with his warm, brown eyes and said, "My dear Alex, I'm honored by your proposal, but I have no resources to buy into your agency, as much as I would like to do it."

"Give me one dollar, please," I said, extending my hand to receive the bill. Puzzled, he reached into his pocket and came up with a dollar. I took it, stood up, and said, "Welcome, partner, you just bought 30 percent of General Tours. Here are the papers confirming your ownership." The contract I had asked my attorney to prepare changed the company's hands and changed the course of our lives. Years later, I repurchased his shares for a price reflecting the then-existing market value of the company. It helped him to retire in Israel, which he chose as his home.

Satisfied that my company was under prudent management, I turned to my marital problem, which had reached a breaking point. Our relationship had become dysfunctional. The years of suffering during the war were at last taking a toll on Natty's psyche, creating an imbalance in her behavior. In her eyes, I could not do anything right, and I was constantly ambushed by her threats of suicide, which she finally attempted by swallowing the contents of a vial of sleeping pills in my presence. At the hospital where her stomach was pumped, the attending physician recommended that we consult a marriage counselor. I insisted that it be one of Natty's choice. After a number of joint and individual sessions, he recommended a divorce rather than reconciliation in order to salvage our ability to lead normal lives.

We distanced ourselves from each other. I arranged for Natty to take one of our tours, Capitals of Eastern Europe, with an educational group escorted by a professional lecturer of history and arts. After that, she would spend a few weeks with her family in Portadown in Northern Ireland. I left home, never to return.

I sailed on the *Dalmatjia* accompanying two couples, Jeanne and Irwin "Robbie" Robinson, publisher and editor of the prestigious travel publication *Travel Weekly*, and Sarah and Sam Nadelman, the general manager of Swissair in the United States. We sailed the waters of the Adriatic and Mediterranean seas, disembarking at various ports for land excursions. Two of these stopovers, both in Egypt, stand out vividly in my memory. Upon our arrival in Alexandria, the government tourist authorities invited us to an elaborate late-breakfast reception in the prestigious former British colonial governor's mansion, which required a jacket and tie. Before entering the dining room, we used the facilities of the men's lounge. I was nearly finished using the urinal when I suddenly sensed the movement of something crawling at my feet. I recoiled in horror to see the curly black-haired head of a very young boy who vigorously began to shine my shoes. Another boy pushed a stool behind my back, forcing me to sit down, and before I knew it I became the beneficiary of the best shoeshine of my life. Sam and Robbie shared the same experience, and when we generously tipped the young entrepreneurial teams, the shine on their smiling faces matched the shine of our highly polished shoes.

The other memorable stopover was at the Nile Hilton Hotel in Cairo, where we spent one night following our arrival from Alexandria. While enjoying an after-dinner coffee at the hotel's cellar nightclub, a gypsy fortune-teller offered her services to the men in our small group. We never found out why she excluded the ladies. Robbie was first and scoffed when she told him that he would soon sell his business and that his son would successfully follow in his professional footsteps. "That's rubbish. She is wrong on both predictions." The facts would later prove that she was absolutely correct. He sold *Travel Weekly* to

Ziff Publications at the time she predicted. His son became a successful publisher of various specialty magazines in California.

Upon studying my palm, she told me that I would live to the ripe age of ninety-one. "Well, if you know that, why don't you tell me how old am I now?" I challenged her.

"Mister, no ask question," she said in broken English. "I say what I see. You run away from home." I shrugged over this statement of the obvious. "You run from old woman wife. You no return to she." Closing her eyes, she described a scene at the New Year's party in our friend's house—me dancing with the hostess and Natty watching us—as her face twisted in an expression of jealousy mixed with hatred. The detailed accuracy of the incident left me breathless. "You marry two more time. A brunette woman, you know, she your new wife." I was tempted to ask for a closer description of my prospective wife, but having been rebuffed once, I held off. "You make very good business. You very lucky man," she concluded. I was impressed by the accurate reading of my current situation and was surprised by her prediction. My companions shook their heads and smiled, amused. Except for Ada, not a soul knew about my decision not to return home to Natty.

The gypsy woman moved to Sam's palm next, but quickly dropped his hand, asking to be paid for her efforts. "Not until you finish your job," he insisted. Reluctantly, not wanting to forfeit her reward, she proceeded to tell Sam that within two years he would lose five members of his close family. She wouldn't elaborate on her reading and stood up to leave. I had a feeling that she would have left even if Sam, whose turn it was to treat us that evening, had not paid her.

After a full-day sightseeing trip by car along the Suez Canal, we reached Port Said to rejoin our ship for our next stop, Beirut, Lebanon. After dinner, the Robinsons retired to their cabin. I was unsettled by the fortune-teller and invited the Nadelmans to join me for some after-dinner drinks. Sarah wouldn't let Sam drink, knowing his low-level alcohol tolerance. I insisted. Sarah relented and said, "Alex, you are in a strange mood. Are you feeling well? Is something upsetting you?" Without thinking, I revealed that Natty and I would indeed be divorcing and that the fortune-teller surprised me with the accuracy of her clairvoyance. I realized too late that I had committed a blunder. By granting the fortune-teller credibility, the gruesome prediction for his family greatly upset both Sam and Sarah. The color of Sam's face turned pale. He became very agitated and summoned the waiter, ordering a bottle of chilled vodka. On his insistence, Sarah retired to their cabin while the two of us, joined by the purser of the ship, exhausted the ship's entire supply of vodka for the remainder of the cruise. That night, the ship ran into a violent storm. In the morning, none of the passengers showed up at the dining room for breakfast except Sam and me. We were the only passengers who slept through the storm, being too drunk to feel its effect. The entire contingent of waiters welcomed and treated us as heroes, while we took pride in our new discovery of the best remedy against seasickness. The tragic part of the story was that Sam indeed lost five family members, including Sarah, within the time the fortune-teller predicted.

My legal separation from Natty took place shortly after my return. Our divorce was hardly amicable despite my efforts, as well as those of Ada and her husband John, both of whom supported our parting of the ways.

Natty moved to a smaller apartment and continued her social activities with her friends. According to Ada, she regained her composure and found inner peace. I too regained my inner peace; my adrenaline started flowing again, resulting in an increase in business, expanded coverage of new destinations, and my personal involvement in conducting familiarization tours for travel agents and special interest groups. Being a bachelor again, I combined my escorting chores with a renewed interest in members of the opposite sex, leading to short, intense romantic liaisons, exhilarating sexual experiences, and long-lasting friendships.

Women constituted the vast majority of the American travel agents' community. They were the hardest working and most knowledgeable and respectable professionals of any service industry. Many of them considered a familiarization tour a well-deserved relief from the rigorous daily working routine. Some saw it as a license to let their hair down and enjoy themselves socially. My status as a recently divorced single man made me a natural target for attention and advances. As proper as I tried to be, traveling two to three weeks together was conducive to some intimate relationships. Some of the ladies were just too appealing to ignore. Naturally, these relationships were conducted in a most discrete and inoffensive manner.

One memorable experience occurred on a trip in Yugoslavia during a visit to Sveti Stefan on the Montenegro coast, a delightful little seaside resort. The peninsula of Sveti Stefan consisted of a tiny hill jutting into the sea, with a small church at the top connected to the mainland by a narrow neck of sand, creating beaches that stretched behind houses abandoned since the nineteenth century. In the Middle Ages, the peninsula was ringed with walls as a defense against pirates. Skillful transformation had modernized some of the houses and turned Sveti Stefan into a village of individual guest cottages.

On our first night, a severe storm knocked out the power lines, submerging us in total darkness. Fulfilling my duties, with a flashlight to guide me, I visited every cottage to make sure that everyone of our group was comfortable and equipped with candles and matches. Deanna F. was one who had refused to stay alone under the circumstances, demanding that I keep her company. The violent storm that hit the island was meek in comparison with the storm of passion in which Deanna enveloped me that night. The flickering candlelight provided a romantic setting until the first light of the morning penetrated the slats of the window shutters.

CHAPTER 23

PEOPLE OF STATURE

1
Haskel Tydor

I regained my equilibrium, became socially and sexually active, and again enjoyed the gift of life. Still, my unhappiness had not been eliminated, nor had the haunting questions of my survival diminished. Why me, why do I deserve the benefits of life when so many had been denied that chance? The images of my parents, my brother Ignac, and the other close members of my family kept flashing before me. I spent many hours looking at photographs of my family recovered from my uncle Maurice's shoeboxes. It was there that I found our maternal family tree, confirming the early American immigration of some of our family members in Illinois, Wisconsin, and Ohio. This included the Harrises, whose name my parents had adopted. It was also there that I found the letters and postcards my mother wrote her brother, asking him to help find me, the son she missed so much.

Reading my mother's pleading postcards tore my heart apart. I shared my feelings with Haskel. He became my soul-searcher and confessor. His small physical stature would not match his towering character, his wealth of moral fiber, and his reverence of God. He never advertised his deep religious beliefs, never tried to impose them on others, and was extremely tolerant of those who did not share them. He never looked down upon them.

Haskel lived up to my expectations. He administered my office with authority that belied his mild manners and gentle personality. While he did not expand the business, he managed to keep it steady and healthy. He complimented me for my professional and personal attitude toward the Germans, Poles, and

Russians. "You have every reason to hate them for what they did to you. By not yielding to hatred, you became a better human being." I told him about my paternal grandfather's message, "Never let hatred enter your heart," which has guided me throughout my life.

Shortly before my departure for Yugoslavia, he solidified the reservation department by hiring Eva Neumann, a college graduate in her late twenties, with travel agency and airline experience. Good-looking, smart, quick, and witty, she brought a surge of energy to the company. Fluent in French and German in addition to English, she broadened the client base and very quickly improved our sales by her uncanny ability to turn inquiries into bookings. She caught my attention, and I started to rely on her ability and enthusiasm. She was a skilled and natural salesperson and became recognized as an outstanding speaker and lecturer at educational seminars. We developed an intimate romantic relationship. She was the woman the fortune-teller in Cairo described to me as my next wife.

Eva and I worked well together. Her sales and marketing capabilities made her a known personality in the travel industry. Representing General Tours at educational sales seminars for travel agents across the country, she traveled to every major city in the United States, winning universal acclaim as a leading industry speaker.

In the summer of 1969, I married Eva with Haskel Tydor's blessings.

Our 1969 wedding picture. From left, Haskel and Shirley Tydor, Stanley and Zosia Stebel, Eva and I, Eva's mother Edith, and stepfather Dr. Paul W. Sack.

Monsignor's Rojek's blessing continued and extended to include Eva. 1978 Letter from Monsignor Rojek to me and Eva, Monsignor with the then-Archbishop of Krakow Karol Wojtyla, and Mother Superior of the Order of the Felician Sisters.

Haskel was an interesting person. In the 1950s, as a survivor of the Nazi death camps of Auschwitz and Buchenwald, he was part of a delegation of grateful American Jews who visited the White House to express their gratitude to President Eisenhower for liberating them. A beautiful scroll especially prepared for this occasion was to be presented to the president. Haskel proposed that he recite a Hebrew prayer for the president just after that. The leader of the delegation preferred that they act as Americans, not as Jews, and was opposed to the idea. The meeting held in the Oval Office went smoothly, the scroll was presented and received with appreciation, and it was time to go. At that moment, without warning and in defiance of the head of the delegation, Haskel spoke up.

"Mr. President, we Jews have an ancient prayer that calls for God's blessings on the head of our government. I would like to offer that blessing upon you. Do I have your permission?"

The head of the group and others objected, fearing embarrassment, not knowing how a Christian president would react.

"Indeed you have," the president said. He got out of his chair, stood erect, and bowed his head. Ignoring the discomfort of the other members of the delegation, Haskel put on a skullcap, opened a prayer book, and intoned the ancient Hebrew prayer, while the president listened to the sounds of the alien words. Then Haskel repeated the prayer in English.

Teary-eyed and visibly moved, President Eisenhower said in emotion-filled voice, "Thank you very much." The delegation was moved by the president's reaction, which underlined the true meaning upon which America was built: that one could be a Jew, or any other minority, and a true American at the same time.

Haskel's wife perished in Auschwitz. He devoted himself there to saving the camp's starving children by forcing adult prisoners to donate part of their meager daily rations. His motivation was to assure the survival of the young to preserve the future Jewish generation. He led a group of them after liberation on their journey to Palestine. He fought for and witnessed the birth of the State of Israel. He remarried, and his wife Shirley bore him a daughter, Judith, in whom he instilled his faith and beliefs. She made him a proud grandfather of two girls, preserving his quest for the continuation of the future Jewish generation.

I was comfortable speaking freely of my happy moments and the good fortune I enjoyed but also experienced nagging feelings of guilt for my survival and all the gifts life had bestowed upon me. As an attentive confessor, he consoled me with his deep belief in God's ways.

While I didn't match the intense depth of his religious conviction and unquestioned faith in God, I took solace in our long discourses that filled many hours of our leisure time.

I summarized them in a poem, which I wrote following his death from cancer in 1992.

REFLECTIONS ON LIFE

I lost a friend, much older in age
And wise beyond his years and times
Respected scholar and philosopher, whom I engaged,
In countless discussions to the wall-clocks chimes

The subjects did vary, as did our mood
From religion, history, politics to what's evil and good
The death-camp tattooed number, which his strong arm bore
Added meaning, depth to his profound wisdom that much more

He experienced tragedy, suffering to extremes
Yet never lost his faith in God and the human kind
He never imposed on others his views and beliefs
But, as a living example expanded other's minds

He lived simply, modestly spreading goodwill around
Loving his daughter, son, their offspring, adoring his wife
To reach a ripe age before departing, Heaven bound
Leaving me with these memories and reflections on life

"One is never sure of life, as long as one lives"
He was saying with a twinkle in his gentle eyes
Followed by another saying, head tilted to one side
"No one has ever yet left this world alive"

"Life is the biggest bargain, you got it for nothing"
Was another quote he found in his studies
"But it is up to you to give it some meaning"
Otherwise you join the vast ranks of "nobodies"

Life is full of puzzles, challenges, mysteries, he mused
And, "Just when I knew all life's answers—
They changed the questions," and as if on cue
We burst out laughing—how true, how true

"When life gives you lemons, make lemonade"
"Face your problems one tomorrow at the time"
"Keep smiling and people will reciprocate
And their smiles will make your spirit climb"

We agreed on a lot, in substance and platitudes
Except for the one answer I looked for in vain
The one that divided us in our attitudes
And which caused me deep anguish and pain

The senseless tragedy of the Holocaust
My own survival, with all loved ones lost
His acceptance of the inexplicable mystery of God's ways
Against my anger and grief, which despite time's passage, persistently stays

He told me, my survival was meant to be
A sort of redemption, with God placing on me
The burden of filling my loved ones with pride
While they're watching over me from the Great Divide

"Make life count, you have but only one
As long, as you inhabit this earthly planet
Take all you can, but give back and then some
To greet them in the Unknown with a proud "I have done it"

Yes Haskel, my friend, I heard you and heed your advice
Stretching every moment of days, months and years
Giving time, energy, brain power as my sacrifice
To those who brought to my life meaning and cheers

And on the day, when I join you in the Universe
I hope we shall once more have time to converse
As we did in the past, to finally derive
Life's true purpose and essence in our reflections on Life.

In memory of my friend and mentor Haskel Tydor
December 1993.

2
The Men of Intourist

On September 11, 1956, President Eisenhower gave a speech at the People to People conference in Washington DC about "building bridges between peoples and countries." It was two years after the Geneva peace conference, and with Eisenhower's green light, I began close cooperation with the Soviet tourism monopoly Intourist.

I dealt with its functionaries ranging from local and national guides to administration and operations staff, from their protocol department to the top executive branch. I came across mediocrity, ignorance, hostility, ever-present suspicion, stubbornness, indoctrination, and plain stupidity. From others, I found a desire for understanding and cooperation, intelligence, respect, and friendship. My encounters were too numerous to describe in these pages. They have filled another book I have written.

Victor Kuzmich Boychenko, a man I got to know, respect, and admire, carried the title and position of First Deputy Chief of the Main Administration for Foreign Tourism of the USSR. In fact, he was the "boss" of Intourist, equivalent to a corporate president answering to his chairman, Mr. Nikitin. A war hero, Boychenko was awarded the Gold Star, which always adorned the lapel of his suit, representing the highest award for bravery on the battlefield. He earned it as a young fighter in the Red Army at the Ukrainian front. When he found out that I was the recipient of a similarly prestigious Polish decoration, the cross Virtuti Militari for my actions during the war, my status rose appreciably to that of comrade in arms.

He was a man of many talents, many faces, reflecting many moods. They could be read in his eyes. They were brown, warm, and friendly, but would turn into ice or fire on any given occasion. Victor had a fair knowledge of English, moved with supreme confidence and authority, and felt equally comfortable in the company of high-ranking international government officials as with a group of plain tourists. His staff respected, adored, and feared him. When he was the host at many occasions, he was at his charming best. His alcohol tolerance was better than average, and I earned the distinction of being able to match him drink for drink. This earned me his respect, which on some occasions I was able to convert to business advantage.

But the real test of his ability to perceive other people's values and his willingness and ability to compromise his regime's imposed philosophy occurred in the mid-1960s, when I led a group of thirty American travel agents on a familiarization tour of Russia.

As the engines of KLM's Electra became silent at Moscow's Sheremetevo Airport, we looked out of the plane's windows to be greeted by a huge sign in large white letters on a red banner proclaiming: "Welcome to the Soviet Union."

Two young soldiers wearing green border-guard insignia climbed the lowered steps of the rear exit and positioned themselves on each side of the doorway. Their young baby faces were a striking contradiction to their stern looks and robot-like movements. As they collected passports from the deplaning passengers, they looked with severity and suspicion at each face, comparing it with the passport photograph. Once on the ground, the passengers were assembled into groups, and an Aeroflot female escort led them into the terminal about 150 feet away from the plane.

I led my group toward the plane's rear exit. The guard extended his hand for me to surrender my passport. I shook my head to indicate my refusal to do so. I became overwhelmed by the desire to make a statement, to take a stand against Soviet intimidation, to challenge their mistrust toward foreign tourists.

I pointed to the sign "Welcome to the Soviet Union" and said in Russian, "I'm not in the Soviet Union yet. Aboard the plane, I'm still in Holland. I wish to step down on the Soviet soil as an American citizen, which my passport signifies. After deplaning, as your guest, I'll honor your rules, surrendering my passport. But not before."

My group was aghast at my action. They saw themselves and me carted away to prison at any moment. This thought crossed my mind as well, yet I decided to brave it out, to make my point and retain my leadership and credibility with the group as well as with the authorities.

It is remarkably strange how one's ego can overcome fear and summon courage to fight against overwhelming odds. The guards were dumbfounded. They could not perceive my point, nor could they change their procedure. We reached an awkward impasse. An alert stewardess summoned the plane's captain, who, after a tense conversation with me, summoned his KLM ground service manager, who in turn contacted the Soviet authorities. A solution was reached. The soldiers moved to the bottom of the steps, and we touched the ground before we surrendered our American passports.

With Victor Boychenko

It was most gratifying to me to see the initial fear and apprehension of my group give way to an expression of approval and pride. This incident sent a message and established a precedent for the future, marking an early understanding among the Soviet officialdom, that intimidation was counterproductive to the development of tourism, especially from the United States.

I recalled with fondness my father, whose advice to me in my early life proved to be so effective: *Never fear obstacles. When you face one, be confident and try to get through it. If you can't, try to go around it. And if that doesn't work, fight it and bring it down.*

There were many more incidents that paved the way to improvements in tourism between our countries. History has recorded many positive changes since that incident at the Moscow airport. My Soviet friends became my Russian friends. The communist officials became capitalists, but the Intourist old-timers still refer to me using Boychenko's term, *molodyets*. It translates to "gutsy fellow," which Boychenko bestowed on me after the incident at the airport. This showed his broad understanding of the underlying elements for successful development of international travel and goodwill.

Boychenko retired prematurely due to health problems caused by the wounds suffered in the war. I have the highest esteem and respect for his role in the cause of promoting peace through tourism, a concept he understood, accepted, and implemented despite the rigidity of his government policies.

He was fortunate, by choice or chance, to have an ally in Leonid Philipovich Khodorkov, his vice president. I thought very highly of Leonid, considering him by far the most intelligent of all his predecessors. He had a deep understanding of tourism, having advanced through the ranks from his early position as a guide. Of medium size and height, he had the appearance of a well-dressed college professor. His unaccented English was loaded with nuances and catchy phrases. His face was finely tuned with keen, intelligent eyes. He had a vision of the immense benefits tourism had to offer, matched by a sharp sense of reality of the environment in which he functioned.

In the late '60s, the tour business from the United States to the Soviet Union was generated by a handful of American tour operators. The destination was neither popular nor desirable and couldn't compete with the countries of Western Europe. As a result, the flow of tourism to Russia was more like a trickle. My company decided to take drastic action to remedy this situation. We worked out a plan to jump-start the market from its state of lethargy.

We would engage in funding an aggressive promotional campaign of low-cost, quality tour packages with frequent departures, while Intourist would provide these services at the lowest possible cost to us. Under these conditions, I was prepared to guarantee a volume of several thousand tourists, which would exceed the entire current annual production from the combined tour operators in the United States.

Leonid said that unless he were to make a similar condition available to the other tour operators selling tours to Russia, this would amount to a General Tours monopoly. I could not suppress my laughter at the irony of his mention of monopoly. When I pointed out to him that we were not just like other sellers, but rather were aggressive promoters, and that no other tour operators approached him with such risky, daring proposals, he changed his tune, saying that his Board would most probably refuse or make him personally responsible for the results.

Leonid and Luba Khodorkov

"You understand that if you fail, I'll lose my job," he said.

"Yes I do, and if I fail to produce, I'll lose my company," I replied.

Our handshake sealed the deal, and the rest is history. With Leonid Khodorkov as my Russian ally, we broke the border of a bureaucratic fear of change from the officially established basic rules and traditions, and forced the creation of a business philosophy and environment that recognized the realities of the marketplace and the need to adapt to it.

Our success put the Soviet Union on the map for American tourism in a most daring and risky breakthrough.

3
United States Tour Operators Association

The end of World War II marked a surge in international travel between the United States and the rest of the world, particularly Europe. Transatlantic steamship travel was supplemented and eventually overtaken by airlines. Speed and the flexibility in getting to and between places quickly became an important factor in passengers' selections.

The number of travel agencies all over the country mushroomed to serve the traveling public. The American Society of Travel Agents, or ASTA, was founded as the trade organization representing the interests of retail travel agents. Missing in this upsurge was an organized group to represent creative tour packaging operators, who turn travel into tourism.

Several failed attempts were made to create such an organization until 1972, when a group of ten operators located in California organized a regional association under the name of USTOA–United States Tour Operators Association. A few years later, a number of tour operators were invited to a meeting in New York with the purpose of broadening the association's membership nationally to focus on integrity in tourism. An editorial by *Travel Trade* editor and publisher Joel M. Abels urged the group to take meaningful action to demonstrate sincerity and commitment to a high standard of ethics and professionalism of the members' tour operators. On behalf of my company, I took an active part in the discussions, offering creative suggestions, and to my surprise I was nominated for the positions of vice president and president-elect of the newly expanded national association. Overwhelmed and handicapped by my sense of shyness, I declined the honor. I honestly did not feel capable or ready for the enormous task of leadership the position would require.

The booming voice of Mike Alford, president of California-based Unitours, suddenly reverberated through our meeting room. "Who the hell do you think you are, making all of us look stupid by suggesting we are choosing the wrong man? You better believe in yourself to match our belief in you. I'll pretend I did not hear you!"

The laughter that broke out gave way to words of concurrence with Mike. Bullied, humbled, challenged, and inspired, I accepted the honor. With that one simple statement, Mike Alford helped my professional career by giving me the confidence and opportunity to discover my own inner strength and qualities I was not aware I possessed. It helped me become one of the tour industry leaders, and my firm General Tours among the most respected American tour operators.

Ron Armstrong, the newly elected president of Spacific Tours, could not fulfill his duties since his company's business responsibilities kept him in Australia and New Zealand most of his time. I became the acting president of the organization. If that wasn't a challenging task, I don't know of any other that was. Conducting the Board of Directors meetings in a room filled with competitive superegos was tough. The roster of participants read like a "Who's who" in the world of tourism:

Mike Alford; Paul Herman of American Express; Jimmy Murphy of Brendan Tours; Tom Maupin, founder of Maupintour; Jessie Upchurch of Percival Tours; Bill La Macchia of Funway Holidays; Paul Albrecht of Globus-Gateway; Arthur Frommer of Arthur Frommer International; Ed Hennessy of Cartan Travel Bureau; Jules Cortell of Europacar Tours; Ronald Harris of Hemphill Harris Travel; Francis Luk of Pacific Delight Tours; Ed Hogan, founder of Pleasant Hawaiian Holidays; Arthur Tauck Jr. of Tauck Tours; Bob McGregor of Trade Wind Tours; Norman Sosner of Hawaiian Holidays; Zev Melamid of Tower Travel; and Tyler Tanaka of Japan and Orient Tours.

H. Don Reynolds, executive vice president and the only salaried officer of our association, a lawyer and former enforcement chief of the International Air Transport Association, was at my side to provide legal counsel and help to keep the meetings in focus. Often his short temper interfered with this mission, increasing the pressure on me. The basic problem we faced was building confidence and security for the travel agents and their clients who purchased our products. We defined four main objectives:

First, to inspire our own members that USTOA could play a viable role in the industry. Second, to establish external credibility by creating a financial security bond as a guarantee of our financial integrity to the public in case any of our members should become insolvent. Third, to hold and promote an annual conference where worldwide associate and allied members, such as suppliers of air, sea, and land travel services, lodging and transportation facilities, marketing, and other related services, would meet and network with the principal decision makers of our active member companies, helping both sides develop personal and business connections. Last, but not least, to make our voice heard by the agencies of governments in the United States and abroad on issues affecting the tourism industry.

To accomplish our goals, I needed the full cooperation of the Board of Directors. I remember one meeting in which intense arguing became intolerable. I stood up and opened all windows in the room. As we all shivered in the cold December air, in answer to protestations, I announced that I had to let in the cold breeze to cool off the tempers and freeze the egos in the room. With my message absorbed, I earned the respect of my peers. I went to some length explaining my rationale that we must consider ourselves not competitors, but independent entrepreneurs who happen to be operating in the same field of endeavor, working toward common goals and benefits.

"Compromise and move forward" became the motto of my term as the head of USTOA.

We managed to create a $100,000 Consumers' Payment Protection Fund to protect members against any major loss through bankruptcy; this eventually grew to one million dollars per each member company. To bolster our visibility through increased public relations, I was charged with the task of finding the right person for the job. I narrowed my choice to a Boston attorney with a broad knowledge of the tour operator sector of the industry.

On a late Friday in August 1978, I went to my office for some cleanup work. Don called to ask me to interview a young man for the vacant position. I reminded Don that I had pretty much made my choice. Don persisted, and out of respect for him, I relented. An hour later, a young man with a slightly Chaplinesque stride walked into my office. Dirty blond hair, flipping over his collar, framed his boyish-looking, smiling face. When he spoke, his slight Southern accent was charming, completing my favorable first impression of Robert E. Whitley. He knew the requirements of the job from Don and delivered a verbal presentation of his qualification for it. We engaged in a pleasant conversation about his past jobs and experience in tourism. I suggested that he call the following Tuesday, allowing me time to consult with my fellow directors. Shaking his head from side to side, he looked at me with intensity and said, "Oh, Mr. Harris, I can't wait till next week. I just can't go home to my family without this job. It is right for me, and I'm right for it. I must have your approval today. I know how much your peers respect you and would honor your decision. I promise that you will never regret hiring me."

What impressed me most was Bob's determination, bordering on *chutzpah*, to get the job. We shook hands and ended the meeting in an embrace of friendship that began that moment and lasts to this very day, extending to his wife, Carol, and his children, Kelly, Scott, and Shaun.

We worked well together during my presidency. Later, I was chairman of the government affairs committee, earning my induction as a life member of the association. We fought many battles, survived many crises, and overcame many obstacles to achieve most of the goals we had initially set forth.

Our progress was noticed abroad. The Russian tourist monopoly, with which my company was heavily involved, met my ascent in the industry with a cool reaction. The Kremlin's paranoia about an American conspiracy to harm the Soviet Union, a paranoia that resembled a communicative disease, seeped through all government establishments. No American was totally trusted, and

I found that the more influential I became in the industry, the less trusted I was by my Russian partners. They resented the position of power that could possibly be directed against them by organizations like USTOA. In response, I pointed out that the more influence tour operators would have on our government, the more it would lead to improvement of relations and understanding, enhancing tourism between our countries. I quoted the American governor, ambassador, and statesman Averell Harriman on relations between our countries: "We have choices of cooperative coexistence, competitive coexistence, or confrontation."

It took me a long time to persuade my Russian tourism partners to accept the first choice. My point was weakened when, as part of a boycott on travel to the Soviet Union in protest of its invasion of Afghanistan, President Carter prevented the American team from competing in the 1980 Olympics in Moscow.

Unfortunately, the president misinterpreted and disregarded the American spirit and the conviction that freedom of travel was not a privilege but a right. And Americans would not be deprived of their rights. There is no way to curb people's curiosity and their desire to travel. Americans would not allow themselves to be locked in, separated from the rest of the world, not being able to explore, learn, and compare. Once more, Mark Twain's remark that "the best way to learn about one's country is to visit another" came to mind.

For my company, President Carter's decision was devastating. Having contracts under deposit from many leading U.S. corporations for groups of their invited guests, executives, and employees, we were looking at a banner year. Under direct pressure from the White House, these groups canceled their travel plans. Many of the top corporate executives, realizing the unfairness of the president's decision that was forced upon them, were too embarrassed to ask for the refund of their token deposits. Nonetheless, we faced a dire threat to our existence, losing not only monies we had sent to the Soviet Union but also prospective passengers. Our projected turnover of about twenty million dollars was now down to zero.

When some of my friendly advisors suggested I declare bankruptcy, my disappointment turned to rage. The vivid image of my father's confrontation with his young playboy associate—and Father's words, "I would rather be dead than bankrupt"—flashed through my mind. I decided to fight for the survival of my firm and took my case to Washington.

Accompanied by Bob Whitley, by then the executive vice president of USTOA, we visited the offices of senators involved in commerce and tourism. We had no success in obtaining their assistance or intervention on tourism's behalf. The office of Lloyd Cutler, White House general counsel, directed us to

Philip Klutznick, the secretary of commerce. We met with his general counsel, and I used every argument about why our segment of industry needed and relied on our government's assistance. He was unimpressed. At one point I said, "If instead of tour operators, I were here to represent farmers, would you be just as adamant in your attitude?" With a broad smile, in the most brazen display of callous indifference, he replied, "You don't have the voting power of the farmers' community."

He must have recorded the looks of disgust and shock on our faces. Changing to a friendly smile and a softer tone, he said, "Mr. Harris, you are an outstanding businessman, and the reputation of General Tours, as we know it, is among the finest in the industry. You should have no problem to find a buyer for your company."

Our interview was over. Later that evening, I attended the festive and ceremonial Annual Tourism Industry Unity Dinner. Watching the color guard, I placed my hand on my heart during the national anthem, with my feelings of anger giving way to hope.

After dinner, at the bar of the Hilton Hotel, I ran into David Elmore, co-owner of Russian Travel Bureau, my competitor and the officially appointed ticket agency for the Moscow Olympics. He also looked tired and depressed when we greeted each other. A tall, handsome man with a trace of silver in his hair, he conveyed strength and energy. He commented on his day's fruitless efforts with his congressional contacts. I recounted my experience at the White House and the Department of Commerce, saying, "I have had it with this business."

He spontaneously responded, "Alex, would you consider selling your company?"

"The way I feel now, I would probably consider it."

"Great, I'll call you on Monday. I hope you are serious."

We concluded the sale of the company in May, with my company joining Elmore's conglomerate First Family of Travel. I retained my position as president, with all my executives under contract at their old salaries and the company's management and operation unimpaired by the change.

My chairmanship of USTOA's government affairs committee gave me the opportunity and a voice to tackle problems negatively affecting tourism.

I formed a travel and tourism coalition with a broad representation of all segments of our industry. Among the issues we successfully battled were the activities of foreign state-owned government tourist offices, which enjoyed immunity from U.S. taxation and our judicial system while competing in the U.S. market with American tour wholesalers. Our immediate target was the consulate of New Zealand. We managed to have the State Department adopt and circulate an official policy statement to foreign embassies and consulates in the United States, advising them that selling travel was not permitted as part of a diplomatic or consular operation. The Russians held this action against me as it affected their own plans of direct competition in the marketplace.

When one of the vice presidents of Intourist tried to implement such a plan, I organized a group of American tour operators dealing in the Russian market to actively oppose such a move. We took our fight to Moscow, where we formed the American Soviet Tourism Society (ASTS). We prevailed, and the originator of the plan was dismissed from Intourist.

I served several terms as president and chairman of this organization, later renamed the American Tourist Society (ATS), with Donald R. Reynolds our executive vice president. Don and I developed a friendship based on our respect for each other, our shared sense of humor, and a deep understanding of the value of our mission. We aimed to promote tourism in the areas of East and Central Europe, the Baltic countries, and the Red Sea/Mediterranean region under the slogan "Bringing The World Together."

Another issue our committee took to task was our own State Department's travel advisory system. We again prevailed when it was revised, eliminating the term "advisory." It was simplified and streamlined to "fairly inform and subsequently warn" the American public of adverse conditions in particular areas of affected countries, rather than a blanket warning about the whole country. In the process, we convinced the Department to limit the duration of its warnings so that when the cause of the original warning began to diminish, the public was accurately updated about improved conditions in the country. In this way, a country would not lose a whole tourist season unnecessarily. It humored me to be called by my business friends and associates the "industry's watchdog."

My toughest fight was when I introduced the concept of "open borders" to my peers at USTOA. I received a lukewarm reaction, with some members suspicious of my motivation. I explained over and over again that I did not advocate abandoning border controls or surrendering any country's sovereignty. My purpose was to have the ruling bureaucracies remove the psychological barriers on freedom of travel and to adopt an official policy encouraging international tourism. It took me several years to finally have USTOA issue an Open Borders Policy statement at its annual meeting in Hawaii on December 12, 1983.

USTOA recognizes Canada at our association's first Annual Conference in New York in 1978. Ed Hennessey, Cartan Travel; Ray Desjardine, Canadian Tourist Authority; Me; Bob Whitley, USTOA.

4
Cord Hansen-Sturm

For over half a century, motivated by the explanations and definitions my father ingrained in me so deeply in my formative years, I devoted my efforts to broadening international tourism beyond physical, political, psychological, and intellectual borders.

I believed that if we could break down barriers between feuding societies, we could help eradicate the destructive power of ignorance and hatred. I believed that contact with people and confrontation across the table beat the alternative of going to war, which I viewed as no more than an act of desperation. Thus, despite the fact that I had suffered as a prisoner and a gulag camp inmate in Russia, or maybe because of it, I became obsessed with providing what I thought to be an antidote to the still-prevailing cold war atmosphere by opening and generating a tourist flow between the West and the East—or to be more precise, between the United States and the Soviet Union and the communist-ruled countries behind the Iron Curtain.

The average Soviet citizen and Eastern European living under the communist regime, subjected to the heavy anti-American propaganda, was robbed of the freedom to travel to the United States unless he or she was in a special group under the supervision of the communist secret service's watchful representatives.

Americans, comfortable in the safety and protected freedoms of our democracy, which many took for granted, had little interest in traveling to destinations considered politically undesirable by our governing institutions. I could only hope to make a small dent in that attitude, to rally people as well as the authorities on both sides of the political divide, to reduce the hostile climate and correct the harbored misperceptions about our two societies, and to raise the level of trust and knowledge about one another. Travel offered the most effective opportunity to see how those others looked, lived, and thought, to get to know their problems, misgivings, and fears. Conversely, I wanted to let them get to know America as a peace-loving and friendly nation embedded in the principles of democracy.

The search and pursuit of these ideas, which took priority over my commercial interests and values, accounted for the energy I found to make General Tours the leading specialist in travel and tourism to destinations branded as unpopular. I conveyed the "nothing is impossible" approach to my staff, making them believe that they could and would make a difference, and by doing so they would raise people's consciousness above the ignorance and prejudice of countless others.

In Cord Hansen-Sturm, I found a great ally and supporter of my mission of peace through tourism. As vice president for strategic planning at my company, he inspired and assisted me in my endeavors. He shared the belief that the way to peaceful coexistence was enlightenment through travel. Cord joined the company in the late 1970s after his departure from American Express. He formerly had served as an economist with the State Department, a member of the staff at the American Consulate in Moscow, and a staff member of various U.S. government agencies. An author of many papers on travel and information flow, he argued travel's benefits to the U.S. economy, intelligence, and foreign relations. His bulky Viking physique was matched by a brilliant mind, courage, and persistence that strengthened my efforts.

We worked well together. We spent hours composing letters to the various departments of our government, as well as to the governments of countries behind the Iron Curtain, until the moment the Berlin Wall came down.

In the Georgian Republic of the Soviet Union with Cord Hansen-Sturm standing behind me as we admire the 13th century Metekhi Church perched on a cliff overlooking the Kura River.

Cord inspired me to extend our efforts to other parts of the world. We were instrumental in creating the South American Tourist Organization (SATO) by writing its principles and bylaws.

With Cord at my side, I joined a group of leading tourism executives in actively promoting the importance of tourism to the economy of the United States. This resulted in President Reagan signing the Proclamation of National Tourism Week. It was fun sitting in the East Room of the White House witnessing this significant ceremony.

My greatest satisfaction and pride, however, was the government's new Open Borders Travel and Tourism Policy. As chairman of USTOA's government affairs committee and with Bob Whitley's support, Cord and I lobbied Washington for its adoption. After years of hard work, the U.S. undersecretary of commerce, Rockwell Schnabel, announced a new Open Borders policy on February 7, 1990.

Our success gave me the good feeling that I had started, in my own way, to pay back the favors and blessings the industry had bestowed upon me.

This capped my long years of efforts to break down the borders of isolation and prejudice. In Cord, I found the perfect partner who gave me added strength toward this mission. He holds my gratitude and respect.

My business friends would sometimes challenge my enthusiasm. "How can you be so optimistic in the face of the reality of the cold war and the insurmountable differences that still divide our two worlds?" they would ask.

To this I had only one answer, which represented my deep personal belief: that there are no insurmountable differences and that optimism was an integral part of our industry.

Open Borders Policy adopted by the U.S. Department of Commerce

5
Ram Kohli

I had been accused of masochism for the tendency to pick and market difficult destinations. I considered it a personal challenge to remove borders isolating societies. I proved the validity of my attitude by the success of my mass-charter movements to Russia and East Africa and an attempted movement for India, which unfortunately didn't survive the waving sea of the Indian government bureaucracy.

I fell in love with Africa, finding its wildlife devoid of greed, jealousy, and oppression. The sight of a herd of zebras returning to pasture, thirty yards away from a pride of lions feeding on a zebra kill from a few minutes earlier, became symbolic of the law of nature governing the animal kingdom. My repeated travels to Kenya, Tanzania, Uganda, and Ethiopia, as well as South Africa's Kruger Park, became an obsession.

My constant quest to explore new areas for my company to market brought me close to Ram Kohli, the U.S. representative of one of India's foremost Indian tour companies, Travel Corporation of India (TCI). At the time, India wasn't an easy sell, but the pioneering spirit we shared—matched by Ram's enthusiasm and drive—started to produce some results.

India, in addition to its own abundance of elephants, tigers, and other game, also offered an irresistible appeal of ancient history, variety, culture, and natural beauty. Ram had been instrumental in my visiting his country in depth to discover its habits, ambitions, and, most important, its people. Ram's wife Deepak amplified this beauty. Their two sons, Rajeev and Rohit, were brought up under the strict discipline Ram had imposed. I enjoyed visiting them in New York in their Fifth Avenue apartment, where I became their Uncle Alex after exchanging vows of brotherhood with Ram.

We have often celebrated our relationship in our travels throughout India with toasts of fine scotch. I've enjoyed staying at the luxurious home Deepak, a most gracious hostess, and Ram maintained in New Delhi. Ram and I traveled throughout India, to Agra and its world-renowned wonder, the Taj Mahal; Jaipur, teaming with life; and Benares (Varenasi), with the holy Ganges River, which, following revered custom, we took a dip in.

We spent time in Shrinagar, before it became unsafe in the wake of turmoil between India and Pakistan. We were lodged in splendor aboard a luxurious water barge and spent time admiring the magnificent carpet weavers at work. We visited shops displaying hand-carved wooden screens used as decorative partitions, and I couldn't resist the temptation of buying one. On my trip to Nepal, I had the opportunity to view Mount Everest from a four-passenger helicopter flown by an experienced American Vietnam War veteran pilot. Landing on one of the clearings on the mountain slope, intermingling with the sparse inhabitants, I felt lost in the immense space surrounding me, wishing for the tranquility of the moment to last forever.

Ram humbled me by his assurances that I have been a kind of role model for him. Viewing his career, I'm proud of his success and his establishment of Creative Travel in New Delhi. Ram became involved in industry associations, accumulating a voluminous number of awards and positions of leadership in the travel industry.

As the twenty-first century arrived, I was proud to nominate Ram as the American Society of Travel Agents' (ASTA) International Travel Agent of the Year, and he was selected in recognition of his industry involvement, creativity, and long-standing professionalism. Unintimidated by adversities, displaying a highly developed sense of humor, Ram has always managed to reach his intended goals.

On my fiftieth anniversary with General Tours, he surprised me by throwing a lavish party in my honor at a leading Indian restaurant in New York. I was honored to receive a letter from President Clinton commemorating the occasion.

Ram refers to me as his "Big Brother," and I reciprocate by calling him my "Little Brother." We truly feel a deep bond and warm relationship. Deepak and their two sons, who are actively running and expanding his business, are an integral part of this family relationship. Being with Ram has always been easy; his sharp sense of humor and natural curiosity, and wise observations of people and places, makes him a wonderful companion.

I further strengthened my bond with India through our relationship with Andy Bhatia, longtime sales manager of Air India, based in New York. Ram and I share the warmest feelings for this man of patience, tact, dignity, loyalty, and grace.

My fiftieth anniversary with General Tours in 1998. Me, Bob Drumm presenting President Clinton's letter, Ram Kohli, and Andy Bhatia of Air India.

THE WHITE HOUSE
WASHINGTON

July 24, 1998

Mr. Alexander Harris
Chairman
General Tours, Inc.
Keene, New Hampshire

Dear Alexander:

    I am delighted to commend you for your 50 years of dedicated service to the travel and tourism industry. America's strength as a nation has always depended on citizens who understand the value of hard work and commitment. Your steadfast devotion serves as an inspiring example of caring and leadership.

    Best wishes for continued success and every future happiness.

Sincerely,

Bill Clinton

President Clinton's congratulatory letter

6
Pave and Nazli—The Rebuild Dubrovnik Fund

In 1991, when civil war struck Croatia, my favorite ancient city of Dubrovnik, the jewel of the Adriatic, was badly damaged through artillery shelling by Serbia. The bombardment resulted from the long-standing ethnic and nationalistic tensions that spilled over when the Serbs in Croatia rebelled against the new Croatian government. Sixty percent of Dubrovnik's terra-cotta roofs were destroyed, nine sites burnt to the ground, and virtually every major monument was damaged to some extent.

The travel industry in the United States was appalled by this act of aggression on a city that was a spectacular world tourist attraction, included in Unesco's list of World Heritage Cities. It bore no strategic or military threat to anyone.

The late Earlene Causey, a past president of ASTA, led the nonprofit Rebuild Dubrovnik Fund and Pave Zupan Ruskovich, head of the Atlas Travel Agency headquartered in Dubrovnik and later Croatia's minister of tourism. The other founders were Atlas' U.S. representative, Nazli Weiss; Otto Ruesch of Ruesch International, the late financier; William Davis Jr., a Washington-based attorney; and myself as national secretary. Luminaries of the film industry, and leaders in tourism as well as cultural and educational institutions, joined our Board of Directors. Actor Michael York became the Fund's honorary chairman.

Our mission was to preserve the city's cultural heritage through charitable contributions raised to repair the damaged parts of the city, restore the traditionally used terra-cotta tiles on the roofs of buildings, and to resurrect tourism, the livelihood of many of Dubrovnik's citizens.

Pave, with her quiet yet forceful personality, brought prestige to the organization. Tall, good-looking, and with beautiful manners, she was extremely effective at combining the image of the perfect lady with that of a dedicated, efficient executive commanding respect. I enjoyed working with her and treasure the friendship we developed.

Nazli Weiss became the driving engine of the Fund. She inspired us with her tireless efforts and dedication to the project, prompting the Board members to make use of their connections to advance the cause. I count Nazli, an exotic beauty of Afghan/Indian parents, and her husband Jeff of Russian/Polish/Jewish heritage, among my closest, most respected friends. I have been able to facilitate promotion of the Fund, with my friend Bob Whitley's help, through the annual Croatian sponsorship of the farewell lunch at USTOA's annual December conference and marketplace gatherings. It became an annual feature and tradition that gave Pave—and later, her successor Niko Bulic—a forum to promote tourism to Croatia in a most effective way. The entertainment provided for these lunch meetings was of the highest quality. We have all fallen in love with Tereza Kesovija, an internationally famous Croatian national singing star. Tereza entertained us for a couple of years, each time bringing the audience to tears of joy.

The "Buy a Tile," a contribution campaign for the terra-cotta tiles, was a smashing success. Large contributions by American Express and others boosted the Fund's resources, allowing it to pay contractors for their work. The campaign also helped restore the Marin Getaldic Elementary School, the Pile Bridge, the Miha Pracuta 11 Palace, the Dordic-Mayneri Palace Chapel, steps leading to the Jesuit Church and Seminary, the St. Blaise statue at Revelin Fortress, central heating for the Dubrovnik Symphony Orchestra building, The Stardom [Placa], the kindergarten in Cilipi, and facades facing the Stardom.

Funds for the restoration of the old synagogue were the result of a one thousand-dollar donation at a fund-raising reception and dinner at the home of Otto and Jeanne Reusch. Dr. Bruno Horovic, the president of the Jewish community of Dubrovnik, honored us with a visit. In his acceptance speech, he did not fail to mention that it took a good Catholic like Otto to spearhead a fund-raising effort on behalf of a Jewish cause.

The copy of the original plaque listing the donors' names, which hangs at the entrance door to the synagogue study, adorns my den, along with the commendation signed by the Lord Mayor of Dubrovnik, the Honorable Vido Bogdanovic.

My real reward came while visiting Dubrovnik to receive his commendation. I walked the streets, which had been severely damaged not long before. I viewed the buildings and relics, once again justifying their inclusion in the list of World Heritage Cities, with the strange sensation that the buildings smiled at me.

I consider the members of the Rebuild Dubrovnik Fund as people of stature. I feel privileged to have joined them, repaying in a small way my debt to society.

Dick Friese, the publisher of *Travel Agent* magazine, summed up the significance of these actions as transcending the objects themselves. "They represented the spirit of the American travel industry—the recognition that the beauty and culture, and if I may add, the well-being of people of the world, should be preserved as a matter of moral principle and responsibility for the future."

In 1998, I received a plaque from Vido Bogdanovic, Lord Mayor of Dubrovnik. Next to me is Nazli Weiss, Bob Whitley, and Pave Zupan Ruskovic, Croatia's Minister of Tourism.

CHAPTER 24

BEATING THE ODDS

The strain of my arduous activities and the millions of air miles flown for close to forty years of intense travel finally caused my body to rebel, forcing me to slow down.

My unscheduled 1985 trip was in an ambulance to Manhattan's Cabrini Hospital, with what was diagnosed as a mild heart attack. Transferred to the New York Cornell Medical Center Hospital, the renowned cardiologist Dr. Isadore Rosenfeld and his son-in-law Dr. Harvey Goldberg took charge of my health.

Seven years later, I landed again in the hospital. Harvey's voice brought me up to the reality of the moment. In a most casual way, he broke the news that my arteries were 90 percent clogged and recommended an immediate quadruple heart bypass operation. Other cardiologists and surgeons reviewing the results of my tests supported his opinion.

"What are my odds to survive?" I asked Harvey.

"They beat the odds you had surviving the gulag and fighting the war. You will be in the care of a fine surgeon, one who operated on my father-in-law. I have full confidence in Dr. Jeffrey Gold."

I trusted Harvey, who had been caring for me for some time now, showing good judgment and an understanding of my personality. He proved it in 1987 when, during my routine checkup, he noticed an elevated blood pressure and a change in my behavior. He questioned what was bothering me. Did I suffer from financial difficulties, marital problems, or tourism-related pressures that were obviously affecting me?

Tourism, despite its pitfalls, had been good to me. I was married to it. It provided the vehicle that filled the purpose of my life. The existence of this bond had become stronger than my relationship with Eva. Working side by side with me for years as my vice president of marketing, she had become tired of the tensions and pressures the job required. She strived for a career of dog breeding and training and eventually became a professional kennel owner. I liked dogs from the day when, as my fiancée, Eva surprised me with a boxer puppy for my birthday. We named him Boris and enrolled him in breed and obedience competitions where he won a double championship as Ch. Eldick's Alexander the Great CD. When Eva expanded her canine family to nearly twenty members, expecting me to join her full-time at the expense of my business, I declined. When I confessed to Harvey the differences in our continued life goals, Harvey casually said, "Today is Wednesday. Why don't you call me on Monday with your decision about your marriage so that I'll know how to treat you?"

I was surprised by his calm as well as the enormity of his request. I was being challenged to solve in a few days what normally takes a long period of frustration, indecision, and procrastination. I gave him a look of shock, only to find his look of determination and a smile of encouragement.

Saturday, during breakfast, I told Eva that we needed to have a serious conversation. She replied, "I think so too." Within the next hour, we agreed to file for divorce to pursue our interests and live independently. Our 1988 divorce was amicable, and to this day we maintain close contact. I retained a fondness and a warm feeling of gratitude for her contribution to many years of happiness and the great role she played in the development of my company.

"Thanks. Now I know how to treat you," were Harvey's first words when I told him on Monday about the agreement to dissolve our marriage.

Yes, I trusted Harvey, and looking at him from my bed I said, "Okay, Doctor, set up the date, and let's get me unclogged." A triple bypass operation took place on March 12, and on March 25 I returned home with renewed hope for a full and happy life. The outspread wings of my mother's love had protected me once again.

Backtracking to my divorce from Eva, after the initial period of sadness and reflection, I began enjoying relationships with a variety of women. Residing now in my Manhattan bachelor loft, I experienced several romances varying in intensity and depth, but none serious enough to make it permanent. At the same time, I realized that I was not cut out to live as a bachelor. I needed a structure in which I could openly share my feelings with a person I would love and care for, someone who would understand and respond to my needs and help to create a framework that would give meaning to my life.

One evening, my buddy Bob Whitley asked me to join him at a cocktail reception given by the Singapore Government Tourist Office. I wasn't in the right mood. "Come on," he urged. "If you don't like it we'll leave, walk over to Harry's Bar at the Waldorf, and get us some drinks." That sounded fair to me.

At the reception, my mood improved as I exchanged greetings with familiar industry friends. At one point, Bob steered me to the table of Judy McDaniel, an assistant general manager, and two junior executives of TBI, a tour company owned by the Japan Travel Bureau. Following Bob's introductions, we joined their table. I sat looking into Judy's blue-green eyes, feeling an overpowering electric current running through my body. Her beauty overwhelmed me and I blurted out, "You are the most beautiful woman I have met in the travel industry." I felt subconsciously that using the term *travel industry* rather than *the world*, an old cliché, would strike a responsive cord. The noise of the crowd and music prevented any conversation, and we parted early.

We still went to Harry's Bar for a few drinks. Bob made fun of my high-school boy reaction to Judy while acknowledging my good taste. Judy, an Episcopalian raised in Southwest Colorado, traced her heritage to England, Ireland, Germany, and Denmark; and I, a European-born Jew, was now an American in my adopted country. But the differences in our ages and backgrounds had not kept us from bonding emotionally. Our acquaintance would become a courtship and a warm relationship. I had a premonition that this chance meeting would bring a change to my life.

Judy cemented it by her unselfish concern and the warm feeling she displayed during my most trying moments following my triple bypass heart surgery. Her face and Ada's were the first images that penetrated my consciousness when I opened my eyes after the surgery. It took me quite a while to realize that they were real, standing by my bed in the recovery room.

At the start of our relationship, these two women I loved bonded quickly. I respected Ada's approval of Judy, knowing that she was an acute judge of people. She had perceived Judy's inner values, which I discovered later: her unselfish caring for people, her spirit of generosity and goodness, her loyalty, and her zest for life. Added to these attributes were her beautiful looks. Black hair framed the light complexion of her well-shaped face, with an upturned nose, a broad, charming smile, and blue eyes turning green in different exposures to light or mood. A pert figure, standing five feet tall, she was a delightful sight. I enjoyed the sound of her quick, tiny steps as she moved around. As tiny as they were, she still could outpace anyone. Her voice carried a permanent smile, yet she would sound serious and efficient in the business environment. The sound of her contagious laughter projected happiness, and her knack for easy chatter made her a pleasant, enjoyable conversation partner.

I felt grateful for her daily evening visits to my hospital bed, which she kept despite her heavy working schedule. Some evenings, overwhelmed by exhaustion, Judy would rest her head on my shoulder and fall into slumber for the entire time of the visit. The closeness and intimacy of those moments endeared her to me beyond description. I felt loved, trusted, and cared for, experiencing the unsurpassed beauty of falling in love.

In April 1992, a month after my surgery, a letter from ASTA heightened my emotional recovery. I was to be inducted at the 62nd World Conference in Cairo, Egypt that September. I felt proud and humbled. My entire office personnel was elated at the news. I assured them with all sincerity that they earned and shared this highest industry honor with me.

Judy kept emphasizing that I must regain my strength to be fit for the trip to Egypt. I surprised her with my announcement that I felt fit enough to accompany her on her May trip to Durango, Colorado, to participate in the wedding of her younger sister, Joan, to Tom Kuhn. She insisted on hearing my cardiologist say that I could travel by air and tolerate Durango's 6,500-foot elevation. Yet she was happy about my desire to meet her family and was relieved when Harvey gave us his blessing.

Nine weeks after my triple bypass heart surgery, I was winging my way across the United States to meet the large family contingent of my sweetheart. Eight years later, I married her and was welcomed into their midst. Durango's oldest respected attorney, Larry McDaniel, Judy's father; his life companion, Lena Brittelle; her brothers Freddy, Gerry, Robert, and Gordon; their spouses; and, of course, her sister, Joan, and the groom Tom, accepted and approved my relationship with Judy. As time went on, acceptance turned into a close and warm feeling that spread to include Uncle Bob, aunts Phyllis, Barbara, and Doris, as well as numerous cousins, nieces, and nephews. Our annual visits to Durango were our year's highlight, and hosting family members on their visits to New York became our favorite events.

Joan's wedding to Tom took place in a picturesque mountain lake setting, and on Tom's insistence it was kept in Scottish tradition. I joined the group dressed in traditional Scottish garb with all its paraphernalia, borrowed from Bob Whitley. I also joined Tom's young friends in a game of volleyball. Since we were playing at an elevation of more than seven thousand feet, Judy was angry at my foolishness. But I felt strong, happy, ready, and eager for my September trip to Egypt.

With my new extended family—standing third row, right next to Judy

Judy and I on our wedding day at Blue Lake Ranch in Hesperus, Colorado, July 2000.

CHAPTER 25

THE HALLS OF FAME

The first impressions upon arrival in Cairo are the Egyptian extremes. A bustling city with fast-moving buses overflowing with riders, a multitude of cars and taxis with their horns blasting away, contrasts with the quiet of the vast desert, its slow-moving camel caravans, and the pyramids, proclaiming eternity.

As one of the earliest members of ASTA, I attended many of its impressive World Congresses. This one in 1992 started with a ceremonial opening by Egypt's President Hosni Mubarak.

The huge exhibition hall was filled with stands featuring travel-related products and services from worldwide regions and countries. The crowds of delegates milled around enjoying the entertainment offered by many of the exhibitors, greeting many industry friends, and making new acquaintances before collapsing from pleasant exhaustion. Festive dinners with entertainment sponsored by leading companies rounded out the busy days.

One evening activity hosted by *Conde Nast Traveler* magazine took us to a huge tent set up in the desert. We passed an honor guard dressed in white burnouses, perched on camels, lined up on both sides of the road, rifles across their backs and burning torches in their hands. This scene, with the pyramids illuminated by powerful searchlights in the background, created an image and a moment never to be forgotten.

An eight-man band entertained us as dinner was served. I had the pleasure of sharing the table with Donna Tuttle, undersecretary for tourism at the U.S. Department of Commerce, who was sitting with her daughter, Alexandra. Donna was instrumental and effective in cooperating with the private sector of the industry to elevate tourism to a higher level of recognition and importance in the bureaucratic maze of government priorities. She earned my respect and gratitude. Toward the end of the dinner, the heavy curtain behind the band opened up, revealing the spectacular view of the brightly lit pyramid. Donna and I enjoyed a dance on the parquet floor covering the desert sand. It was an evening to remember.

Donna Tuttle—Undersecretary of Tourism
at the Department of Commerce, 1983 to 1988

The following night, several thousand members of the ASTA Congress were driven to the desert for a barbecue dinner. Five thousand carpets covered the desert floor. Low tables and taborets were in abundance for us to enjoy the meal in comfort. Omar Sharif, the international movie star, was one of our hosts. I wouldn't try to guess how many female travel agents were close to fainting as he circulated, greeting us all. He flashed a seductive smile and let himself be hugged by the more daring ladies.

Four stages raised at the corners of the carpeted area accommodated troupes of performers from different regions of Egypt. A center stage hosted a military band. Forty-eight soldiers staged a military display at the edge of the carpeted area, culminating in a charge with their drawn swords in the air, galloping on camels across the desert and kicking up a cloud of dust. It was yet another spectacular evening.

On September 25, the Hall of Fame induction ceremony took place in the immense auditorium of Cairo's Convention Hall, with speakers and screens located outside the fully packed hall area for the overflow of attendees who could not be seated.

I was rehearsing my acceptance speech in a room adjacent to the stage designed as an Egyptian temple, supported by huge columns on each side, with the sphinx and pyramid images serving as background. An usherette appeared to take me backstage while the story of my life was being flashed on a screen mounted at the top of the stage. I listened to the narrative and pinched myself to make sure that it was real. We walked backstage gingerly, avoiding a mass of cables and wires. The usherette parted the backstage curtain to lead me to the current ASTA President Phil Davidoff, who presented me with an impressive-looking crystal obelisk, a replica of the Washington Monument resting on a black base with my name and description of the award embossed on a silver plate. He then directed me to the lectern with the microphone.

I realized that the moment was real indeed. Here I was, standing humbly in front of thousands of my industry peers on their feet applauding, waiting for me to offer my thanks for the highest honor they were bestowing on me. It felt *awesome*.

The blinding flashes of the press photographers ceased, and after properly addressing the ASTA officials and the thousands of delegates, who gave me such an encouraging welcome, I began my speech.

It took me *forty-five hours* of the fiercest battle for Berlin in World War II to win the highest Polish military award, the Cross Virtuti Militari. Conversely, it took me *forty-five years* on the battlefields of tourism to earn this highest award you have bestowed on me today. I thank you from the bottom of my heart and want you to know that I feel I must share it with each and every one of you. My success is your success. I may have created the tours, but it was you who sold them to more than a quarter of a million Americans who have visited Russia and the scores of thousands who visited Poland, Czechoslovakia, Hungary, and other countries behind the infamous Iron Curtain of history. I thank you.

When, very recently, I stood at Moscow's Red Square, on my trip there, I did some reflecting on my past in this industry. My thoughts went back to the early 1950s when, with your support, I started organizing group tours to the Soviet Union and the other countries of Eastern Europe. It was a rocky road paved with great risks and political dangers with the only assets being faith, perseverance, and the deep conviction that *one cannot imprison the human spirit forever.*

President Eisenhower recognized that, and it was his White House endorsement that encouraged me in my work to create and develop tourism to these destinations.

At this time, it is only proper to acknowledge a Russian official, whose vision of the future made him risk the security of his position in helping me in drastically changing the system of restrictive policies of the Soviet tourism institution. I'm sure it will pay off since Russia and all the countries of the old Eastern Europe will experience an unprecedented boom in the near future. Thank you, Dr. Leonid Khodorkov.

I also thought about the organizations and institutions, which I have helped to create and which in turn gave me strength, ideas and friendship. My special thanks go to Bob Whitley, president of the United States Tour Operators Association and Don Reynolds, executive director of the American Tourism Society. Thanks are also due to my ASTA peers and mentors, George Brownell and Francis Goranin, and to my ex-wife Eva Harris, my collaborator for many years. My time is too short to acknowledge the many others who have earned my gratitude.

Travel demand is *irrepressible*, and unless our society becomes completely dehumanized, there will always be the need for human advice, human support, and human service. And that means an absolute need for *you*—the women and men who supply it to the traveling public. Even the most sophisticated electronic systems need that human touch to push the button, to reach a target, to put men in space, and to guide the most complicated devices.

I've been so proud to be part of this wonderful industry, and so grateful to you all to be recognized for my part in it. I wish you success and God's blessings in your private and professional lives. Thank you

My speech concluded, I acknowledged the ovation that followed, feeling that I had struck a chord of understanding and approval with my audience.

I lost count of the number of hands I shook when I descended the stage. Congratulations came from friends and many well wishers I barely knew.

ASTA President Phil Davidoff presenting my ASTA trophy and guest speaker, correspondent Peter Arnett

ASTA
American Society of Travel Agents

TRAVEL INDUSTRY HONORS

★ Travel Hall of Fame ★

The Travel Hall of Fame was established in 1971 during the 41st World Travel Congress in Sydney, Australia. The objective of the Travel Hall of Fame is to recognize and honor permanently those individuals whose careers have made an enduring impact on the development and expansion of the travel and tourism industry. It is the highest honor the travel industry can bestow.

Candidates for the Travel Hall of Fame must meet the following eligibility requirements in order to be nominated.

- The individual must have made a significant contribution to the travel or tourism industry;
- It is suggested that the honoree have completed the work for which he/she is being honored;
- Representation in the Travel Hall of Fame can be from any domestic or international segment of the travel or tourism industry;
- Current national or local officers of ASTA or members of the Society's Awards Council are not eligible to be nominated.

The members of the Travel Hall of Fame are:

Year	Members
1972	Gilbert Grosvenor, Conrad Hilton, Timothy O'Driscoll, Juan T. Trippe
1973	William Allen, Neil Armstrong, C.R. Smith, Lowell Thomas
1974	Miguel Aleman, Robert Hemphil, James Michener, Edward Rickenbacker
1975	Max Adrian Blouet, Donald Wills Douglas, George Eastman
1976	Wayne Parrish, Frances Knight Parrish, Sir Frank White, C. Kemmons Wilson
1977	Som Nath Chib, Amelia Earhart, Tetsuzo Imumaru, Brendan O'Regan
1978	Eugene Fodor, Jose Melia, William Allan Patterson, Wilbur and Orville Wright
1979	Dr. Arthur Haulot, Sir William Hildred, Capt. William Matson, Irwin Robinson
1980/1	Sir Samuel Cunard, Eric Friedheim, Charles Lindbergh, Mohan Oberoi, Harvey Olson
1982	Dr. Christopher Kraft, John Lewis, J. Willard Marriott, Per A. Norlin
1983	Thomas Cook, Elrey Jeppeson, Joop Strijkers
1984	Edward Carlson, Henry Flagler, Lord Charles Forte, Sen. Daniel Inouye
1985	George G. Brownell, Jr., Walt Disney, Thor Heyerdahl
1986	Elwood Ingleduc, Lars-Eric Lindblad
1987	Christopher Columbus, Donna Tuttle, D.E. Woolman
1988	Charles Gillette, Sir Edmund Hillary, Charles B. West, CTC
1989	Joseph R Stone, Roy and Estelle Kelley
1990	Walter "Freckles" Smith, Milton A. Marks, CTC, Arthur Tauck, Jr., Arthur C. Tauck, Sr.
1991	Ted Arison, Tom Maupin
• 1992	Alex W. Harris, CTC, Mohammed El Sakka

ASTA Travel Industry Honors

List of Subsequent Inductees

1993 Edward and Marilyn Hogan
1994 James Dubin
1995 Warren Titus, Charles Kuralt, Karl Baedeker
1996 Murray Vidockler, Marco Polo
1997 Tyler Tanaka, J.W. Marriott, Jr.
1998 Vasco de Gama, Frank A. Olson
1999 M. William Dultz, Curtis L. Carlson
2000 Fred Kassner
2001 Joel Abels, Lord Marshall of Knightsbridge
2002 Mario Perillo, Gordon "Butch" Stewart
2003 James Murphy
2004 Mathew Upchurch
2005 Alan Fredericks
2006 Don Daly

My peers congratulated me for my determination, persistence, and tenacity—intertwined with a polite and gentle, diplomatic approach, matched with toughness when needed—traits that were instrumental in reaching milestones in international understanding through tourism.

*   *   *

I was flattered, proud, and amused reading several quotes from interviews with Richard P. Friese, publisher of the prestigious magazine *The Travel Agent*. I humbly considered these quotes, in his publisher's letter column, among my most important rewards.

"Several weeks ago I found out that Alex Harris was recuperating from major heart surgery. Normally it's cause for concern when a friend is down with a serious heart problem. But in Alex's case you have a feeling that everything is going to be okay, because Alex Harris truly has the heart of a lion. In fact, whenever I see him I'm reminded of the motto inscribed on the Italian 20 lire silver piece. 'It's better to live one day as a lion than a hundred years as a sheep.'"

Ending his editorial, he wrote,

"The Lion has a small American flag on his desk and an American eagle displayed on his wall. Nobody has to explain to Alex what freedom is all about. It may sound crazy, but Harris is as Yankee as you can get. And in the words of Ralph Waldo Emerson, "The Yankee is one who, if he gets his teeth set on a thing, all creation can't make him let go.""

In another editorial, he wrote, "In Yiddish he might be called a *mensch*. In Spanish he is *simpatico*. Or as Sarah Lee might put it, nobody couldn't like Alex Harris. You see, Alex Harris just happens to be one of the nicest men ever to have graced the travel industry."

It was another big surprise when on May 14, 2005, I was selected to receive the prestigious Ellis Island Medal of Honor, bestowed on ethnic Americans who have distinguished themselves as outstanding U.S. citizens and are acknowledged for the contribution they have made to the country.

After a ceremony conducted with great pomp and military honors, we dined at Ellis Island's famous historical Great Hall. Later, aboard the ferry on our way back to Manhattan, we experienced another surprise as fireworks honoring us burst into the air over the Statue of Liberty. My memory drifted to the cold morning of February 18, 1947, when my eyes opened in awe and wonder upon sighting the beautiful statue from the deck of the MV *Ernie Pyle*. I mouthed a silent prayer of gratitude to America for adopting me and giving me the opportunity to repay in some measure the privileges she offered me. It is my fervent and humble hope that I have been worthy of this precious gift of survival.

Now, at the sunset of my life, my conversion from a European refugee to a full-fledged American complete, I reflect on my life history since that worker's strike in Lodz and the angry words hurled at my mother, "Don't you know better than to walk the border of freedom and oppression?"

Yes, Mother, I have walked it and contributed to breaking borders between oppression and freedom, devoting my life to keeping them open for others.

Indeed, travel does break borders. To quote Hans Christian Andersen, "To travel is to live."

My journey from the Gates of Hell to the Halls of Fame gave a true ring to his words.

EPILOGUE

The sun casts its last golden shadows on the towering skyline of Manhattan, slowly descending behind the far reaches of the New Jersey horizon. From the windows of my 34th floor apartment, I admire the reflection of the sunset in the peaceful waters of the East River. Sitting in my favorite swivel armchair, sipping my favorite scotch, I marvel at the accuracy of the remark made by actor Paul Newman, who said, "There is only one way to live in Manhattan: above it."

I take in the view below me, Third Avenue forming a straight arrow stretching south all the way to its end and beyond. The rush hour traffic is in full swing. The long white beams of the cars' headlights facing north become an imitation of a diamond-studded bracelet, and the reflection of the changing red and green lights of the traffic signals are like rubies and emeralds. The brightly lit contours of the four bridges—Williamsburg, Manhattan, Brooklyn, and Verrazano-Narrows—create graceful shapes of sparkling pearl-like necklaces. In my right eye, I catch the imposing tower of the Empire State Building, completing New York's panorama.

In my reflective mood, I count all the blessings and lucky breaks with which Providence has treated me:

Surviving World War II, becoming an American citizen, being privileged to do work I enjoyed while turning it into a worthwhile mission. Meeting royalty, heads of state, people of fame and stature. Traveling the world over, earning accolades and awards, recovering from triple bypass heart surgery, enjoying the bliss of domestic life with Judy, helping those in need. Developing professional and devoted personal friends, who for several decades comforted me in moments of distress, provided a warm social environment, and relaxed and humored me.

My thoughts roll back to 1993. Bob Drumm, an industry friend and former tour department manager for Pan American Airways, acquired the company from John Noel, who had purchased it from Dave Elmore's First Family of Travel and owned it for a short period. I was pleased and grateful to accept Bob's offer to continue my involvement with General Tours as its chairman.

We bonded and began a close friendship marked by mutual respect and affection. Under his stewardship and that of the most capable and devoted executives and staff, the company's reputation continued to grow, enhancing its standing in the industry while carrying out its traditional mission of travel as a weapon of peace and maintaining a spirit of charity and involvement in humanitarian, environmental, and cultural causes.

After the collapse of the communist Soviet Union in 1991-92, when the country experienced food shortages, our company introduced the "Feed a Friend" project, an assistance program in which all General Tours clients traveling to Russia would bring food packages for schoolchildren in St. Petersburg and Moscow. When the food crisis subsided, Bob changed the program to "Meet a Friend," expanding it to all destinations visited on our tours, offering and maintaining the spirit of direct contact and friendship between peoples. I love and respect him.

The darkness of the evening envelops my living room. I mix myself another drink and return to my comfortable chair. Outside, bright lights appear in millions of windows, illuminating the Manhattan skyline. Above the buildings, the flashing dots of planes suspended in the air, lining up for landing at La Guardia and JFK airports, appear like sparks breaking the darkness of the horizon. I have always loved to watch the streaks of the moving airplanes, the bloodline of travel and tourism.

Peter Greenberg, the travel editor for NBC's "Today" show and a nationally syndicated radio talk show host on "Travel Today," emphasized the importance of travel, stating, "Indeed, travel really is the last best hope. It unites more than it divides. It builds more than it destroys. And perhaps more importantly, it gives us almost unlimited options in our personal and professional lives. Travel is a special gift we give to others and hopefully ourselves. It is more than just freedom. It perpetuates freedom. Travel catapults you to the threshold of a dream and beyond it. It needs to be eternally encouraged as well as protected and defended."

Arnie Weissmann, editor in chief of *Travel Weekly*, wrote, "Travel is the straightest road to cross-cultural understanding, and cross-cultural understanding is the best hope for lasting peace."

In my heart, I carry everlasting gratitude to my grandfather, who instilled in me the rejection of hatred and the importance of tolerance; and to my father, who drilled into me the respect for honesty and inspired me to defy borders of isolation and ignorance.

Unknown to them, they were responsible for my devotion to the cause of tourism as the weapon of peace, and to my becoming a builder of understanding and friendship, a role I clung to as a rock of consistency in a sea of change.

As midnight spreads its wings over the city, signaling my time for bed, I take one more look at its skyline. The void, which the loss of the Twin Towers of the World Trade Center created in Manhattan's horizon, is the final image of the evening, provoking an overwhelming sensation before I fall asleep. I close my eyes and mouth a prayer of fervent hope that the United States will never abandon the spirit and guarantees of our Constitution and the Bill of Rights, never give in to fear, causing abrogation of these sacred rights, and never adopt a policy of physical, spiritual, and emotional isolation from the rest of the world's community, similar to the one the communist Soviet Union imposed on its citizens for three quarters of a century.

Benjamin Franklin's words, which I have stored permanently in the top drawer of my memory filing cabinet, come to mind: "Those who would sacrifice liberty for security deserve neither liberty nor security."

I conclude my prayer with a wish for mankind's return to a state of sanity abandoning fear, hatred, and violence. With full realization that the experiences of my life may be buried in the dust of time, I hope that the principles and values that motivated me and by which I lived will stay alive forever.

Twin Towers as viewed from my apartment

Twin Towers hit on September 11, 2001

Twin Towers destroyed

IN GRATITUDE

I feel deeply motivated to recognize and convey my respect and gratitude to those who contributed to my efforts in my professional and personal journey through life. I remember with fondness the late Arnold Mandelbaum, my vice president of operations who was always calm and composed in carrying out the company's tour operations.

Bruce Kanfer, his successor, continued his well-orchestrated, smooth, and efficient operation, always working well with the staff, tour directors and in particular with our capable, reliable financial executive John Fonte. They both cooperated with Lynne Anfang Stern, who succeeded Eva as Vice President and the company's manager.

Lynne knew my habits, requirements, and motivations, as no other person did. Her tall, well-shaped figure moved around the office with grace and authority. Her rich jet-black hair framed a strong pretty face with an upturned nose and hazel green eyes. They would blaze with anger and disapproval at those who had failed in their performance, to become soft and smiling at those deserving praise. She was as good a manager of the company as she is today as a wife and a mother of three lovely children. Her friendship is a precious gift to me.

Another contributor to the firm's prosperity was the executive vice president, Norman Harrison. A chiropractor by profession, he switched to travel as an organizer of medical tours and seminars. He was an unrelentingly tough businessman, yet on a personal level we had some good times and interesting experiences in traveling together in the Soviet Union, China, India, Iran, South America, and Africa. We parted when the company reorganized in the early '90s.

The steamship companies' executives and hard-working reservations staff made up the first group of people who shaped my early career. I worked closely with United States Lines, Cunard, Home Lines, Holland America Line, Italian Lines, and French Line.

The rapid development of international air travel created the biggest impact on the growth of the company and my professional life. The roster of persons

I encountered and befriended would fill too many pages. While I treasure the times spent and memories shared with each of them, I'll limit myself to mentioning those with whom I enjoyed a long and meaningful relationship. Regrettably, some of them are no longer among us.

The late Gus "Mize" Miezejewski of KLM-Royal Dutch Airlines, my Polish drinking buddy, heads a list of Poles who became my close friends. Monsignor Arthur Wojciech Rojek; the Pauline Father Michael Zembrzuski; Walter Zachariasiewicz; the directors of the Polish National Tourist Office in New York, Leszek Mokrzycki, followed by Jarek Novak and then Jan Rudomina; the consuls general of the Republic of Poland in New York, Jerzy Surdykowski and Agnieszka Magdziak-Miszewska. Krzysztof Gerula and Pawel Lodzinski, round out my honor roll of Righteous Poles.

Yan Yones and his successor George Menrath, both of Sabena Belgian Airlines, carried on the tradition of close cooperation between our companies and remained personal friends.

Pan Am's late Vice President Jim Montgomery provided me with a vast circle of friends: Edna Harkins, Dave and Helen McAninch, Jerry Healy, John McGhee, Hans Mirka, Jerry Murphy, Nick Slovak, Dick Boynton, and many others. I enjoyed knowing Pan Am's chiefs, General William S. Sewell and his predecessor Najeeb Halaby, whose daughter Lisa became Queen Noor of Jordan.

Pan Am's office in Moscow, under Erastus Corning III, became my American beachhead. With his lovely wife Rosanne, their home became my island of tranquility in a turbulent and often hostile sea.

The late Joram Kagan, El Al's manager, with his charming wife Marysia, turned our business relationship into a close friendship. I respect both for their intelligence, wit, and penchant for history and cultural events. We spent quality time together, occasionally joined by their son Ali.

The late Paul Herman, an American Express executive, and his wife Marion were another couple I enjoyed socializing with. I considered Paul, with his highly developed intellect, to be one of the most knowledgeable men I have encountered in my professional life.

In 1996, General Tours purchased TBI Tours, the company Judy worked for. Over the years, she introduced me to a number of her associates and executives. It helped me to better understand and appreciate the Japanese and their culture, history, and customs. I was impressed with the etiquette of propriety and grace in their social relations and respect for protocol and honesty in business dealings. I developed friendly business and personal relationships, cultivated on and off the golf course. I remember with warmth and fondness Paul and Marina Oyama, Koichi Fukuroe, Noriharu Takazawa, and Naotaka Odake.

The travel agent community, whom I recognized in my ASTA Hall of Fame induction speech, means a lot to me, especially some of its leaders such as Mike Spinelli, Richard Copeland, and Kathy Sudeikis.

The members of the travel industry press gave my company and me extraordinary coverage. Their stories, which I always acknowledged with gratitude, inspired me and helped the company reach a high level of recognition and acceptance. Their friendship and encouragement increased my dedication to continuing my life's mission. These efforts were recognized when on December 14, 2004, *Travel Weekly*, the leading travel trade publication, honored me with a Life Achievement Award.

The enormous contribution of the press to the cause of tourism is legendary, as are the names: Irving "Robby" Robinson, Eric Friedheim, Joel Abels, Dick Friese, Carl Ruderman, David and Doug Golan, Alan Fredericks, Arnie Weissmann, Jim Shillinglaw, Maria Lisella, Jim Ruggia, Bob Sullivan, Clifton and Doug Cooke, Nadine Godwin, Kate Rice, Dina Long, David Cogswell, John Stone, Michael Mulligan, Jim Glab, Laura Del Russo, Judy Elster, Charlie Gatt Jr. and son Peter, Mark Murphy, Ruthanne Terrero, Hal and Laurel Herman, and many others who could fill pages. My apologies to those I have inadvertently omitted.

To round up the compliments, I must include the public relations, advertising, and marketing firms and suppliers of various essential services that were of help in making General Tours known to the public and to the travel agent community, especially Stu and Paula Herman, Linda Kundell, Mira Birman, Karen Hoffman, Sandy Dhuyvetter, and others.

In the '60's, Peter Rotholz, Morton Louis "Morty" Meyer, and I created a company called Welcome Service USA, Inc., to provide airport transfers for airline passengers arriving in New York. Our timing was premature, and the company dissolved. Morty's son Danny became an outstanding success in the restaurant business, recognized for his organizational genius, innovative food, and excellent service and hospitality one can rely on in any of his many establishments in New York City. He has been acclaimed as America's most innovative restaurateur.

I'm grateful to successive heads and staff of the various foreign government tourist offices, especially the German National Tourist Office, including Udo Grebe, Knut Haenschke, and Michaela Klare, and George Vella. I was honored to be appointed to their Travel Advisory Board; their families became my friends. I also thank Deborah Renner of Lufthansa. Being awarded Honorary

Citizenship of Munich and the Medal of Honor by the City of Heidelberg are my treasures, and I thank Gertrude Schaller, Beate Weber, and Nils Krosen. His Excellency Akel Biltaji of Jordan, closely connected to His Majesty King Abdullah II, became my admired and respected friend, and as Jordan's Minister of Tourism, governor of Aqaba, and senator, he vigorously promoted the Mediterranean/Red Sea region through the American Tourism Society.

The U.S.-based director of the Jordan Tourist Board for North America, Ms. Malia Asfour, capably carries on its important mission.

Don Reynolds, ATS's executive vice president, selflessly contributes to its existence and development under the motto "Bringing the World Together," as does ATS's President Michael Stolowitzky, who as a young teenager trained with me in the Eschwege DP Camp. Phil Otterson brought a fresh breath to the organization with his clarity of vision and boundless energy.

The SKAL Club, a professional organization covering 87 nations with membership approaching 2,500 tourism leaders who promote global and regional tourism. Steward Low, Paul Abramson, Mona Aramburu, Warren Buckner, Jeannie Dalton, John Ruzich, Susan Shapiro, Joan Duran, Robert Hussein, Charles Librader, Peter Lintner, Joseph Rotante, Mok Singh, Roy Stepanian, John and Rena Udell and many important others have contributed to my appreciation of travel as a binding force of friendship.

In the early 1960s, American Express's Rutger Rosenberg perceived the importance of enhancing tourism to countries behind the Iron Curtain. He chose my company as an American Express preferred supplier of services to that part of the world. I was honored by having been invited to serve as a member of the Tourist Committee of the American Soviet Trade and Economic Council (ASTEC), chaired by Howard Clark and later James Robinson, both chairmen of American Express. Vince Campagna and Don Daly, as well as American Express Chairman Roger Ballou, Lorig Yephairian, and Donna Flora, carried forward the traditional ties between our companies.

The images of new friends who have enriched my life flash before my eyes: Jackie Turner, Jerri Ross, Geoff Bannister, Sande Davidson, David and Mary (Rabbitt) Mackie, Maryanne and Dirk Van Dongen, cousin Ernie Turner and Isabel Rimanoczy, Premal and Paule Shah, and a host of others, headed by Judy's siblings, including the extended members of her large family she brought into my life.

My fellow tour operators, competitors, friends, and members of USTOA kept my company alert and provided the challenge for us to perform to the utmost of our talents and capacity.

And last but not least, thank-you to the management and staff of tourist offices in the many countries abroad, and especially those in Russia and East/Central Europe, many of whom, despite the rigidity of their regimes, opened their minds and hearts while contributing to the development of international tourism to bridge the gap dividing the two hostile worlds.

RECOGNITIONS

In the five decades of promoting tourism to the Soviet Union, Eastern Europe, China, India, East Africa, and other parts of the world, Harris and his company brought about many changes to facilitate tourism, while at the same time collecting lasting memories, recognition, and many awards.

*1974	Named Tour Operator of the Year to Eastern Europe by the Annual World Travel Awards.
*1975&1976	Awarded the coveted ASTA (American Society of Travel Agents) African Travel Trophy for pioneering East Africa as a new air charter destination.
*1976	Received an award from the Soviet Ministry of Tourism
	Received a Presidential citation from ASTA
	Received an award from PATA (Pacific Area Travel Association).
*1981	Awarded Cedok's (Czechoslovak Government Tourism Office) 60th Anniversary Commemoration Medal, presented by Director Joseph Vacl.
*1984	Invited to President Reagan's White House for the "First National Tourism Week." The theme "Travel—The Perfect Freedom" echoed Harris' work.
*1985	Received the prestigious Noah Award, established to recognize individual achievement and to promote such achievers as role models and mentors for the industry.
*1992	Awarded the highest travel industry honor by being inducted into the American Society of Travel Agents Hall of Fame.

*1996	Awarded Poland's Order of Merit by President Aleksander Kwasniewski.
*1998	Received a certificate of appreciation for his role as national secretary of the Rebuild Dubrovnik Fund, presented by the Lord Mayor of Dubrovnik (Croatia), Vido Bogdanovic.
*1998	Received President Clinton's commendation on his 50th anniversary in the travel industry.
*2000	Selected as one of twenty-one men and women to form World Travel Market Tribute 21, part of the World Travel Market's twenty-first anniversary, recognizing those individuals who have made the most contributions to travel and tourism worldwide over the past twenty-one years and continue to be distinguished leaders in travel heading into the twenty-first century.
*2002	Awarded the Onore de Amerigo Vespucci from *Traveling Times* for an "indelible and enduring impact made on the travel industry."
*2004	Awarded a Lifetime Achievement Award by *Travel Weekly*, the leading Travel industry trade publication.
*2005	Awarded the Ellis Island Medal of Honor presented to outstanding American citizens, from all walks of life, who have distinguished themselves within their specific ethnic groups and are recognized for their significant contribution to this country. Both the United States Senate and House of Representatives have passed resolutions officially recognizing the Ellis Island Medal of Honor, ranking it among the nation's prestigious awards. His name has been included in the Congressional Record of the 109th session of the House of Representatives.
*2006	Awarded the Heidelberg Medal in recognition of membership and chairmanship of the New York Heidelberg Club.
*2007	Received World Tourism Award from World Travel Market in London, honoring individual efforts in opening tourism in new markets worldwide.

978-0-595-45415-0
0595-45415-1

Printed in the United States
124417LV00001B/232-249/P